Voices from Babylon

Or the Records of Daniel the Prophet – A Biblical Commentary of Visions and Prophecy

By Joseph Augustus Seiss

"With the ancient is wisdom." – Job xii. 12.

Published by Pantianos Classics

ISBN-13: 978-1-78987-323-8

First published in 1879

Contents

Preface

The name of Babylon stands for the oldest of earthly cities and the first and most illustrious of earthly empires. It filled a large place in the early history of our present world, and possibly may figure again in its final years. According to its native etymology (*Bab-El*), it means *The Gate of God.* Gates, in Oriental times, were the places of judgment. It was in the gates that authority spoke, whence the laws and ordinances were given out, and where causes were heard and decided. As the places of public concourse, they were also used by prophets and sages for the delivery of their messages to the people. And it is a singular fact that the great prophetic judgment upon the succession, career and final termination of worldly sovereignty was given out from the original head of world-empires, and from a primal capital whose very name denotes *The Gate of God.*

Equally striking is the further fact that the holy prophet through whom these divine decisions and fore-announcements were made was not only an illustrious sage and courtier in this Gate of God, but that his name (*Dan-i-El*) means *God's Judge.* Thus, by a group of coincidences which could hardly have been accidental, we have God's judge in the Gate of God giving forth the predeterminations and decrees of God with regard to the whole course of earthly political power.

These Voices of God from the Gate of God, through the judge of God, it is the object of this book to describe. The intensity of their interest to our day and generation, when fairly and fully interpreted, cannot well be exaggerated. Daniel is peculiarly the prophet of the latter days. Augustine speaks the language of all Christian antiquity, as" well as of all the prophetic foreshowings, where he says: "As the world approaches its end errors will increase and impiety and infidelity will abound;" and Daniel is pre-eminently the man of God to instruct and stay the heart of faith in evil times. Such was his office to God's erring people in his own day; such was the effect of his prophecies in the period of the Seleucid deceivers and oppressors; and such his Book is meant to be to us as the shadows of the coming judgment gather upon the world. Nowhere does the Spirit of prophecy and miracle stand out more illustriously in the eyes of men than here. Nowhere is there a more marvellous demonstration to mankind of the power, providence and presence of God in human affairs than in this Book. By astounding wonders, themselves luminous with celestial and moral teachings, the attention is drawn to the prophet's utterances, and by the accurate fulfilment of his predictions through the entire roll of the ages since, those miracles are ever more and more confirmed. And it is hard to conceive what sort of divine manifestations could be better adapted to encourage and establish God's people in these latter days, to fortify them against the materialistic and deceptive philosophies in vogue, to nurture that fulness of faith which alone can withstand the Antichristian storms whose tempestuous darkness is already thickening around us, or to enable suffering devotion to look beyond all present adversities and perturbations to that heavenly light and eternal calm which kept the spirit of the prophet, and which are at length to take possession of this afflicted and misruled earth.

Unfortunately, however, these Voices from Babylon have not been receiving the sort of attention to which they are entitled. Modern theology in general has so dwindled and sunk away from the original and proper faith of God's Word that the spirit of this Book has become estranged and uncongenial, if not offensive, to it. Criticism, instead of endeavoring to bring out its sublime teachings, has labored rather to encourage unfounded suspicions of its genuineness, to reduce its terms and imagery into conformity with a few flat and self-invented prepossessions, or to deplete it by way of apology for its presence in the holy Canon. Even when taken in hand by earnest believers, the treatment has mostly been either so superficial and partial as to belittle while attempting to expound and exalt, or so polemico-scholastic as to destroy all proper exegesis, or so very deferential to the shallow rationalism of the worshippers of human progress as to stifle the very soul of the prophet's crowning presentations. What the world and the Church need with regard to this Book is, that it be released and emancipated from all such imposed clogs and fetters; that the great Daniel be made to speak for himself in the majesty of his own inspired words; that those sublime foreshowings vouchsafed to him by the God of heaven be recalled and restated as they were, and were meant and received at the beginning; and that the invincible demonstrations which forced their way to victory over the pagan soul of Nebuchadnezzar be let forth again in all their divine reality upon the proud, skeptical and God-defying spirit of this evil age.

The treatment of these sacred Voices in the following Lectures is but little in the vein of most of the commentaries and treatises on the subject. Whilst the best and worst of modern criticism and exegesis on Daniel have been consulted, and much of real worth has thus been found and appropriated, the purpose has rather been to restate the contents of the Book in the direct import of its own terms, and thus to revive and vindicate the older and truer conceptions of the Church with regard to these magnificent prophecies.

There can be no question that all doctrines legitimately claiming the authority of Holy Scripture must ultimately rest on the grammar of the languages in which the sacred revelations are given. What is against the laws and usages of those languages as employed by the Holy Ghost can never be the true meaning. Grammatico-historical criticism cannot therefore be dis-

pensed with in ascertaining the teachings of Biblical writers. All right interpretation of the divine Word is unavoidably bound to it. No mere theological
or traditional arguments are competent to establish an article of faith, or to
refute w4iat claims to be one, without being able to ground itself clearly upon a "Thus saith the Lord" grammatically determined. Due attention has accordingly been given to this requirement, and a new critical translation of
the Book of Daniel, embodying all known results of any worth in that de-
partment, is appended to these Lectures.

But something more, and of equally indispensable necessity in all right exposition of the sacred writings, is required. *"No prophecy of the Scripture is of
any private interpretation."* 2 Pet. i. 20. As no such prophecy is from the individual will or wisdom of the writer, so neither is the composition in which it
is given an isolated thing to be treated by itself alone. As the sacred writers
were all moved by "the same Spirit," their several productions are only so
many parts of one organic whole. Though each has his own particular standpoint, surroundings and objects, which must never be lost sight of, yet no
individual presentations are disconnected from what others have written on
the same subject. The utterances of one dare not be put over against the utterances of another, nor the one be exalted to the depreciation of the other;
but all must be taken together, as equal in authority and dignity and as mu-
tually explanatory.

There is also a correspondence, analogy, interior coherence and harmony
of Scripture with Scripture as to the substance of every subject, which, if
once truly reached at one place, evokes a common response and attestation
from every other place, and thus begets a clearness of conviction beyond all
that the most elaborate discussions can impart. Nor can any interpretation
be the true mind of the Spirit which will not fairly construe with the analysis
of all the passages relating to the same topic.

It is upon this basis and method of ascertaining the purport of God's revelations, rather than on mere scaffoldings of individual textual criticism, or on
any artificial system of theological architecture, that the main reliance is here
placed.

The critically-revised translation is principally the work of the author's
friend and co-laborer, Rev. R. F. Weidner, A. M., whose special studies in ancient Oriental languages and Biblical criticism well qualify him for such work.
That he has done good service in this case will be recognized and acknowledged by all competent to judge of such matters. The *Index* to the whole has
likewise been chiefly prepared by him.

Thus constructed and thus completed, this book is offered to the public,
with the earnest prayer that it may be blest of God to the instruction and
edification of many souls, and to the praise and glory of His own great and
ever-adorable Name!

Philadelphia, Epiphany Season, 1879.

Lecture First - The Forming Prophet; or, Daniel in the Royal College

Daniel 1: 1-21.

IF God will, I propose to give at such intervals as may be convenient a course of somewhat special Lectures on the *Book of Daniel.* It is a part of Holy Scripture, perhaps the most interesting and valuable of all the prophetic books — one remarkably well suited for the determination of some of those questions which modern skepticism has raised, and one very full of just such truth as is most suitable for the consideration of men in our day, whether believers or unbelievers.

Quite a number of the brightest lights of our modern world, as distinguished for their erudition as thorough in their piety, have devoted some of their best efforts to the study of this Book, and given their united testimony to its excellence, its instructiveness and its value as a clue to the knowledge of God's purposes and dispensations as they run through the whole course of time. Though many critics have arisen who have brought all the apparatus of modern learning, and much "science falsely so called," to the work of discrediting it as the production of the great man whom it claims as its author, the result has been to exhibit with augmented clearness, and to establish all the more firmly, not only the genuineness and authenticity of this Book, but the certainty of its inspiration, the importance of it in the canonical record, and the centralness of its place in the revelations of God to man. "Happily for the present age," says Wordsworth, "the shafts of a skeptical criticism, which a few years ago were discharged in a volley against the Book of Daniel, appear now to be almost spent. Its quiver seems to be empty. The attacks made upon this Book with much eagerness and activity have stirred up able champions of the faith, and thus, by God's providence overruling evil for good, the assaults of unbelief have been made the occasions and means of strengthening our belief in the genuineness, authenticity, and inspiration of the Book of Daniel, and have secured to the Church those spiritual blessings which may be derived from a careful study of it." A few passages may have crept into the text on which some reasonable doubt may rest, but the limits of them can be clearly defined, and their elimination, if we must needs let them go, not only does not touch a single item of importance in the Book, but tends to set out in far more intelligibleness, consistency, conspicuity and elegance the grand and noble presentations of the great prophet-statesman of Babylon whose name it bears. With all that an inimical criticism and a perverted erudition have been able to accomplish, we may still take up the exclamation of Bishop Newton: "What an amazing prophecy is this, comprehending so many various events, and extending through so many successive ages, from the establishment of the Persian empire, upward of five hundred years before Christ, to the general resurrection! What stronger and more convincing proofs can be given or required of a divine providence and a divine revelation, that there is a God who directs and orders the transactions of the world, and that Daniel was a prophet inspired by Him! No one could thus declare the times and the seasons but He who hath them in His power."

And, as Sir Isaac Newton, "who explored the firmament with unwearied wing, and made an apocalypse of the stars, felt that he was sounding a greater depth and rising to a loftier height when he sat down, a patient student of this Book, to ascertain the mind and make plain to less gifted souls the meaning of the Spirit of God which herein speaks, it surely cannot be beneath us, or a waste of time and energy, or anything less than a pleasant duty and a high privilege, to devote ourselves with some degree of specialness to what God has here caused to be written for our learning upon whom the ends of the world have come. May the God of Daniel guide and help us in the attempt!

It has been the pleasure of a certain class of minds to assume that we know almost nothing of Daniel, the Hebrew captive and exile, to whom this Book is ascribed. The evident reason has been, not that ample records are wanting, but that the admission of those records carries with it the infallible certainty of miracle, inspiration, and prophecy, of which many would like to be rid. The skeptical Gibbon enunciated a larger and deeper truth than he was perhaps aware of, when, unable to see any escape from the contemporary evidence for a fact, or from its miraculousness if true, he said, *"The stubborn mind of an infidel is guarded by a secret incurable suspicion."* And it is this "suspicion," incurable save by the subduing influence of the Holy Ghost — this wilful shutting of one's self up against unwelcome truth— this foregone conclusion against the possibility of miracles and inspired prophecy — this exaltation of a supercilious rationalism against everything above it — which has been the spring of all the adverse criticism on this Book, and the cause of the difficulty in finding authentic information concerning "Daniel the prophet." The truth is, that we know more of him than we know of Adam, Noah, or Job — as much as we know of Joseph, Isaiah, Ezekiel, or Herod the Great — and nearly as much as we know of Moses, David, St. Paul, or Napoleon.

There are three Daniels spoken of in the Scriptures — one, a son of David, born in Hebron of Abigail the Carmelites, referred to in 1 Chron. iii. 1; another, a son of Ithamar, who went up with Ezra after the Babylonish captivity, and of whom we read in Ezra viii. 2 and Neh. x. 6; and the third, the great Daniel, the prophet of God, who lived one of the most original and extraordinary of lives, and wrote one of the most important and remarkable books of the inspired Canon. It is this last alone with whom we have here to do.

This Daniel was descended from one of the highest Jewish families in the last period of the Hebrew monarchy. He was almost certainly of royal blood, born at Jerusalem during the days of Jeremiah. He was among the captives whom Nebuchadnezzar, then at the head of the Babylonian armies, carried away from Judea to the Chaldean capital on the Euphrates. He was then a boy about fourteen years of age.

Of all the Jewish youths thus, transported, he was the foremost in every quality both of body and mind. He was without blemish, comely in person, skilful in wisdom, cunning in knowledge, quick of understanding, and having ability in him. And as it was the custom of Oriental monarchs to select the most likely of their captives taken in war for their own particular service, Daniel's royal blood, culture, and excellent physical and mental recommendations soon pointed him out as one destined so to be employed. The better to fit him for the king's service, he, together with three other Hebrew youths, was put under the charge of the Babylonian eunuchs to undergo a special training of three years.

It had been prophesied by Isaiah to Hezekiah: "Of thy sons which shall issue from thee, which thou shalt beget, shall they take away, and they shall be eunuchs in the palace of the king of Babylon." Isa. xxxix. 7. The inference is, that in Daniel this prediction was fulfilled, as Josephus also states, and that in suffering and privation he was formed for the place in which he became so conspicuous and notable.

An attempt was likewise made to obliterate his Judaic prepossessions and opinions by assigning to him a different name. It has been observed that while the king of Babylon liked Daniel's pleasant face and scholarship, he did not like his religion. As men of the world delight in the erudition, eloquence, and attainments of Christian ministers, if only spared these continual appeals to conscience and the everlasting urgency of the Gospel in its claims to the practical mastery of the heart and life, so the king of Babylon would gladly avail himself of Daniel's science and grace if he could only separate from them everything relating to Daniel's God. Daniel's name had in it a reference to Jehovah, as also the names of his three Jewish comrades. As this would be to them a constant reminder of the worship of their fathers, and something of a standing protest against the gods and idolatries of the Chaldeans, it was anything but agreeable to the proud court of Babylon. Hence other names were given to these youths. *Daniel* means *God's judge;* so this name was changed to *Belteshazzar,* which means *Bel's prince,* or he whom Bel, the chief god of Babylonian worship, favors and exalts. *Hananiah* means *Jehovah's gift;* so this name was changed into *Shadrach,* which means *the king's friend. Mishael* means *the incomparableness of God;* so this was changed to *Meshach,* which means *the gentle one,* or the one devoted to the Goddess Shesach. *Azariah* means *Jehovah our help;* so this was changed to *Abednego,* which means *the servant of the star,* or of the god Mercury. In other words, all four of these names were completely heathenized by cutting out of them all references to the God of Israel, and inserting corresponding references to the idol gods of Babylon.

There might seem to be but little in a name, but it is not a matter of total indifference. A fortunate or unfortunate name may have an important effect on the history of him who bears it. The very sound of the designation by

11

which one is perpetually called will have its influence, and cannot be without some moral effect, either favorable or unfavorable. Whole histories and vast circles of ideas are often treasured up in a name; and names should never be given without consideration. If they can be made suggestive of noble principles, examples, or memories, so much the better. Parents may be shaping the destinies of their children and affecting their whole life by the names they fix upon them. In the vocabulary of heaven we have reason to believe that names are the significations of things. God wished His Son to be called Jesus, because He was to save His people from their sins. And when the court of Babylon wished to blot out from these Hebrew youths the memory of their fathers and of the worship of the God of Israel, the very first thing was the changing of their names to correspond with the object desired.

But the expedient in this case did not succeed. Babylon began too late with these youths. Their names were changed, but their principles did not yield to the enchantment. Early instructions are not so easily obliterated. The impressions of childhood are always the most lasting. They engrave themselves upon the whole formation of the man; they constitute the mould of one's being. They may be weakened and overlaid but not extinguished. They are like words spoken in a whispering-gallery, which may not be heard near where they are uttered, but are produced in far-distant years and go echoing along the remotest paths of life. A child's heart is plastic, and the form to which it is once set is the hardest thing in the world to change. These youths had been brought up in the knowledge and worship of the true God, and had been taught His word and law; and their early teachings abode with them and remained proof against all the subtle seductions and expedients of a heathen court. They quietly took the new names assigned them, for they could not help themselves. Those names were indeed lies as applied to them, but they were obliged to submit, as the good and pious of every age have had to bear the ill names which the world has put upon them. It is not possible for God's people to escape the reproaches of the wicked. Paul was called a madman, and Christ himself was called a glutton, a winebibber, and a devil. Both meekly endured it in the blessed consciousness of its utter falsity. And so these Hebrew youths took the base cognomens dictated by their heathen conquerors, but under those offensive names still lurked the holy teachings of their childhood. Tyrants might change their names, but their hearts remained loyal to the God of their fathers. Teach your children the fear of the Lord and the truths of revelation from their earliest infancy. Even if they cannot fully understand them, imbue their young natures with them; and in after years, when you are no longer present to direct, they will be like the lodestone to the mariner in navigating the trackless sea. It may seem like casting your seed upon the waters, but some of it will find a lodgment where it will grow to beautify and bless long after your voice has become silent in the grave.

It was not long before a test occurred to prove how firmly rooted in their hearts were the sacred teachings which had been early imprinted upon these youths. The more to draw and attach them to their royal conqueror, the king appointed them a daily provision of meat from the royal table and of the wine of which he himself drank. It was a mark of most particular favor and condescension — a regal generosity — intended to win their hearts and excite their admiration, gratitude, and affection for their master. One writer thinks it was as much as to say, "If you will become priests of our temple, we will give you an endowment from the state." It was at least a token of gracious preferment to impress them with an idea of their sovereign's goodness, and to show them what they might expect by loyally identifying themselves with Babylon's king and Babylon's institutions. It was a most enticing appeal to the ambition of these young men. In the king's school, chosen for the king's service, and fed and feasted from the king's table with the food and drink of which the king himself partook, it would be difficult to imagine what could more stir and inflame the aspirations of their youthful hearts. What might they not hope when thus noticed and honored from the throne?

But, whilst duly sensible and appreciative of the royal favor, "Daniel purposed in his heart that he would not defile himself with the portion of the king's meat, nor with the wine which he drank." To partake of these royal viands was, to him, contrary to his religion and his conscience. It was the common custom among the heathen, when they sat down to a meal, to offer or dedicate a portion of the provisions and drink to the gods. In the place of our asking a blessing, they had a ceremony of acknowledgment or dedication to their household deities. Paul refers to this, and, on the ground of Christian principle, forbids participation where eatables are thus devoted to idols. The Jewish law was still more rigid, and strictly prohibited certain classes of food altogether, and other classes also if not prepared in a prescribed way. There was no security, therefore, that, in every mouthful he might take of this meat, and drink from the table of the king, Daniel would not be violating the laws of his God. The question consequently was, whether he should consult his conscience or his appetite and comfort — whether or not he should let his religion go and accept common cause with idolaters — whether he should relinquish fidelity to the throne of his Maker or risk his good standing with the king, who was disposed to favor him. Had he been one of those easy-going Christians of our day who are ready to make any worldly pleasure, gain, or convenience an ample excuse for setting aside any claims or duties of religion, we should never have heard of any scruple on the subject; but then we never should have had the illustrious Daniel. It takes sterner stuff to make saints, prophets, and holy princes than that which shuts its eyes and asks no questions, and is content to accommodate itself to almost any thing; and any place. Abraham's conscience would not let him stay in Ur, though his going out would lead him he knew not whither. Moses' conscience would not allow him to accept Egypt's throne and riches, though it sent him an exile for forty years in the wilderness. Paul could not permit himself to confer with flesh and blood, though at the sacrifice of everything earthly. And any one who would be a true man of God must be willing to risk all, and even life itself, rather than go against conscience and the clear will of Jehovah. The worldly-wise may call it squeamishness, and sneer at it as a straining at gnats, that Daniel resolved not to defile himself with the viands of the king's table; but it was the great foundation-stone of all his greatness. Principle is never small. It is even greater when exhibited in little things than in matters so imposing that there is scarcely room for trial. And he that is faithful in little is thereby also faithful in much. The man who has no regard for pence is not to be trusted for pounds. Our own history has shown us how a mighty revolution and the creation of a great and glorious nationality may be wrapped up in a box of tea. Daniel took his stand for God, conscience, and righteousness even in the little matter of his meat and drink, and thus laid the groundwork of a character which passed untarnished and unscathed through seventy years of political life, which outlived envy, jealousy, and dynasties, and which stands out to this day the brightest on all the records of humanity. We wonder and gaze with awe upon him as we contemplate his sublime career.

Elevated from his early youth to the presidency over all the colleges of Babylon's wise men, then to the judge's bench, then to the headship of all the governors of an all-conquering empire, and holding his place amid all the intrigues indigenous to Oriental despotisms through three successive monarchies; honored during all the forty years of Nebuchadnezzar's reign; entrusted with the king's business under the insolent and sensual Belshazzar; acknowledged by the conquering Medo-Persians; the stay and protector of his people under every administration through all the dreary years of their long exile; dwelling with the great in the most dissolute as the most grand and powerful of all the old heathen cities; invulnerable to the jealousies and envies of plotting satraps, and maintaining himself unspotted to the end as a worshipper of Jehovah in a court and empire made up of idolaters, — Daniel's life presents an embodied epic of faith and greatness, and exhibits one of the rarest pictures ever shown in any mere man. And yet the whole of it had its root and beginning in his youthful resolve not to defile himself with the portion of the king's viands!

Josephus resolves the whole matter into the wisdom of a vegetarian diet for success in study. But Josephus wrote as a sycophant and a craven. He knew better, but wished to avoid reflections upon the idolatry of the emperors and people whom he desired to propitiate and please. Had he possessed a spark of Daniel's devotion and honesty, he never would have perpetrated such an absurdity. The question was not about what sort of diet is most conducive to learning, but about the requirements and commands of God with respect to things offered to idols and contrary to the Law. It was not a question about vegetable food or of total abstinence from vinous drinks, but one of loyalty to his Maker, to his conscience, and to the ordinances of Heaven. It was not a question of dietetics, but one of high religious principle and duty. Daniel might have kept himself to pulse and water all his days and never been more of a man than Josephus was; but he had learned the statutes of Jehovah, and kept himself devoutly to them. Hence the blessing of his humble fare, and of himself in the use of it, which turned deficiencies into successes, weaknesses into power, and adversities into glorious triumphs. It is not meat and drink that make men prosperous, wise, and great. It is not the eating of the king's portion, nor abstinence from it, but solemn, self-sacrificing devotion to sacred principle, which develops Daniels, Hananiahs, and noble masters of wisdom and saints of God.

But it was not in offensive self-assertion that these youths declined the king's viands. An obtrusive piety is never of God. True religion is always courteous, modest, and anxious to avoid unnecessary collisions. With all its inflexibility it is always amiable and kind. There be some who seem to think they cannot be faithful without being rude, or true to God without harshness toward men. But here we have all the modesty and politeness of genuine refinement, and all the courtesy of an accomplished courtier, with all the steadfastness of the most devoted piety, evincing the genial sincerity, and heralding in its simplicity the future greatness of the man. Daniel showed no acerbed temper. He did not fly into an indignant passion about his religion and his God. He did not break out in declamation against Babylonian ways and idolatries. He did not feign himself insulted by the offers of his king because they did not harmonize with his views and feelings. There was no bravado, no insolence, no defiance. That would have been as wrong as to eat of the king's meat. It would not have recommended him or his cause, and could only have made matters worse. Therefore, with the modesty of a true man, with due regard to the situation, and with that humility of spirit which considers the rights and feelings of others while yet faithful to principle, he put the whole thing in the shape of mild and gentle *request* that he and his three friends might be permitted to live on pulse and water, if only by way of experiment for ten days. And such entire confidence had he in God's favor to those who honor His statutes that he cheerfully stipulated to accept whatever should be judged right if at the end of that time he and his friends did not prove as fair and fat in flesh as any of his schoolfellows who had no scruples about the portion of the king's meat.

In all these particulars we behold the sound and refined religious character of the man, and the putting forth of those shoots of moral stamina which made Daniel one of the noblest and most successful of men.

And what an illustrious example have we here for the imitation of all young men! You have been indulging many a fond and anxious dream of success, honor, and greatness in the world. You would like to do something good and noble for yourself and for your race. You are often absorbed with thinking over plans, movements, and methods of operation by which to conciliate the favors of fortune, to reach distinguished positions in life, and to leave behind you some good record when your race is run. If it is not so, I would not give much for your prospects. And as you think, all the warmth and zeal of your young nature kindles at what you propose to accomplish and make of yourself. I find no fault with this. It is all right enough, and what becomes youthful years. I would have you think with all seriousness, make up your plan of life with the deepest fixedness of purpose, and then pursue it unswervingly through thick and thin, never faltering and never surrendering. Your life will come to nothing without this. True and great men and great and honorable successes never come by accident. And one all-conditioning thing in a successful life is deep-rooted and inflexible devotion to correct religious principle. This made the Daniels, the Pauls, the Luthers, and the Washingtons of history. He who leaves out of his plans and purposes an honest and devout regard for his soul, his God, and eternal judgment, leaves out the very seed-grain from which all true greatness and all real success grow. You may not like such sentiments. You may think it merely professional in me to state them as I do. You may consider it manly and independent to throw off restraints and shackles of this character, and despise them as only in your way. But let me tell you that all the proper success and glory of your life is wrapped up in them. You make a sad and deplorable miss-shot of your being if you propose to realize your golden dreams without them. There is no right life in merely caring for this dying body and pandering to its appetites, while the soul and its high being are wilted by starvation and neglect. It is not right life merely to till the earth, and cover its hills with cattle, and make its fields glad with harvests, while all the sublime domain of the immortal spirit is left to waste and desolation. It is not right life merely to build houses, cities, and railways — to unchain the imprisoned spirit of steam — to dig up metals and pound them into shapes — while the moral nature is abandoned to chance or stagnation, with all its nobler treasures neglected, overlaid, and lost. It is not right life merely to become rich, famous, or even learned, if the momentous things of God and immortality are disregarded or despised. What matters it to pass with sublimest brilliancy through the few years of stay on earth if it must end in an eternity of darkness and despair? With tremendous urgency, and for ever, rings out that unsolved question of the Master of all wisdom: "What shall it profit a man if he gain the whole world, and lose his own soul?" Better fail a thousand times, and fail in everything else, than attempt to shape for yourself a life without God, without hope in Christ, and without an interest in heaven. No one can afford such an experiment. It will unmake you if you try it. It will turn your life into nothingness and your being into an ever-greatening curse. You may think it independent, dignified, and noble, but you can no more succeed in it than you can dwell with devouring fire.

What young men generally are mostly concerned about is *capital.* They think if they only had *capital* they would accomplish wonders. And so they can, if the word be taken in its right sense. They understand by it a full and heavy pocket, but, properly, *capital* does not mean balances in bank, bonds, and letters of credit. Its true meaning is *a right head.* If you have this, you are prepared for the business of life, and equipped to make the most of it, no matter about other things. If only *the head* is right, and the man is not awry or wrong in his upper departments, he has *capital,* and may be sure of triumphant successes. But a man who ignores God and disregards the statutes of Deity and moral right, is not in his right mind. He mutilates his being; he damages his manhood; he mars the nobility of his nature; he throws out of

16

gear his intellectual constitution; he puts from him that very *capital* out of which alone his life can become a success. A man who has not learned to know, feel, and obey the Truth, who fails in a just recognition of his Creator and his Creator's will, who lives only by veering impulse, without a settled faith and aim adjusted to the verities of his position in the universe, can by no possibility have reason and sanity on his side. He is more or less beside himself. His *head* is not right. He is in measure a weakling, an imbecile, a moral cripple, a spiritual dwarf, disabled from the noblest activities of a proper man; and he never can be great. What men need to make them *men* is a firm anchorage on God, a modest, sincere and unflinching adherence to the laws of righteousness, and such a devotion as would at any time rather live on pulse and water with a good conscience than to sit down at the table of the king with a debauched soul. With such *capital* it matters not what seeming odds may be against a man. The laws of the universe are in his favor. No storms or revolutions can ever wreck his good fortune. The throne of Heaven stands pledged to keep him in safety. And beyond the hills which bound our present horizon — beyond the stars which look down so lovingly amid these anxious night-watches — beyond these competitions, doubts, struggles, aches and ills, when this world's bloom is gone, its pleasures past, its fortunes worthless, its chaplets withered, its joys and sorrows over — there still remains a realm of light, beauty, victory, and glory, where they that have sown to the Spirit shall of the Spirit reap life everlasting.

Lecture Second - The Vision of Empire; or, Nebuchadnezzar's Dream.

Daniel 2: 1-35.

IT is well worthy of notice that the three principal events in the primeval history of man connect with the confluence of two rivers, a very celebrated mountain which those rivers drain, and a very celebrated plain which those rivers water. Where the Euphrates and the Tigris join is where Eden bloomed, where man was made, and where his dreadful fall occurred. The mountains from which they descend include Ararat, where the Ark of Noah lodged when the all-engulfing flood subsided. The plains through which they meander to the sea are the plains of Shinar, where the race halted in its first migrations after leaving the Ark, where the great defiant tower was attempted to be built, and where the Lord interposed to confound the language of men and to scatter them abroad upon the face of the earth.

The date of the Flood has been much debated and variously represented. But if we take the mean of the two reckonings given in the two principal versions of the ancient Scriptures, or the best deductions from the historical and monumental remains of the various original tribes and peoples, or the indications embodied in the Great Pyramid of Gizeh, by each of these methods we are brought to the concurrent date of two thousand eight hundred years before Christ, or near about four thousand six hundred and seventy-eight years ago. It was in the sixth generation from Noah, about three hundred years after the flood, that the great dispersion of his descendants occurred, for it was in the days of Peleg that "the earth was divided." But in two generations earlier than Peleg we already read of the city and kingdom with which the history of Daniel connects, and the culmination of which was represented by Nebuchadnezzar. There is no older known city — no older known kingdom — than Babylon. From the tenth chapter of Genesis we learn that Gush, the son of Ham, begat Nimrod; that "he began to be a mighty one in the earth;" that "he was a mighty hunter before the Lord," whose doings became proverbial in all after-time; and that *the beginning of his kingdom was Babel [Babylon], and Erech, and Accad, and Calneh, in the land of Shinar.*

The name and fame of this Nimrod, under whose administration the building of the Great Tower was undertaken, still resound all over the Mesopotamian region and live in the traditions of the people whose forefathers deified and worshipped him as a god. Many of the remarkable mounds and ruins of that ancient country are named after him. The ancient Chaldean astronomers placed him in the heavens as the constellation of Orion. The present inhabitants of the regions over which he reigned never mention his name but with reverence and awe. And up to the time when the tenth chapter of Genesis was written there was no other model of greatness and dominion to which mankind were so accustomed to refer as "Nimrod, the mighty hunter before the Lord."

The disaster of the confusion of tongues, while it caused the leaving off of the building of the city for a time, did not destroy the kingdom which this man founded. The names of not less than twenty-six Babylonian monarchs have been exhumed within the last quarter of a century, the earliest of them dating back very near to the time of the Dispersion itself. From these recently-recovered remains it now appears that a certain *Ismi-Dagon* was on the Chaldean throne one thousand eight hundred and sixty-one years before the birth of Christ, and that he was preceded by at least four monarchs, whose names have likewise been recovered. The oldest of these was *Urukh,* whose kingdom must have been very great and his reign long, for his name is upon the foundation-bricks of the greatest buildings in some three or four of the most distinguished of the ancient cities of that country. Even his own signet-cylinder has been found. His son *Ilgi* reigned after him, and very many others whose names have been discovered, indicating the existence of a Babylonian empire extending, in one form or another, from Nimrod down to Nabopolassar, the father of the Nebuchadnezzar who figures so largely in this book of Daniel.

Nebuchadnezzar was not yet properly the king of Babylon at the time of the taking of Jerusalem, when the Jews were carried into captivity. In the opening of the account Daniel calls him "king," but it is partly by anticipation, as he became sole king at the death of his father, two years afterward, and partly because he was at that time something of a coregent with his infirm father, having been assigned the royal charge of the armies which he so victoriously led. Daniel had been two years in the school of the eunuchs when Nabopolassar died; and it was two years after Nabopolassar's death, the second year of Nebuchadnezzar's sole regency, that the things; narrated in this second chapter of Daniel occurred. The second year of Nebuchadnezzar's sole regency would then be the fourth from the time he began to share the regal administration, thus leaving no room for the difficulties and cavils which have been raised respecting the chronology of these events.

The greatness of Babylon and of the Babylonian empire is attested on all hands. This chapter treats of it, not only as the very head of all the great world-powers, but as a *head of gold,* to which other empires are only as silver, brass, iron, and clay. For a period prior to Nabopolassar it was a tributary to the Assyrian kingdom, which had its seat at Nineveh, Nabopolassar being at first only a sub-king of that dominion. But he instituted a rebellion, in which, by the co-operation of the Medes, he succeeded, made the grave of the great and glorious city of Nineveh, and annexed the Assyrian empire to Babylon, to which it had of old belonged. The triumphant expeditions of his son extended the Babylonian dominions still farther, even to the utmost bounds of the earth. When Edom and Moab and Ammon and Tyre and Zidon sought to concert with the king of the Jews against Nebuchadnezzar, God, by His prophet Jeremiah, pronounced all such efforts vain. "I have made the earth," said He, "the man and the beast that are upon the ground, by my great power and by my outstretched arm, and have given it unto whom it seemed good unto me. And now I have given all these lands into the hands of Nebuchadnezzar the king of Babylon, my servant; and the beasts of the field have I given him also to serve him. And all nations shall serve him, and his son, and his son's son, until the very time of his land come; and then many nations and great kings shall serve themselves of him. And it shall come to pass that the nation and kingdom which will not serve the same Nebuchadnezzar the king of Babylon, and that will not put their neck under the yoke of the king of Babylon, that nation will I punish, saith the Lord, with the sword, and with famine, and with pestilence, until I have consumed them by his hand." Jer. xxvii. 4-8. All the nations to which Israel might look for help, including Egypt, are embraced in this description; but Arabia, Kedar, and Hazor did not lie too deep away to be also reached by Nebuchadnezzar's victorious armies. The Indian histories tell of his power and successes eastward. Libya and Iberia were subdued by him. When Ezekiel pronounces the destruction of Egypt, he tells Pharaoh that he will meet in the grave "Asshur, and all her company; Elam, and all her multitude; Meshech, Tubal, and all her multitude; Edom, her kings and all her princes; the princes of the north, all of them; and all the Zidonians, fallen by the sword" — the sword of this same resistless power. The conquest of Tyre and Zidon naturally also involved the Phoenician colonies in Africa and Spain; so that Philostratus declares Nebuchadnezzar's dominion "advanced to the Pillars of Hercules." He subdued Egypt, and set up over it a king subject to himself. Meshech, and Tubal, and all they of the north quarters, and their bands, are mentioned among the peoples brought under him, which would extend his dominion to the Caucasian Mountains, over the countries around the Black Sea, the Sea of Azof, and the valleys of the Don and the Dnieper, including much of the present empires of Russia and European Turkey.

The enormous public works which he wrought sufficiently corroborate these accounts of his victories, resources, and vast dominion. He adorned and exalted Babylon with a magnificence befitting the metropolis of so mighty an empire. He built an enclosure around it so thick and high as to embody more solid masonry than the Chinese Wall. It took in not less than one hundred and thirty square miles. Through this wall were one hundred passage-ways, secured by ponderous gates of solid brass. Inside these walls were two palaces, themselves very wildernesses of architectural magnificence and artistic adornment, besides the famous artificial mountains and mighty temples, the mere ruins of which have left piles still one hundred and forty feet in height. Near to this city he made a reservoir one hundred and thirty-eight miles in circumference and twenty fathoms deep, into which to drain off the river and retain its waters. He lined the Persian Gulf with great breakwaters against the irruptions of the sea. He cut various navigable canals, one of which remains to this day and is still called the "King's River." He walled up the sides of the Euphrates all along its course to the sea, casting up enormous embankments, some of which exist to this present. And all the great cities of Upper Babylonia he rebuilt, adorned with magnificent temples, and exalted with works which still tell of him to the antiquarian and explorer.

Having made all these mighty conquests, become invested with the sole authority over the great empire of Babylon, and settled down now as the sublime lord of all this realm, riches, power and glory, Nebuchadnezzar began to think over his affairs. Being a man of breadth and seriousness of intellect, he was led to consider very profoundly the situation of things and to wonder about the end of all this magnificence, how he got it, what was involved in it, and what was to be the future history and outcome. He was yet young. All the known world was at his feet and subject to his will. He had been wonderfully successful and had reached very dizzy heights. Glory and dominion unparalleled were his. What was he to do with it? To what landing was this proud ship of state to come when once his little span of life was measured? What was to be in the hereafter? These were the "thoughts" that came upon him. They came up even into his bed. His very sleep was disturbed as he thus contemplated the unknown and inscrutable Beyond.

We are not informed whether there was anything in all this akin to the experience of King Richard III., of which Shakespeare makes him say —

"Methought the souls of all that I had murdered
Came to my tent; and every one did threat
To-morrow's vengeance on the head of Richard."

But it could hardly be much otherwise. We may be sure, at least, that these invading *"thoughts"* had reference to the security and destiny of himself and his throne, including all the mysterious implications besetting such an administration. Out of these "thoughts" God also framed for him a dream-picture of the whole matter, which disturbed him yet the more when the morrow came, even though he could not remember so as to describe it.

A bright and mighty image stood before him with the outlines and lineaments of a man. The form of it was lustrous and terrible. The head of it was glittering with gold. The breast and arms were shining silver. The chest and thighs were glowing brass. The legs were pillars of iron. And the feet and toes were mingled iron and clay. A mystic stone, self-moved, rolled down from the mountain and struck the image on its feet, breaking them to pieces and grinding the whole image to dust, which the winds blew away, while the stone developed into a great mountain and filled the whole earth! It was the image of worldly empire, from its beginning, through all its varying fortunes, down to the end of time, and of the supernal power which is then to supplant it. The king could not describe the vision when he awoke. It went from him with his recovering consciousness, as it had framed itself to his thoughts when he uneasily sank into those slumbers. But the awfulness of it was upon his soul. It was such a strange and overpowering intermingling with his thinking, and seemed so evidently a supernatural answer to his questions, that it stirred him profoundly. If in the power of man to recall that vision, he determined that it should be recalled and its meaning ascertained. Nor was it mere curiosity, but sober seriousness, which moved his anxiety.

Nor can I but admire the earnestness of this man in this matter. It is just what ought to press most urgently upon the heart and conscience of every young man as he moves out into the cares and responsibilities of life. Especially if our efforts have brought us great successes, honors, greatness and power, it should much occupy our thinking to know where we are, how it is likely to go with us, what rocks and quicksands may be encountered in our voyage, what precipices and dangers may be before us, how best to secure what is made dependent upon our will, and how to steer that thines may have an honorable and happy outcome. It belongs to every one's proper manhood to exercise himself well in this very way, and to be earnestly anxious in this very line. Many are born into this world, and live through it, and die out of it, and even take prominent part in its affairs, who never seem to become conscious of themselves, or to think whence they came, what they are, or what is to come of them or the things on which they are spending their energies. And though God comes to them with many a brilliant vision, many an imposing dream, and many a word of useful information, they let it go as if it concerned them not. Eternal Wisdom condescends to put the sub-

21

limest teachings within their reach, but they care not to know what they are or what is to be in the future. Let this heathen king rebuke and shame their brutishness. Not all his honors, greatness and power could divert him from solemn thought of what was to come. Upon his royal couch he seriously moralizes and thinks. He reasons and wonders and inquires about the end. And when sensible of some mysterious tokens from the Deity, he will not rest till he learns the import of the vouchsafed revelation. All the masters of sacred wisdom are summoned to help him to an understanding of the heavenly intimations. It was noble in him, and evinced the seriousness and dignity of a true man, who will rise up in the judgment and condemn those who never cast a thought upon the solemnities of life or care to learn what God has vouchsafed for their guidance to a happy destiny. Very incompetent, however, were the helpers to whom the king betook himself for the recovery and explanation of his dream.

It was the custom of ancient monarchs to gather around them the best representatives of science and learning that could be found. It helped to dignify their thrones. Babylon especially had her orders of wise men, priests, and hierophants, supported by the state and held in the highest honor. The history before us calls them the magicians, and the astrologers, and the sorcerers, and the Chaldeans.' It would be useless to attempt to define exactly what was the office, pretension, or sphere of duty pertaining to each of these several classes. It is enough to know that they were the recognized keepers of the highest wisdom, the skilled dealers with all recondite things, the men set to ascertain and interpret the messages and will of the gods, the educated teachers and mediators on all subjects relating to the supernatural, the sacred, the invisible, and the divine. Among them they professed to know the mind of the gods, to read fortunes and events from the stars, to obtain oracles from the unseen powers, to explain dreams, visions and omens, to charm spirits, cure diseases, and procure supernatural interferences and aids. They had reduced their sciences into systems, rules, and methods, by which they claimed to do great wonders. The libraries of such practitioners at Ephesus — which, upon their conversion by the preaching of Paul, they publicly burned — were valued at fifty thousand pieces of silver.

All these scientists, priests, diviners, and representatives of wisdom and spiritual power the king summoned to the work of divining his dream and interpreting its meaning. And so earnest and resolved was he that he made it a matter of life or death to them. He demanded of them either to make known unto him what had been shown him, as also the interpretation thereof, or be cut to pieces by the public executioner and have their houses destroyed. In vain did they remonstrate that he was asking too much, and tasking their science and power beyond reason. He was only angered and infuriated by their prevarication and delay, and gave forth the decree that they should all be slain.

Much blame has been lodged against Nebuchadnezzar for this, as having been quite too harsh, unreasonable, and despotic. That there was something of caprice and inhuman tyranny in his nature is not to be denied. That there was a decided tinge of cruelty even in this case is also to be admitted. But Oriental despots were always cruel, and the same features show themselves to this day among Persian, Indian, and Turkish rulers. I do not defend it, but neither do I share the feeling that the king was so seriously at fault. It may be true that the demand was an uncommon one; that no king or dreamer had ever made such a requirement before; that no wise man, magician, or astrologer had ever performed such a task as he laid upon these loud pretenders; and that none but the gods could do what he required. Still, they professed to speak for the gods in other things. They claimed to be able to divine the mind, will, and purposes of the eternals. They held their places, honor, and living on the plea of being in communication with the spiritual powers. Even in this instance they alleged their ability to explain exactly what the vision meant if only the king would make it known to them. And if they were really in communication with the gods, and could infallibly tell what the dream meant, they could by the same means just as easily tell what the dream itself was. So the king reasoned, and with perfect right. If they could not, from communications with the gods, tell him what his dream was, he justly argued that neither could they tell him what it meant. In other words, they stood revealed to him as a set of impostors, whose pretension was all deceit and sham, and whose claims were nothing but a gigantic lie. In that case they merited his intensest resentment and richly deserved the severest of punishments. Bloody and extreme as the sentence was, it was founded in justice. Sincere as some of these men may have been, their profession was a deception and an imposture so far as regarded the exercise of any power from God. I sympathize therefore with the king's estimate of the matter. If he showed something of cruel harshness, he showed also his correct logic and sound sense. The matter for which he called them came fairly within their province. Not to be able to meet it was to forfeit all right to their proud place and influence. Whatever else they may have been, yet as exponents of the gods or as mediators of the sacred powers they were a failure; and, being a failure, they were a fraud; and, being a fraud, it was right that they should be punished and swept away. And one day more would have made an end of them had it not been for the youthful Daniel, who came forward as God's true prophet, answered the king's demand, and saved the necks of these traders in imposition. If people cannot do what they profess to do, and what they have their living and their honor for doing, they ought to suifer; and that government is at fault which does not punish them.

But the thing has much deeper and farther-reaching implications. It furnishes demonstration of the incompetence of all mere human resources, learning, and power to ascertain the mind and will of God apart from His own revelations. Here was the full-grown heathenism of more than a thousand years. Here were the combined strength and wisdom of the most noted schools in the highest acme of their glory. Whatever ability existed in priest or savant, astrologer or necromancer, wise man or magician, apart from the anointed servants of the God of Israel, was here concentred and embodied. If these men failed, it was the laying prostrate of all the wisdom, power, and art of man. The case was legitimate. It was propounded by proper authority. It presented a fair test which they could not disregard, evade, or escape. Not only the honor of their profession, but their very lives and dwellings were put under forfeit. Every possible condition existed to bring out the utmost that could be done. And fault or failure in a trial so fair and so complete could only be because it is not in man, nor in all the science of man, nor in all his occult arts, nor in all his command of oracles, incantations and priestly devices, nor in all his calculations of the stars, his consultations of the living or dead, his rites of inquiry of devils or of gods, nor in anything that lies within his reach or control, to ascertain the mind, the will, and the purposes of Jehovah.

But fail they did; and themselves confessed the failure before the face of all the empire. "The Chaldeans," the most renowned and exalted of all the orders of Babylon's sages, "answered before the king, and said. *There is not a man upon the earth that can shew the king's matter;...there is none other that can shew it before the king except the gods, whose dwelling is not with flesh.*"

I look upon these venerable colleges of sages, savants, priests, mantologists, and philosophers. I consider how much they were above and beyond all the rest of the heathen world. I trace how Phoenicians, Egyptians, Greeks, and Romans copied their systems, adopted their sciences, and followed their arts and inculcations. I see in them the full-orbed sun, around which all the mythologies and theologies and philosophies and religions and wisdomtreasures of the whole pagan world revolved and derived their light. And when I read these words, formally given out by their very chiefs in the name of them all, and sorrowfully pronounced in the audience of the imperial majesty of the earth as the utmost they could do to save themselves from summary destruction, I see a veil of darkness drawn over all the wisdom, strength, and science of man which makes me shudder as I gaze. It shows me, in one single sentence, that all the astrology, necromancy, oracles, dreams, and mantic revelations of the whole pagan world for six thousand years is nothing but imbecilities and lies. It proves to me, in one brief utterance, that all the religions, arts, sciences, philosophies, attainments, and powers of man, apart from God's inspired prophets and all-glorious Christ, are but emptiness and vanity as regards any true and adequate knowledge of the purposes and will of Jehovah or of the destinies of man. It demonstrates to me, in a few words of sad despair, that all the learned theorizings of this world's wouldbe wise, from Babylon's magicians down to the Hobbes, Herberts, and Voltaires of the last centuries and the materialistic skeptics and pantheists of our own day, are but rottenness, rubbish, and damning falsehood, in so far as they conflict with the revelations which the Almighty has given by His own anointed prophets. It is to the modest Daniels and to the humble Nazarenes, after all, that the proud world must come to learn the true God and to find out His mind and purposes. It is upon these that the self-glorifying wisdom of man must, after all, lean to save itself from being cut to pieces and blotted from the earth. And without these there is an impenetrable eclipse upon all the illuminating powers of our world, and nothing remains but despair and death even for the wisest and the best.

I fear, my friends, that we do not half appreciate the unspeakable treasure which God has given us in the Holy Scriptures. I fear that even our most considerate, pious, and devoted believers do not begin to comprehend the desolation which would swathe the world if it were not for what God's prophets and evangelists have testified and written for our learning. Have you ever thought what would be the result if these sacred testimonies were to be stricken out of being, with all that rests on them or has sprung from them? Have you ever considered what an utter obliteration of the highest intellectual and moral life of the race would attend such a calamity? Have you ever reflected how it would silence every preacher of righteousness and salvation, abolishing at once his office and his text, stop every work of mercy and philanthropy that would bind up the wounds of suffering humanity, and quench every fond hope of the recovery of our afflicted world, the restoration of our dead, or a home in heaven when this poor life is over? Ah me! Extinguish the Bible and its teachings, and no star remains to cheer the tossed mariner on this troubled sea — no chart by which to direct his uncertain way — no known haven or blessed shores for which to steer! Extinguish the Bible and its teachings, and the last appeal of the down-trodden and oppressed, the last check to the aggressions of power, the last bonds of restraint upon man's depravity, are gone, clean gone, giving carnival to every lust and freedom to every beastly passion, without corrective, without limit, and without end! Extinguish the Bible and its teachings, and light and comfort wilt away like Jonah's smitten gourd, and leave man to drag out a hopeless orphanage while years continue, and then to gather himself up to die and perish like the brute! Extinguish the Bible and its teachings, and des})air and wretchedness must settle on all hearts, as on the vanquished Chaldean sages under the decree of their inexorable king! Ay, did men but understand it, there is no possession on earth like the deliverances which God has given us by His holy prophets. Treasure, then, the sacred record of them. The Bible is the Book of books.

"Within this ample volume lies
The mystery of mysteries.
Happiest they of human race
To whom their God has given grace
To read, to fear, to hope, to pray,
To lift the latch and force the way;
And better had they ne'er been born
That lead to doubt, or read to scorn."

Lecture Third - The Succession of Kingdoms; or, the Four Great Sovereignties

Daniel 2: 36-46

WE have seen that the great Nebuchadnezzar, king of Babylon, dreamed a dream. It was one of the most original and significant dreams ever presented to the contemplation of man. It exceedingly impressed and startled the king to whom it was vouchsafed. But though deeply affected by it, when he attempted to recall it, its features proved so obscured to his recollection that he could not tell what it was. Satisfied that it was something very extraordinary, and that something divine was in it, he appealed to the ministers of religion and to the most famous adepts in science and divinity — the magicians, astrologers, sorcerers and Chaldeans — to recover it for him and to give him the proper interpretation of it. But none of them were of any avail to him. And though he put them under pain of being hewn to pieces and their houses reduced to ruins if they did not tell him what it was and what it meant, they were obliged to confess that all their science and powers were totally incompetent to do for him what he required. Infuriated at their failure in a matter so entirely within the province of their professions, he gave forth the decree that they should all be slain and their houses destroyed. And so sweeping was the edict that it also involved Daniel and his three friends.

When notice of this bloody decree had come to Daniel, he wondered that the king should be so summary in his action without further inquiry. He and his friends, though involved in the sentence, had not been at all consulted, and why should they be put to death for the false professions and incompetency of others? Daniel had a considerable liking for Nebuchadnezzar, because he was a really great man, and because his thinking was in general correct and just; but here was a case of manifest wrong, at least so far as he and Hananiah and Mishael and Azariah were concerned. Hence his surprise. Hence also he went in to the king — to whom he seems to have had ready access — modestly expostulating against the premature execution of the decree, and pledging himself to make known to the king all that he desired. It was a very bold thing for Daniel to do, for as yet he was in total blankness as to what the king had dreamed or as to what was the meaning of the vision. He himself seems to have been no little shaken when he came to realize what he had taken upon himself. It had about it the air of the greatest presumption, which it would be very wrong to imitate except under corresponding circumstances. It reminds us of young David going out to fight the great Goliath of Gath, from whom all the mighty warriors in the army of Saul shrank away. But in both these instances we recognize a divine impulse quite above the reasonings and courage of mere man. Daniel had confidence in the power and presence of God and in the divine sufficiency. He had had some personal experience of God's prospering providence, and felt the pre-intimations of the high office for which he was destined. The case also presented indications that God was specially concerned in the king's vision, and hence would not fail to bring it all out. The superior honor of God and His confessors, as over against the deities of Babylon and their priests and servants, was also so clearly at stake that there was good reason to hope that it was a case in which the Almighty would not fail to interfere to help out those who put their trust in Him.

In order, therefore, that the divine help might not fail him in this emergency, Daniel concluded to lay the matter before the Lord, and urged his three friends to unite with him in supplications that God would be gracious to him, enable him to fulfil his pledge to the king, and thus save him and his fellows from the doom that impended. There is nothing like prayer. It is the ready resource of the saints in every time of need, and never fails to secure the most blessed results. The Christian poet did not overstate its worth and power when he said,

"Prayer moves the Hand that moves the world."

Neither did it fail in this instance, for then Mas the secret revealed unto Daniel in a night vision." The dream which had been taken away from the king's recollection, that the imbecilities and deceits of pagan priests and prophets might be detected and the servants of Jehovah exalted, proved to be this: There stood before him a great image in the likeness of a human being, whose "brightness was excellent," but whose "form was terrible." The head of it was gold, the breast and arms silver, the abdomen and thighs brass, the legs iron, and the feet and toes mingled iron and pottery. Gazing upon this image, he saw a mystic stone from the mountain supernaturally fall upon the feet of the figure, shattering them to atoms and grinding up the whole fabric, so that the iron, the clay, the brass, the silver and the gold became like the chaff of the summer's threshing-floor, and the winds carried them away; but the stone became a great mountain and filled the whole earth.

The king at once recognized the whole description, and was so thoroughly convinced of the true and real inspiration of Daniel that he bowed down before him and reverently acknowledged him to be a prophet of the most high God. And it is the explanation of this dream that we are now to consider.

I. You will observe that Daniel regarded the dream as a communication from God. It was common for the Almighty to communicate with men in this way. "In a dream, in a vision of the night, when deep sleep falleth upon men, in slumberings upon the bed, then He openeth the ears of men and sealeth their instruction." Job xxxiii. 15-17. God said to ancient Israel, "If there be a prophet among you, I the Lord will make myself known unto him in a vision, and will speak unto him in a dream." Num. xii. 6. Jacob was promised his portion in a dream. Joseph was foreshown his subsequent exaltation in a dream. It was in a dream that God appeared to Solomon and bade him ask what he wished. And so in hundreds of instances, both in the Old Testament and the

New. Many believe that similar experience is constantly occurring. Nor would I undertake to deny it. There is a divine promise concerning the latter days, that God will pour out His Spirit upon all flesh, and the young men shall see visions, and the old men shall dream dreams. Acts ii. 17. Most frequently "a dream Cometh through the multitude of business" (Eccles. v. 3), yet there are instances in which we have reason to believe that God does still interpose to instruct, warn and admonish people through the agency of dreams. We are not to look for illumination in this way where we have the Holy Scriptures to guideus; neither are we to believe or follow our dreams in anything contrary to God's written word. It is easy to become superstitious in such matters, and to do ourselves and others much mischief by observing signs, omens, and supposed revelations. But in this case the dream was from the Lord. Daniel says of it, "God in heaven maketh known to the king Nebuchadnezzar what shall come to pass — what shall be in the latter days." It was originally from God to the king, and when he failed in ability to recall it, it was God who made it known again to Daniel.

Nor is it to be thought strange that God should select a heathen king to be the organ of such a mighty revelation. He had in like manner employed Pharaoh to give warning of the famine that was about to come upon the world; and in both instances the proceeding contemplated the bringing forward of His own chosen messengers as the only interpreters. Besides, the possession of political power and dominion connects very closely with the Almighty. Great potentates, whatever may be their personal character, still are, in a sense, God's agents, servants and appointed administrators. "The powers that be are ordained of God." Rom. xiii. 1. And it is not incongruous that a universal monarch, in the highest glory of the world's original kingdom, should be the seer of the course and end of all secular dominion, particularly when earnestly concerned about the matter, and when God's own chosen prophet was to be the interpreter of it, to the great discomfiture of the necromancers arid blind guides of heathenism.

II. You will notice also that Daniel regarded this dream as very momentous. When it was made known to him he broke into exultant adoration, not so much because he was the honored servant to whom it was revealed as for what it signified. It showed such a majesty above all the majesty of earth, such a plan in the course of all human governments and dominion, and such a power to handle and order all the potencies of time, that his soul was ready to break away from him when the mighty showing flashed upon his understanding. It set every emotion and energy within him on fire. He thanked and praised the God of his fathers for having answered his prayers and given him such wisdom, but first, and above all, for the showings of the dream itself. Sublime is the song he uttered: "Daniel answered and said, Blessed be the name of God for ever and ever: for wisdom and might are His: and He changeth the times and the seasons: He removeth kings, and setteth up kings; He giveth wisdom unto the wise, and knowledge to them that know understanding: He revealeth the deep and secret things: He knoweth what is in the darkness, and the light dwelleth with Him."

Such expressions could come only from an understanding of what the dream signified. They tell of new views of the glory and attributes of God and His administrations in the affairs of earth. They tell of a sweep and majesty in Jehovah's plans, and of a satisfactoriness of outcome to them, which had not before been realized in Daniel's previous thinking. They tell of a new world of ideas, exhibiting the intelligence, the efficiency, the calculation, the potent activity, and the just and beneficent purposes of Jehovah in a vastness of stretch, and yet particularity of detail, not before so clearly perceived. As Thomas, in the fulness of his conviction when he beheld the risen Christ, broke out in the recognition of depths and glories in the Saviour's being which till then he had never half appreciated, so Daniel here exultingly broke forth in recognitions of the majesty of the living God, which he had never half comprehended till beheld in the prophetic picture of Nebuchadnezzar's dream. Nor need we look further than his own inspired interpretation of it to find ample justification for all this exultant adoration.

III. You will notice that it gives an outline of the history and destiny of all earthly dominion, from Nebuchadnezzar to the end of the present world, and for ever. The several metals of which the great image was composed designated a succession of universal empires. For this we have the authority of the prophet himself.

The head was "fine gold;" and Daniel said to Nebuchadnezzar, *"Thou art this head of gold."* There can therefore be no mistake in the application of this part of the vision. Babylon was the first and greatest of kingdoms, and Nebuchadnezzar was its sublimest king: the vision therefore begins with him. He and his successors, as long as his empire stood, constituted the head and neck of this image, the head empire of our world. The exalted character of it is shown in the part of the figure which it occupies — *the head;* in the material of which it is composed — *gold;* and in the particular description given by the prophet in his explanation: "Thou, O king, art a king of kings: for the God of heaven hath given thee a kingdom, power, and strength, and glory: and wheresoever the children of men dwell, the beasts of the field, and the fowds of the heaven, hath He given into thine hand, and hath made thee ruler over them all. Thou art this head of gold."

The breast, shoulders and arms of this image were silver. From the finest of metals the descent is to a less valuable one. The gold gives place to silver. The great empire of Nebuchadnezzar is supplanted by another, less illustrious than his. Nor can we be at a loss to determine its identity. Daniel interprets it as meaning "another kingdom," and one which should arise in immediate succession to that of Babylon. Profane history amply tells what kingdom that was, but we need not travel beyond the records of the Bible to identify it. It is written in the second Book of Chronicles that Nebuchadnezzar carried away to Babylon such of the Jewish people as escaped the edge of the sword, "where they were servants to him and his sons until the reign of the kingdom of *Persia*." Even in this Book of Daniel, in the explanation of the handwriting on the wall at Belshazzar's feast, this same power is referred to as of *"the Medes and Persians."* These were two nations, answering to the two shoulders and arms of the image, but bound together as one in Cyrus, the mighty conqueror, constituting what is known in history as the Medo-Persian empire, the second great universal empire on earth. The conquests of Cyrus, the representative of this power, were second only to those of Nebuchadnezzar himself Herodotus writes that 'wherever Cyrus marched throughout the earth it was impossible for the nations to escape him." Xenophon writes that "he ruled the Medes, subverted the Syrians, the Assyrians, the Arabians, the Cappadocians, the Phrygians, the Lydians, the Carians, the Babylonians, the Indians, the Phoenicians, the Greeks ill Asia, the Cyprians, the Egyptians, and struck all with such dread and terror that none ventured to assail him. He subdued from his throne east, west, north and south." Seventy years from the beginning: of Nebuchadnezzar's reign did his dynasty run, till, under his grandson, the sensual Belshazzar, Cyrus gained possession of Babylon and established over it the great Medo-Persian dominion. About two hundred years did this Medo-Persian empire stand; and we need only refer to such of its sovereigns as Cambyses, Darius Hystaspes and Xerxes in illustration of its vastness, wealth and power. But it too was to pass away and to be superseded by another.

The abdomen and thighs of the image were of brass, which according to the explanation denoted "a third kingdom," which was likewise to "bear rule over all the earth." In the somewhat parallel vision given in a subsequent chapter we learn what power is here denoted — to wit, "the king of Orecia," or the Grseco-Macedonian empire of Alexander the Great. A double line of monarchs had been holding petty sway over the turbulent Greeks for more than eight hundred years when Philip of Macedon, against whom Demosthenes so eloquently harangued, subdued the various Grecian states to his dominion. Alexander was his son, in whom the genius and spirit of conquest reigned and wrought with amazing power. It was a little more than three hundred years before the birth of Christ that he set out in his great Eastern expeditions, conquered the Medo-Persians and took possession of Babylon, feeding the strength of his own supremacy with the wrecks and spoils of all the great dominions before him, and then sat down and wept because no more great nations remained to be conquered. The kingdoms of the Seleucidae and the Ptolemies were the principal continuation of the dominion acquired by Alexander, and answer to the two thighs of this image.

It is worthy of remark here that the period of the Persian and Macedonian empires is regarded as the most brilliant in the world's history. Its lists of heroes, poets, painters, orators, statesmen, historians and men of renown are the longest and most illustrious of any known to earthly fame. But while the annalists of this world view it as the golden age, and cannot get done lauding it as the brightest in the scroll of time, God pictures it as an age of *brass* — an age of glare and flare, with but little real merit — and assigns to it only the briefest place in His holy records. When Paul stood on Mar's Hill he referred to this age of blaze and splendor, and called it *"the times of this ignorance,"* and the same estimate is put upon it, both positively and negatively, in all parts of the divine word. What this world holds for gold God knows to be but brass.

But the image had legs, and feet, and toes. These were of iron, except the toes, which were of mingled iron and clay. This, Daniel says, denoted "the fourth kingdom," "strong as iron: forasmuch as iron breaketh in pieces and subdueth all things: and as iron that breaketh all these, shall it break in pieces and bruise." The particular name of this power is not given in the Old Testament, for the time of its rise was after the close of the ancient Canon, and its career belongs mostly to New Testament times. Hence we read in Luke ii., iii. of a dominion which claimed the sovereignty over the earth, of "a decree from Caesar Augustus that all the world should be taxed," and of an emperor called "Tiberius Caesar, Pontius Pilate being governor of Judea." And when we read further of the breaking and bruising wrought under the administration of the Caesars, the crushing of conquered nations, the crucifixion of the immaculate Son of God, the utter destruction of the Holy City, the slaying of all the apostles of our Lord, the ten mighty persecutions which reddened the whole Roman empire with martyr blood, and the threshing, breaking and stamping done everywhere and in all directions by the iron despotism of Pome, — there can be no reasonable question as to the identity of the power denoted by this part of the great image. The Roman empire had two great divisions, the Eastern and the Western, answering to the two legs. It was universal, like the three universal empires which preceded it. It was the strongest of all the governments the world had ever seen, and from all quarters it is characterized as the one superlatively won kingdom. When its armies invaded the islands of Britain, the Scottish chieftain Galgacus said, "These ravagers of the world, after all the earth has been too narrow for their ambition, have ransacked the sea also. If their enemy be rich, they are covetous; if poor, they are ambitious. The East cannot satiate them — no more can the West. To plunder, to murder, to rob, is their delight. Violence they call dominion; and wherever they can make a dreary solitude they call it peace." Gibbon uses the very imagery of the text with regard to the nations successively broken by the iron monarchy of Rome, and tells how "the empire of the Romans filled the world, and when that empire fell into the hands of a single person, the world became a safe and dreary prison for his enemies. To resist was fatal, and it was impossible to fly." "Wherever you are," said Cicero, "remember that you are equally within the power of the conqueror."

Since the Roman there has been no universal empire, nor will there ever be again, after the style of the four great monarchies symbolized in this dream. After imperial Rome had run its course, its territory and power parted into various subdivisions. In the composition of these something of the iron remained, but only in connection with the more fragile element of baked clay, the forms and coherences of which were to be fluctuating and doubtful. His-

31

tory down to our time tells how completely this has been fulfilled. In this severed, variable, "partly strong and partly broken" form the Roman dominion still continues. Under its codes, combined with the brittle intermixture of the will of the governed,' all the nations are still living, and will continue to live to the very end of this present world, when the stone will strike, making: an end of all mere human sovereignty, and setting up in its place "a kingdom which shall never be destroyed, but shall break in pieces and consume all these kingdoms, and stand for ever."

IV. You will notice also that in this foreshowing of the succession of earthly administration there is a continuous deterioration from the beginning to the end. Political economists and statesmen claim that the world has been growing in wisdom and excellence through all these ages, and that the administrations of power particularly mark this progress. And in some respects there has been growth. The great image has gone on filling out as time proceeded. The experiences and observations of man have also vastly increased. His progress over the earth, his acquaintance with its character, relations, elements and adaptations, and his mastery of its natural susceptibilities and powers, have wonderfully advanced. But with all, in God's estimate, there has been a never-ceasing downwardness, depreciation and tendency toward the earth out of which man was taken. The beginning was gold; the next stage was silver; the third was brass; the fourth was iron; and then came iron mingled with clay, until we now have very much more mud than metal. Babylon, the head, was an absolute autocracy; and as a government God likened it to gold. Persia was a monarchical oligarchy, in which nobility was everything, and the nobles were equal to the king in all but office; and as a government God likened it to silver. Greece was essentially an aristocracy, not of birth, but of supposed excellence of mind and influence; and as a government God likened it to brass. Rome was a democratic imperialism — a military dominion, dependent upon the choice of the army and the free citizens, and administered in the spirit of martial law; and as a government God likened it to iron, strong, harsh and frowning, but far inferior to gold, silver or brass. And then, at the last, as parcelled out into constitutional monarchies and more republican forms. He likens it to treacherous clay, incoherently mixed with iron.

Nor is there a government now on earth which is not made up of this compounded pottery. The next stage, according to the vision, is to be the original, God-made mountain *rock,* out of which all these other metals and materials have been derived, even the original and everlasting government of the Originator of all things.

It is therefore the whole history of the world that is comprehended in this vision. Note, then, how all the various actors, agencies and activities that shape human history fulfil Jehovah's counsels. Whatever the motives which actuate them, the passions that sway them, or the freedom and self-direction by which they proceed, they still only act out the programme which God long ago fore-announced. We behold the heroes, conquerors, statesmen and operators of the olden time going forward with their schemes of ambition, making conquests, carving names, building up thrones, monuments, fortunes and glories for themselves, their associates and their children, each busy on his own account, yet each only filling up, unknown to himself, what was projected in the mind of the Almighty for a thousand years before. "We see Hannibal, who had never heard of God's prophecies, begin his wars with Rome, and thus train her soldiers to become the conquerors of the world. We see Scipio, Marias, Pompey and Caesar each take up the place assigned him, and fight or fall or conquer till they make Rome nothing less and nothing more than what Daniel had predicted that Rome should be. We see the eloquence of Cicero, the poetry of Virgil, the odes of Horace, the annals of Tacitus, the pungent satires of Juvenal, the history of Gibbon, all rush forward to produce results and witness to facts which none of them comprehended, but which fill out and demonstrate to a skeptic world what the young prophet in Chaldea said and celebrated — to wit, that *God* changeth the times and seasons, that *He* removeth kings and setteth up kings, that *He* knoweth what is in the darkness and possesseth the light! All these fell into place at the appointed times; and while they thought they were each doing his own work, all were co-operating to accomplish God's predictions. They thought they were the statuaries cutting out the image after their own design, whilst they were but the chisels in the hand of the great Sculptor, unconsciously and unintentionally fulfilling His own grand conception." (See Dr. Gumming *in loc.*)

History, as it appears to man, seems to be only the aggregate of lucky occurrences. The most trifling and ordinary things often determine the characteristics of ages. History takes shape from accidents. A stroke of lightning, killing a young man in Germany, sent Luther to the convent and begot the mighty Reformer,

"Whose *yes* or *no* the wheel of ages turned;
Who balanced Europe on a single breath."

The very existence of Rome hung upon the doubtful fate of two infant boys left in the wilderness to perish. Its fortune was once balanced on the single sword of one of its patricians. At another time its capital was saved by the cackling of the geese which chanced to be fed there. Such things look like very little accidents, and would seem to argue that history itself is accident. But all these accidents had to be fore-calculated in any attempt to tell it beforehand. In this case they belonged as much to the filling out of the predictions as the victories of Cyrus, the conquests of Alexander, or the heroic deeds of the greatest of the Caesars. The smallest things, as well as the more momentous things, are all alike in the contemplations and fore-calculations of Jehovah, and enter equally into His all-comprehending purposes. That the wolves did not eat Romulus and Remus, but suckled them; that the sword of Camillus should accomplish what it did; and that the dull and plodding fowls should be in place to raise their cries, in timely warning of the presence of the stealthy foe, — were all as needful to the fulfilment of Daniel's prophecy, and hence as much fore-calculated by the Eternal Mind in giving this dream to Nebuchadnezzar, as the campaigns of the most famous generals, the marchet of the most massive armies or the results of the most decisive battles. History would have been different without them, and then this dream could not have been true. Thus it follows that everything, and every actor in the world's affairs, soldier and senator, poet and orator, priest and oracle, saint and sinner, has place in the mind and prescience of God, and performs the part required in the working out of plans matured and understood by Him from the beginning. "Oh the depth of the riches, both of the wisdom and knowledge of God! How unsearchable are His judgments, and His ways past finding out!"

Note then, still further, the reality of inspiration and the absolute certainty of supernatural revelations from God to men. This is one of the things at which our modern world is full of stumbling. The old nations accepted it as not only possible, but in every respect so likely and desirable that they never thought of the gods except as willing and ready to make communications to mankind in all cases of importance. So satisfied and confident were they upon this point that they willingly took up with anything that had the remotest semblance of a claim to be considered divine. In the days of gold, and silver, and brass, and even iron, there was no trouble on this subject. The doctrine that it is absurd to believe in communications from God was reserved for the period of earthiness and pottery. It has only come with that sublime development of human genius which gets everything, including itself. and even Deity, from slime and filth. Such consummate wisdom remained to be brought forth only when man bent down from his erect posture and heavenward look for the contemplation of material forces, adaptations, elements and interests as his supreme world of thought and energy. It belongs to that high and superlative science which finds its inspirations in the manipulation, capacities and evolutions of mud! But all such wisdom is but vanity and emptiness. It may please the flesh, but it must starve the soul. It claims to rest on facts. Well, here are facts, and they demonstrate a living God, and unmistakable communications from Him. Here is a piece of composition which no one has dared to assign a later origin than the Maccabean age, but which gives the whole political and social history of man for two thousand years since that time. But it is older than the time of the Maccabees. It was known and acknowledged as a sacred book when Alexander lived and Persia was still in power. Josephus witnesses (*Ant.*, xi. cap. 8) that it was shown to the Macedonian conqueror in Jerusalem when on his Eastern expedition; that the high priest explained to him in person how it foretold the coming of a Greek who should destroy the Persian empire; and that he was so pleased and encouraged by its seeming reference to himself that he agreed to leave Judea untouched and to grant the Jews whatever favors they might ask. This is corroborated by the historic facts that Alexander was at that time personally in Palestine; that he had a special interview with the high priest and other Jewish notables; that the Jews voluntarily agreed to accept submission to him; and that he never did disturb or molest them. This was more than a century and a half before Antiochus Epiphanes. Being at that time in the Canon, it must needs be referred to the period and authorship of him whose name it bears. Ezekiel was the contemporary of Daniel's later years, and Ezekiel mentions him twice with most distinguished honor as an eminent teacher, prophet and servant of God. Ezek. xiv. 13, 14; xxviii. 3. Christ himself quotes from the Book as the production of Daniel the prophet," and not the work of some unknown author in the time of the Maccabees. Matt. xxiv. 15. We have, then, ample reason to accept it, in all its essential parts at least, for just what it professes to be.

And when we find in this Book the whole political and social history of our world grandly and truly sketched, just as it has turned out from that time to this living present, how can we construe it except upon the doctrine alleged by the prophet, that it was revealed to him from the almighty and all-knowing One? Comparing so plain a prophecy with a range of historic facts so vast, so indisputable, and so impossible of anticipation by any sagacity of man, how can we rid ourselves of the conclusion that there is an omniscient God who does condescend to reveal hidden things? Could it just have happened so? How could a young man like Daniel, unacquainted as yet with the great problems of politics and government, stand up in the midst of Babylon at a time when Its unrivalled dominion gave every token of abiding permanence, and assure the king whose sceptre swayed unquestioned over all the known world, that this empire would presently pass away, this glory disappear, this matchless dominion fall a prey to another power, which should in turn give place to a third, and that third to a fourth, and that fourth divide out into ten, and then, amid varied, uncertain and ever-deteriorating changes, run to the final termination of all mere human rule; and all, as far as history has been enacted, turn out precisely as he said, if he was not miraculously helped and illumined by the inspiration of the Eternal? Such a thing would be a miracle more marvellous than inspiration. Yet here are the facts. They cannot be disputed. They stand invincible against both sneers and arguments. You must blot out two thousand five hundred years of earth's history in order to get rid of them. Man has no records besides them. And here is the evidence, equally Invincible, that Daniel foreknew and foretold them as accurately as the events have occurred or the historians recorded them. *How did he get that information?* How could he thus know and declare beforehand what was so improbable to all human likelihood, so impossible for mere human foresight to anticipate? He tells us that *God,* the living God, the God who rules all kingdoms and all history, the God to whose omniscience all things are present, naked and open, *the Almighty,* revealed these things to him; and the seal to his assertion is immutably stamped upon all the records of the succeeding ages.

What, then, are we to conclude — what else can we conclude — but that inspiration is a reality; that there is a knowing God in heaven, whose word has come out upon earth; that His holy prophets were not liars when they delivered and wrote down His messages to men; that there is such a thing as a divine revelation?

Men and brethren, let us not deceive ourselves. There is a God in history, and He hath prophets whom He hath sent to speak His word and will. These living oracles are verily from Him. And if any man have ears to hear, let him hear them.

Lecture Fourth. The Final Dominion; or, the Kingdom of the Stone

Daniel 2: 34, 35; 44-50.

ACCORDING to Daniel's interpretation of Nebuchadnezzar's great vision, it was meant to set forth the history of earthly dominion from the time of the vision down to the end. One image served for this purpose. The history and career of this world's empire, truly considered, presents the appearance of one great man, with a head and neck of gold, breast and arms of silver, abdomen and thighs of brass, legs and feet of iron, and toes of mingled iron and clay. The several metals mark its several great transitions and its constant deterioration, but they all belong equally to one and the same image and history, which spans the whole period of the world, from the first great empire to the time when *"man's day"* ceases and the rule of corrupt mortals ends for ever. Beginning with Nebuchadnezzar, the golden head, all the other parts were consecutively the Medo-Persian dominion, the Graeco-Macedonian dominion and the Roman dominion, the latter dividing out at last into numerous fragments and varying kingdoms, extending down to the present time.

In this fragmentary form, modified with the element of "the sovereignty of the people" — the "miry clay" of government — this Roman dominion still continues. It may sound strangely to modern republican and democratic ears to say so, but it is nevertheless historically true. Though it is now more than one thousand years since the old imperial form of Roman government broke up, yet "from the commencement of the reign of Augustus Caesar down to the memorable year 1806 — a period which comprises a longer term than eighteen centuries — the world has never been without an emperor of the Romans." It is also a fact, which no one competent to speak on the subject will deny, that all the kingdoms, governments and civilized nations now on the face of the earth are still constituted and ruled by the codes, pandects and principles of laws laid down by that iron empire. All the histories of laws prove this. Whatever else the revolutions of the fifth and sixth centuries did, they did not blot out the Roman law." With all the new order that broke over the world, the old Roman law still continued in force as an actual jurisprudence. The Germanic invaders did not destroy the Romans nor impose upon them new codes. Wherever Roman dominion, had been fully established, as in Gaul, Spain and Italy, the remains of Roman institutions, laws and modes of thought continued, and as society gradually became settled were taken as the basis of the legislation that was created for the new nations.

The principles, doctrines and rules of Roman law made up the jurisprudence of Europe. In the twelfth century Bologna had a great law school for the study and exposition of the pandects, the code, the institutes, and the novels which constituted the *corpus* or body of the civil law of the Romans, which spread its influence over Europe and largely affected the judicial affairs of the whole continent; so that the Roman law became the common law of Europe, and thence of all the governments which have since been formed. It is the iron from the kingdom of iron in which that old empire still has being and holds its sway over the earth, though the last of its ancient emperors has been dead for more than a thousand years. Besides, we have occasion to know that there is a pope of Rome, claiming to be the supreme bishop of the universal Church, and dictating canon law to all the world. But it was a Roman emperor who put him into this supremacy. He is the highest ruler on earth at this hour to nearly one hundred millions of the race in all sections of the habitable world, and exhibits the ghostly shadow of the old empire in ecclesiastical form. Look where we will, we still find something of the iron dominion conditioning more or less all the administrations that exist. No new power has been able to take the sovereignty as against it, and never will as long as the rule of man lasts. The kingdom is divided and intermixed with the clay and clamor of the popular will, but the metal which stays all existing governments, the solid material of their laws and administrations, is the iron of old Rome, which thus perpetuates itself in spite of the uprisings, changes, revolutions, marches and countermarches in the political affairs of mankind.

But having reached these days of the mingled iron and clay, when the kingdom, partly strong and partly broken, is endeavoring to maintain and perpetuate itself by all manner of compromises and coalitions, which give way as fast as they are made, we stand upon the margin of events the most momentous in all the history of human dominion. It is in the days of these kingdoms that all earthly political successions are to come to a sudden termination, and be no more. Look again at the prophetic description: "And in the days of these kings [rather, kingdoms] shall the God of heaven set up a kingdom, which shall never be destroyed: and the kingdom shall not be left to other people, but it shall break in pieces and consume all these kingdoms, and it shall stand for ever. Forasmuch as thou sawest that the stone was cut out of the mountain without hands, and that it brake in pieces the iron, the brass, the clay, the silver, and the gold, the great God hath made known to thee what shall come hereafter.'

Here we have a unique and unparalleled power and dominion. To what does it refer? What does it mean? How shall we identify it?

The first point I make concerning it is, that it is truly a kingdom, a government, a tangible sovereignty and dominion over the earth. All the connections and terms of the description show this. It is called a kingdom. It fulfils all the functions and performs all the offices of a great political sovereignty. It falls on other governments, crushes them out of existence and takes their place. As Tillinghast, an old Scotch divine, expresses it: "This is a kingdom, in respect of nature the same with the kingdoms represented by the great image; that is, it is outward, as they are outward, which appears —

"1. From the general scope and drift of the prophecy, which runs upon outward kingdoms. All the first four kingdoms or monarchies are outward, as none can deny; why, then, the Holy Ghost, in speaking of the fifth and last, should so far vary the scope as to glide from the outward kingdom to the inward ought (besides the bare say-so) to have some solid and substantial reason brought for it by those, whosoever they are, that either do or shall assert it.

"2. Because it is not proper to say that a bare spiritual kingdom, considered only as spiritual, should break in pieces, beat to very chaff, grind to powder, the great image — that is, destroy the very being of earthly kingdoms — which work is yet, notwithstanding, done by this stone. Christ's spiritual kingdom may, indeed, by that light and life which it gives forth, much refine and reform outward kingdoms; but when the work comes to breaking, and breaking in pieces — that is, subverting kingdoms, razing their very foundations and destroying their very being — as the kings of this world here, unless we conceive God to do it by a miracle (which is not spiritual), must we also conceive some other hand besides a spiritual to be put to the work.

"3. Because the stone, to the end that there might not be a vacancy in the world, comes straightway in the place and room of the great image so soon as the same is totally broken. For as the great image, while standing, bears rule over all the earth, so, the same being broken, the stone becomes a mountain, and fills the whole earth; therefore must the kingdom of the stone be such a kingdom as was that of the great image — namely, outward; or otherwise the coming of that in the place of the other now taken away could not supply the absence of the other."

Dr. Berg, from whom I quote this argument, regards it "as conclusive that the nature of this fifth power is outward, corresponding to its predecessors, and not merely spiritual." Nor can I see how we can do justice to the prophet's description without so taking it. And if there were no foregone theories against which it strikes we never should have heard of any other idea than that this kingdom of the stone is as really a kingdom as that of Babylon, Persia, Greece or Rome.

Another point I make with regard to this stone kingdom is that, though truly an outward and visible kingdom and sovereignty, it is entirely supernatural. It is a kingdom which *"the God of heaven"* sets up. God was concerned in the setting up of the other kingdoms also, for nothing can come to pass without Him. But the language in those instances is different. Daniel said to Nebuchadnezzar, "The God of heaven *hath given thee* a kingdom, power, and strength and glory;" that is to say, God gave him the natural endowments, the providential surroundings, and the successes of battle and administration by which the dominion of the earth was for the time concentred in him. God gave it to him through the instrumentality of his birth, genius and arms. But there is no such mediation of human activities, accidents and conquests in this case. There is no intermediate agency whatever — no giving to a secondary actor. Everything of this sort is entirely set aside, and "the God of heaven" himself, directly and exclusively, is the setter-up of this kingdom. Barnes properly observes that "though the other kingdoms here referred to were under the divine control, and were designed to act an important part in preparing the world for this, yet they are not represented as deriving their origin directly from Heaven. They were founded in the usual manner of earthly monarchies; but this was to have a heavenly origin."

It is specifically said to be "cut out of the mountain *without hands*." No human agency was concerned in bringing it into being or into the action assigned to it. It is brought forth by some invisible, superhuman power. It moves forward to its work without the help of any other potency than that inherent in its mystic self, by which also it expanded into its vast proportions. Some suppose that the mountain from which it comes is named for the sake of verisimilitude only, and is not to be regarded as significant. But this misses one of the sublimest ideas in the whole representation. I do not agree with Augustine that this primal mountain is the Jewish nation, nor with others that it means the hill-country of Judea. Such notions belong to the littlenesses of interpretation which no greatness of names can ennoble. When we come to **"The Mountain"** in such a description as this we come to the sublime and eternal Original of all things, to the heights, massiveness and eternal permanency of immortal Godhead. Mountains always tell of Deity and His unshaken omnipotence. And from thence this stone comes forth without the aid of created hands. It comes, self-moved from the everlasting granite of the primal heights, to show us that it is most directly and intensely supernatural, heavenly and divine.

It entirely ends and supersedes all human dominions. It suddenly sweeps them away and takes their place. A popular annotator takes its action on the kingdoms of the earth to be "not sudden violence, but a continued process of comminution" stretching through ages. The same is repeated in a recent book of lectures on these prophecies. But this is another of those human glosses imposed on the divine word to save an untenable rationalistic theory. As Nebuchadnezzar saw the vision, the stone "*smote* the image" — *smote* it, as when a man strikes his two hands together or delivers a killing blow — smote it, so that the iron and clay upon which it fell "brake to pieces," as a vessel of pottery is broken when struck by a rock— *smote it,* so that every part of the great image *"brake to pieces together,* and became like the chaff of the summer threshing-floor, and the wind carried them away that no place was found for them." If this is not "sudden violence"— the precipitation of summary destruction— the quick and utter demolition of the thing smitten— there is no power in human language to express it. The whole fabric, from toe to scalp, is summarily shattered to atoms, ground to powder, scattered to the winds, leaving not a vestige of it any more to be found. And as that fabric includes in it all mortal dominion, that kingdom which so shatters it, and takes its place, must needs be supernal, and is neither originated nor administered by mortal hands or conquest.

This kingdom is supernatural in its qualities. It is inalienable and eternal, which cannot be said of ordinary kingdoms. It fills the whole earth, which is not true of mere earthly empires, though called universal. Not one of them, nor all of them together, ever "filled the whole earth."

It likewise abides perpetually with its possessors. Human dominion is ever passing from one potentate to another and from one nationality to another. Monarchs die as other men, and their dominion is left to their successors. The supremacy never remains with one people. They may hold it for a long period, but others are meanwhile developed, and they come and take it, and none can say them nay. But this stone kingdom "shall not be left to other people.' It cannot be alienated from those who possess it. The hands that hold it from the first hold it perpetually. It must therefore be the possession of a people over whom death has no power; for if they were subject to death, it could not be said that the kingdom is never left to other people. Firm as may be the grasp with which this world's monarchs hold their sceptres, death breaks it and the dominion passes; but this dominion is never to pass, and therefore must belong to immortals. Human kingdoms are limited in duration. Everything earthly has a termination. The longest-lived empires dwindle and fade away. There is no mortal rule that has not an end. But this stone kingdom is endless. The prophet says, *it shall stand for ever.*" Whilst, therefore, it has the earth for its theatre, and is a true and visible government and kingdom, it must needs be supernatural. It is on and over the earth, for it fills the earth, and takes the place of what was nowhere but on earth; and yet it is not from the earth, or of the nature of earth, or liable to any of the accidents or changes of the earth, or of the fortunes of mortal man or mortal rule.

What, then, is to be understood by this fifth, or stone, kingdom? Alas that there should be any difficulty or diversity on this the chief and culminating portion of this imperial vision! But great and wide diversity there is, and hence also a vast amount of unsound and erroneous teaching among expositors.

Some say that this stone kingdom is the United States! A learned professor of a theological seminary, recently deceased, has confidently given out that, in his judgment, "there is no possibility of evading the force of the argument which identifies the stone kingdom with the great republic of North America"! With equal conclusiveness he might have said that it is the empire of Russia or the republic of Liberia. Our government is not a kingdom at all, in any proper sense of that word. Neither was it set up by the God of heaven any more than was Babylon, or Persia, or Greece, or Rome, or any other sovereignty that has existed, if we except that of Israel. It has existed one hundred years, and yet it never fell upon the toes of the great image as explained by Daniel, nor shattered or destroyed any kingdom on earth, nor showed capacity for crushing out all other governments. It is not able to govern any one of its own great cities with decent respectability, and how is it to take the rule of the whole earth? It is itself compounded of the miry clay and iron of the toes of that image which the stone is to dash to atoms; and how can it be the stone which does this crushing? So far from being cut out of the mountain without hands, human governments planted and fostered its colonies, and revolution and the power of human arms and passions wrought it into an independent nationality. From the common clay of humanity, by the common processes in the formation of governments, it has come into being, and every year only makes it the plainer that the forces of decay and dissolution are rapidly gaining on the forces of self-perpetuation. Instead of having in it the elements of inalienability and eternity, the power is continually passing from the sovereigns of to-day to other people. Where are the Presidents, representatives and voters of one hundred years ago? There is also every intimation of the ordinary mortality in whatever characterizes our government. Indeed, there is not one feature in all the prophetic description but is contradicted by this notion. I say *notion,* for an interpretation it is not.

More commonly is it held and taught that this stone kingdom is Christianity. This is in the line of the truth, but far short of it. The stone does not here come upon the scene until the time of the clay and iron toes of the great image. When it strikes the colossus, it strikes those toes. It is in the days of these toe-kingdoms that it comes and does the breaking. But Christianity, in its greatest vigor, was set up full four hundred years before the Roman empire was divided at all, and a still longer period before those toes were developed, if indeed they be not still future. Christianity is a religion, a system of truths and moral inculcations — a worship; but it is not a state. To make a political establishment of it is to pervert it. Neither is it in its nature to smite and destroy earthly authority or to take the place of the civil government. It never struck and shattered secular sovereignties; it never broke any kingdom. All its professors are under bonds, as long as this present world lasts, to obey rulers, to submit themselves to kings and governors, and to pray for the maintenance of the civil authority. Taking the sword, they incur the pain of perishing by the sword. By their principles and spirit they may temper and modify governments, but to seek their destruction is treason to their Lord and their own salvation. According to the vision, the appearance of the stone kingdom was followed at once by the complete dissolution of the whole image of temporal dominion; but Christianity has been in the world more than eighteen hundred years, and no damage has it ever done to any human sovereignty or state. The iron empire continued on for four hundred years in all its consolidated power. Its division into its clay and iron toes was not caused by Christianity. And it still lives on in its influences and modern forms, as little in danger of being smitten and annihilated by any power of the Gospel as ever it has been. How, then, can Christianity be this stone kingdom which destroys all other kingdoms? Nay, Christianity is not an outward kingdom at all, and never was intended to destroy or to supplant worldly kingdoms. And it could not if it would. Well, also, has it been asked by one of the defenders of this defective theory, 'If the reference be to the first coming of Christ, how could Jesus be said to strike against a form of the Roman empire which did not then exist? And how can the breaking in pieces of the image symbolize the peaceful character of His mission and the quiet progress of His cause?' In vain has this man labored to make answer to his own questions. Besides, there is not an appointment, commission, or ordinance of Christianity, as we now have them, which has not an end assigned to it. By their own terms these are every one limited to this age, and expire at the coming again of the Lord Jesus. They are in no sense *eternal.* But this stone kingdom is without limit or end. It is to *"stand for ever."* By no possibility, then, can it be Christianity as now in the world.

What, then, is this stone kingdom? It would be passing strange if, having been able to identify so clearly and conclusively the several stages of earthly dominion symbolized by this image, we should, after all, have to give up the great climacteric of the vision as beyond identification. But I do not see why any candid student of the Scriptures should be reduced to so sorry a predicament. The whole Bible, from the first chapters of Genesis to the closing words of the Apocalypse, is full of this stone kingdom. As there is not a road in all England which does not lead up to London, so there is scarce a passage in all the volume of inspiration which does not conduct us directly to this stone, and to the very things which are here so graphically signified concerning it.

Emanuel Lacunza in his day could say, "All interpreters of Scripture, so far as I have had it in my power to examine, tell us that the stone of which this prophecy speaks is evidently the Messiah, Jesus Christ himself, the Son of God and the son of the Virgin. This general proposition is certain and indubitable." Our Lord speaks of himself as "the Stone" — "the Stone which the builders rejected" — the Stone on which whosoever falls shall be broken and which grinds to powder him on whom it shall fall. Prophets and apostles speak of Him under the same designation; and we may consider ourselves on solid ground when we take Him as the head and front of this stone kingdom in Nebuchadnezzar's vision.

As *"The Stone,"* Christ occupies three different relations to three different classes.

To the nation of Israel, Isaiah said that He would be "a stone of stumbling, and a rock of offence, for a gin and for a snare to the inhabitants of Jerusalem, so that many among them should "stumble, and fall, and be broken, and snared, and taken." Isa. viii. 14, 15. We know from the New Testament, and from all history since, how this was fulfilled. He was "to the Jews a stumbling-block," says Paul. He is "a stone of stumbling and a rock of offence, even to them which stumble at the word, being disobedient," says Peter. Thus, the

Jewish people fell upon *"this Stone,"* and were "broken," This is the first relation of this Stone, although not the relation referred to in the prophecy now in hand.

To the Church, or the company of believers in His name, His relation is of another character. He is still *"the Stone,"* but serving in this case a very different purpose. Peter describes it where he speaks of believers coming to their Lord "as unto a *living stone,* disallowed indeed of men, but chosen of God and precious;" and tells them that on Him they, "as living stones, are built up a spiritual house, an holy priesthood," nay, "a *royal* priesthood, an holy nation, a peculiar people." 1 Pet. ii. Whilst carping Jews and unbelievers are dashed to pieces against this Stone, He is the "tried foundation" on which those who receive Him are built. Accepting Him, believers are joined to Him and to one another into one homogeneous body, with one destiny. But neither the breaking by unbelief nor the building by faith and obedience is the thing which was shown to Nebuchadnezzar. That occurred at the first advent, and is going on through all these years until He returns again.

But this Stone has still another relation. Christ himself and all His inspired scribes tell of it. It is His falling upon and grinding to powder those rebellious powers who stand opposed to Him when He comes the second time. At his first coming, and during all the present dispensation, His whole bearing, so to speak, is passive. He is now the meek Lamb, the gentle Saviour, the pitying Redeemer, weeping over the hard-heartedness of men, and not breaking even the bruised reed. Men in their unbelief dash upon Him and are broken, but He does not fall upon them to crush them. Every ingratitude, injury, insult or persecution He patiently bears, and never once resents. But He has everywhere made known that there is a time coming when the measure of suffering, silence and forbearance will be filled up; when this Stone shall take on the activities of judgment; when "the Lord shall go forth as a mighty man, and stir up jealousy like a man of war, and cry, yea, roar, and shall prevail against His enemies." It is of that period He says, "I have long time holden my peace; I have been still and refrained myself; now will I cry as a travailing woman; I will destroy and devour at once," That is "the day that shall burn as an oven, and all the proud, yea, and all that do wickedly, shall be stubble: the day that cometh shall burn them up, saith the Lord of hosts, that it shall leave them neither root nor branch.' Mal. iv. 1. When this Stone came from heaven as the Virgin's son, through the quietness and humility of Joseph's home, no harm did it do to any one. If many afterward made shipwreck upon it, the blame is on themselves, 'for the Son of man came not to destroy men's lives, but to save them." But there is everywhere a time spoken of when He "shall be revealed from heaven with His mighty angels, in flaming fire, taking vengeance on them that know not God, and that obey not the Gospel;" when He will tread "the great winepress of the wrath of God;" when He will "take to Him His great power *and reign;*" when He will "grant to him that overcometh to *sit with Him in His throne,* even as He also overcame, and is set down with His Father on His throne."

Nor can there be a reasonable doubt that we here have the fifth kingdom of Nebuchadnezzar's dream. Here is a wonderful *Stone,* emphatically the Stone, cut without hands from the mountain of eternal Godhead, harmless and passive indeed for many ages, but the while developing into a glorious kinghood, gathering a mighty population infused and disciplined by His Spirit and mystically incorporated with His own person, as a unique and multitudinous empire presently to be revealed in invincible majesty and power. Babylon, Medo-Persia, Macedon and Rome were each many long years in coming to be what they appear in the vision. In each instance these long periods of preparation and gradual formation are assumed in the prophetic delineation, and necessarily implied. So in the case of the stone kingdom also. The period for the gathering of the Church, and the coming of the lively stones into oneness with the great Corner-stone, answers exactly to the preliminary and formative periods of the four empires. And as empires appear in the vision only in the condition and activity of matured and organized kingdoms, so we are to seek for this stone kingdom, not in the time of its formation, but in the time of its maturity, which would be only after the number of the elect is made up, and all are fully in place for what the kingdom as such is to do and accomplish. Christ is the mystic Stone, just as Nebuchadnezzar was that mystic head of gold, the king being put for the kingdom. The power, the dominion and all the populations of Babylon, as a state, were in Nebuchadnezzar as their head and representative; and so all Christians are in Christ, participants in His glory and sharers of His destiny. But the whole thing is only spiritual as yet. Christ was born to be a King, and for this purpose came He into the world; but for the present He is "as a man travelling into a far country to obtain for himself a kingdom, and to return." He is gradually getting that kingdom, in fact. As fast as men are being "born of water and of the Spirit" they are being incorporated into a grand spiritual state. It is unseen as yet, as the Head of it was received up out of human sight; but He is not withdrawn for ever. When the number of His elect is made up He is to come again, bringing His saints with Him. Veiled and hidden whilst His hosts are being gathered, He is then to be uncovered, revealed, seen, manifested in power and great glory. His people are also hidden now. No one surely knows them, and the great body of them is not in the world at all. But the sons of God are likewise to be "manifested." When their royal Head shall come in His glory, and sit in the throne of His glory, then shall they also "appear with Him in glory." And with regard to that stage of affairs the descriptions everywhere answer exactly to what is here seen and affirmed of this stone. It is the Church's royalty and kinghood consummated and realized.

It is a true and proper kingdom. In it is concentred all authority and power for our world. It is to dethrone, break in pieces and cast out of the earth all usurpers, spoilers and resisters of its principles and authority. It is formed and consolidated into a holy and invincible commonwealth by no powers of man, but by the invisible Spirit of God. It is made up of immortals. It is to claim and take and rule the earth as its own possession, redeemed and purchased with the blood of the illustrious *Goel,* who is its everlasting King. It is to extend from sea to sea, and from the rivers to the ends of the land. Nothing opposed to it is ever to be tolerated within its glorious territory. It is never to pass from its possessors — never to revert to another people. Of its glory and peace there is to-be no end. It is the kingdom of the Stone — the eternal representative of the eternal God. And from age to age, through all the ages of the ages, it is to stand and grow and expand, without diminution and without end! There is but one such a kingdom; and it is the sum and fulfilment of all prophecy, the crown of dispensations, the grand consummation of Jehovah's administrations toward our world!

It is of this kingdom that Isaiah prophesied when he so exultingly sang: "Unto us a child is born, unto us a son is given: and the government shall be upon His shoulder: and His name shall be called Wonderful, Counsellor, The mighty God, The everlasting Father, The Prince of Peace. Of the increase of His government and peace there shall be no end, upon the throne of David, and upon his kingdom, to order it, and establish it with judgment and with justice from henceforth even for ever." Isa. ix. 6, 7. It is precisely that which Gabriel announced when he said to Mary, "Hail, thou that art highly favored, the Lord is with thee: blessed art thou among women. And behold, thou shalt conceive in thy womb, and bring forth a son, and shalt call his name Jesus. He shall be great, and shall be called the Son of the Highest: and the Lord shall give unto Him the throne of His father David: and He shall reign over the house of Jacob for ever; and of His kingdom there shall be no end." Luke ii. 26-33. It is precisely that which is celebrated in the thanksgivings of heaven by the great voices that finally cry their triumphant halleluias, saying, "The kingdom [sovereignty] of this world is become the kingdom of our Lord and of His Christ; and He shall reign for ever and ever." Rev. xi. 15.

And yet a modern doctor publishes to the world that this cannot be, because "then it will follow that in the vision given to Nebuchadnezzar *there is positively no allusion to the most important fact in the annals of humanity — the Incarnation*"! Inveterate stupidity! As though the existence and sovereign administrations of a king did not imply that he was born! — as though the sublimest consummation and crown of our Saviour's work does not carry with it every fact involved in the constitution of such a Lord and in such an accomplishment! As well might we set aside what the vision told of Nebuchadnezzar, Cyrus and Alexander, because "there is positively no allusion" as to how or where or under what conditions these mighty conquerors came into existence! How, on such principles, can the vision refer to Caesar, since "there is positively no allusion" to the fact that Caesar came into the world in a way different from other men! I wonder and. am amazed when I see on what slender and silly grounds the professed teachers of God's word allow themselves to be turned away from its sublimest substance, and to be cajoled into the denial of many of its plainest and most pregnant texts. But no such boggling can hinder the fulfilment of the vision to its utmost letter. Twenty-five hundred years have added their seal of demonstration to the truth and accuracy of the prediction as respects the transient empires of this world; and how can it fail in that greater, more important and crowning portion respecting the immortal and eternal regency which is soon to take their place? No matter what reverend unbelief or blatant infidelity may say, let us remember the words of the prophet, that *"the dream is certain, and the interpretation thereof sure."* Our cavilling, skepticism and rationalizing will not alter or hinder the eternal decrees of Heaven. From the beginning of earthly empire Jehovah has made known the coming of a kingdom which shall break in pieces and consume all other kingdoms, and which shall stand for ever — a kingdom of which the God-man is to be the Head and King, the possessors of the authority of which are immortals, and the establishment of which in our world will be the consummation of that redemption to which all dispensations look and for which all the acres wait.

Lecture Fifth. The Golden Memorial; or, Nebuchadnezzar's Great Image

Daniel 3: 1-30.

I TAKE Nebuchadnezzar to have been a man of a deeper, broader and nobler nature than Napoleon Bonaparte. He was as great a warrior, and a much greater emperor. He was a man of larger intelligence, of less selfishness and of a much more generous and earnest mind. He was impulsive and hasty betimes, and even harsh, but his impulses were not mere passions, and were generally founded upon correct reasonings. He was quick in forming conclusions, and very firm in carrying them into effect. He mostly did his own thinking, and spoke and acted officially according to his own convictions, no matter against whom or what they went. He was a heathen potentate, absolute in his authority, but he had a deep religious sense, and was greatly influenced by it, and came the nearest to being a true servant of God of all the heathen kings of whom we have any account. When he beheld evidences of the presence and power of God he noted them, acknowledged them, and fashioned his actions accordingly. He had a conscience, and a strong perception of honor, duty and right. When he gave his word he kept it to the full. When he beheld sham and falsehood he was severe upon it. When he saw the divine Hand he bowed before it, and used his royal place and prerogatives to give others the benefit of what he himself knew and felt. When convinced that messengers of the Most High were before him, he honored them and gave glory to the God of heaven, and was not ashamed to make confession before all men of what his heart believed. He sometimes forgot himself in the midst of his greatness and glory, and took to himself honors which evinced an overweening pride; but when punished for it he frankly confessed it and proclaimed it to the whole empire, that men might know and fear the God of heaven. He never entirely let go the idolatry in which he was reared, but he never failed to hold and confess the infinite superiority of one God, even the God of heaven, over all the idol gods of his kingdom. He was not a saint, but he was nearer to being one than some who profess the true religion and have greater opportunities and fewer hinderances than he possessed.

We cannot but admire his reverent ingenuousness and appreciation under the proofs of the majesty and mercy and help of God in the matter of his dream. Though the sublime head of the greatest of empires, no false dignity prevented him from prostrating himself before the young prophet in acknowledgment of the one Almighty God, and of young Daniel as His true messenger. Such holy services as his heathen education and ideas suggested he at once commanded to be rendered.

Our modern savants and legislators seem to think that the state has no use for the doctrines and counsels of those who make known the mind and will of God; that the teachings of inspiration had better be excluded from the public schools; and that the less the ministers of Bible Christianity have to say or do in matters of education, legislation and jurisprudence the safer for the community. To such, of course, it was a great weakness in Nebuchadnezzar to think and believe that a man in communion with Heaven, and able to declare the rights and purposes of the Lord of kings was a proper person for the government to exalt and honor, or suitable to be made a counsellor, judge and administrator in affairs of state, or fit to be invested with the presidency over all the institutes of learning and schools of wisdom. That God pronounced him the golden head of a golden kingdom is nothing to the point; he did not live amid the wisdom of an age of "miry clay," and how could he be a right-reasoning philosopher? And yet I take his side, and claim that it showed his good sense as a logician, his sound policy as a king and his just feeling as a man, that he bowed adoringly before the Spirit of inspiration; that he acknowledged and proclaimed the worshipfulness and majesty of the God whom it attested; and that he at once constituted the man through whom it came "the ruler [*sultan*] over the whole province of Babylon, and chief of the governors over all the wise men of Babylon."

The facts narrated in the chapter now before us are generally treated as an unmitigated blot upon the character of this monarch. Neither do I intend to defend the transaction; but it is abundantly capable of being construed with the character I have ascribed to him, and without the supposition of a relapse from his favorable persuasions concerning the one Almighty God, or the putting of him down as a wilful and bloody tyrant and persecutor.

That he caused some sort of gigantic figure to be erected on a certain plain adjoining the city of Babylon, that he bestowed vast care and expense upon it, that he regarded it with very particular reverence, and that he made its dedication a very grand state occasion, — are facts very distinctly affirmed. That he expected and commanded all the officials of his kingdom to manifest the reverence for it which he thought to be due, and threatened to punish those who should refuse to regard his wishes and appointments in the case, is equally plain. But when we come to inquire what the figure was, what it was meant to represent, what the king intended by its erection, and what was the precise point involved in the act of reverence demanded at its dedication, the ideas are nearly as numerous and diverse as the commentators, and a great deal of far-fetched guessing has been done.

Some think the figure was a likeness of his father, Nabopolassar; others, that it was a likeness of himself; others, that it was an image intended to represent Bel the great Babylonian deity; others, that it was a new deity of his own; whilst Professor Stuart considers it an obelisk, or plain shaft, with an orb at the summit representing the sun.

The reasons which moved the making of it are also variously surmised. Dr. Gill has pretty well exhausted the common conjectures where he says: "It might be out of pride and vanity, and to set forth the glory and stability of his monarchy, as if he was not only the head of gold, but as an image all of gold, and to contradict the interpretation of his dream, and avert the fate of his empire signified by it; or to purge himself from the jealousies his subjects had entertained of him of relinquishing the religion of his country and embracing the Jewish religion by his praise of the God of Israel and the promotion of Jews to places of trust and honor; or by the advice of his nobles to establish uniformity of religion in his kingdom and prevent the growth of Judaism; or to lay a snare for Daniel and his companions."

To all these notions the Jewish commentators have added still another — to wit, that the king meant hereby to revive what was attempted in the matter of the Great Tower under Nimrod, which had been thwarted by the miraculous confusion of tongues. Any one of these suggestions is about as good as another, for there is not a syllable in the record to prove either.

Searching through the account for a fresh and independent understanding of the matter, it seems to me that every explanation which identifies this golden figure with any of the national gods of Babylon is directly against the narrative. It is nowhere named as representing a Babylonian god, or any heathen god whatever. The Chaldean deities had their particular priests and ceremonies of worship, but they do not appear in connection with the peculiar and novel solemnity of the unveiling of this figure. Three times in the narrative (verses 12, 14, 18) — once by "certain Chaldeans," once by the king himself, and once by the three accused Hebrews — the worship of the acknowledged deities of the empire is specifically distinguished from the adoring prostration commanded in this instance. This "golden-image" business is also given in immediate connection with the preceding chapter, which is so ill suited to the stereotyped conceptions of our every-day expositors that they are necessitated to suppose an interval of perhaps sixteen years between the dream and it, in order to give the king time to forget his vision and to be drawn back again from his semi-Judaism into the full spirit and life of the Chaldean idolatry.

As I read the narrative, this "image of gold," and the extraordinary manner of its dedication, are vitally connected with the king's vision, and related far more to the one Almighty God of Daniel than to any Chaldean deity. It was Nebuchadnezzar's own original thought, suggested by the revelation which was vouchsafed to him from Jehovah, and meant to be an official and national memorialization of that Lord of kings and Revealer of secrets who had thus shown him the character, succession, and fate of all earthly empire. So far from being the result of a change in his mind and feelings, or an obliteration of his convictions as described in the preceding chapter, this whole business was the direct fruit of those convictions, and the way his heathen mind took to express and materialize what impressed him so profoundly. God had shown him a great, bright and terrible image. He had learned from God's unmistakable prophet that it was a divine symbol of God\s wisdom, power and providence in the world, from his own empire to the end of time. It was so remarkable in itself, and so sublimely sacred in all its connections, relations and impressiveness, that it was impossible that he should forget it, or that he should not think of making some memorial of it, particularly as it related, first of all, to himself and his own empire. He had felt it right and due that he should prostrate himself before that spirit of Almightiness which showed itself in his dream, and in the prophet who had recovered and expounded that dream; and why should not all the heads of his kingdom be summoned to do the same? The thing was all mixed up with what we would expect in a vigorous heathen mind under such experiences and convictions; but it was a most natural outcome of a great, honest and original thinker under the circumstances. It was a new, sublimer and more knowing God than all Chaldea's deities which he meant to honor. The figure he set up was not that God, but it was the materialization of the wonderful image which that God had shown him, and which was that God's own symbol of His great power and administrations on the earth. Heathen as he was, how could he better memorialize this Jehovah-power than in Jehovah's own picture of it, of which picture he himself and his empire were divinely said to be the golden head? And with the Jehovah-power thus memorialized after the fashion of its own showing to him in the dream, what more natural than that all his empire, through its constituted representatives, the princes, the governors, and the captains, the judges, the treasurers, the counsellors, the sheriffs, and all the rulers of the provinces," should be officially convened to witness the unveiling of the figure, and to go through the ceremony of falling down before it in lowly homage, as he himself had bowed before the Spirit of that Jehovah-power in Daniel?

This view of the case fully explains every particular in the record, and serves to show, not a debased and oblivious apostasy on the part of the honest-minded king, but that the impression the revelation made upon him became a living power in his soul, which set his great and original genius to work to bring his whole empire into some sort of official accord with it. It was neither the work of a fanatical zealot of Bel-Merodach, nor of a tool of envious idolaters, nor of an arbitrary despot capriciously bent on changing the religion of his empire, nor of a tyrannical and self-deifying egotist, nor of a weakling in the hands of a set of grasping Chaldean priests. On the contrary, it w the work of a great, deep-thinking, honest-minded, self-poised and noble-meaning, imperial man, who had had a true, sublime and unmistakable revelation from the God of heaven, and who, under the devout and powerful impulses which it engendered, yet not entirely released from his heathen methods of thinking, laid hold upon his vast authority and riches to give what he regarded as a due and fitting national acknowledgment and memorial of the great Jehovah-power which had thus communicated with him. Hence this gigantic image of gold set up in a plain quite apart from the Chaldean temples. Hence the special, peculiar and intensely national character of its dedication. Hence the novel ceremonies of the occasion, and the imperial decree that at the appointed signal every office-bearer in the realm should fall down in lowly adoration before it. And hence, also, the very severe penalty foreannounced to come upon any one who should refuse to acknowledge and adore that Jehovah-power under the symbol which that Power had shown him in the vision.

In this view of the matter we are not only obliged to modify our judgment of the king's character, so as to give him far higher credit than that which results from the current representations, but the same goes a great way toward his justification in the severity he used in enforcing obedience to his decree.

Under the clear and full light of revelation and the divine institutes, which Nebuchadnezzar did not have, it is very plain that he made a great mistake, which can by no means be justified or excused on Biblical grounds; but the mistake was in the methods and not in the motives. It was the mistake of defective education, not of intent. He meant it honestly, to acknowledge and glorify that very God of heaven who had so remarkably communicated with him. He intended that his empire, through all its assembled representatives, should thus acknowledge that God in a tangible copy of the image given in the dream. All the depths of his religious nature, experiences and convictions would thus rise up to insist upon the duty and propriety of compliance with what he had so devoutly and honestly arranged and commanded. Was not the God over all gods and the Lord over all kings, who had so fully demonstrated His living power and purposes, to be reverently confessed by all lords and rulers? Was not that image the very likeness of that in which Jehovah had symbolized His divine powder and providence? Had not the king had ample proof that this God is God of gods and Lord of kings? Was it not right, therefore, that every officer of the realm should be required to give this token of reverent acknowledgment to Him?

Besides, taking this figure as the materialization of the great image of the king's inspired dream, there was to him a very sacred identification of himself and his dominion with it. According to the prophet's explanation of the vision, that gold represented Nebuchadnezzar and his divinely-authenticated rule and authority. To refuse obedience to his commands concerning it therefore took on something of the element of treason and rebellion, not only to

Nebuchadnezzar's authority, but likewise to that very Divinity which had so marvellously indorsed his sovereignty as given of God, who, by His own divine presentations, had inseparably connected it with the image the king had thus materialized. Not to obey his solemn and devoutly-intended command would thus necessarily present itself to him as a very great wickedness — a stab at divinely-authenticated sovereignty — a setting at naught of the very golden head of all divinely-invested kings — a casting of contempt upon the most serious and sacredly-founded undertakings of his life, as well as a criminal light-making of all the sacred experiences, convictions and devout intentions of His Imperial Highness. Under such circumstances the man would not have been a man, or at all up to the requirements of the situation, or entitled to the ordinary credit of sincerity and sensibility as an administrator of the government, if he had affixed no stern penalties to a disregard of his orders, or only connived at the transgression of them. If his foundation was wrong, his reasoning was right. Even our own free government permits no man to take office under it without oath on the Holy Testaments of God or solemn affirmation and appeal to the Almighty Lord of all, and annexes very rigid penalties to the violation of the same. From Nebuchadnezzar's standpoint it was but right, and no tyrannical harshness, that he should insist on punishing capitally whosoever should refuse the homage which he exacted. The fault was not in the exaction, but in the heathen error of undertaking to materialize divine things.

On the part of the Chaldeans there could be no scruple against a ready compliance with the imperial edict. They believed in a multiplicity of gods, and were accustomed to worship them in statues, symbols and graven devices. The falling down before this new image, even if it did connect with a new and supreme God, was a matter of no serious account to them, since it involved no abandonment of the old gods and worship of the empire. Even Nebuchadnezzar himself seems to have taken in the God of heaven, not as exclusive of all other gods and worship, but rather as the Athenians set up an altar *To the Unknown God* alongside of many other altars. Even if he did regard the prophet's God as the one Almighty Jehovah, he had not come so far as to disallow national and tutelary gods beside Him. And thus there was nothing whatever to hinder his heathen officials from falling down before this image the same as before any other sacred statue, particularly when their lives depended on it.

But it was different with Shadrach, Meshach and Abednego. From their standpoint, no other gods were allowable, nor the worship of any likeness of anything in heaven or earth. They would therefore have to go against their religion and their consciences to fall down and worship the image as the king commanded. Even though the thing was honestly meant as a great national acknowledgment of the Jehovah-power, they still could not be true to their religious principles and join in this prostration. The Sinaitic law and all the institutes of Moses forebade as well the worship of the true God in graven images as the worship of idols. A pious and faithful Jew could no more bow

51

down to a likeness of God, no matter whence copied or derived, than bow down to the idol gods of Babylon. Therefore, when the rest of the assembled nobles and officers, at the sound of the music, prostrated themselves adoringly before the image of gold, these men remained standing. They did not serve the false gods of their conquerors, and they would not now debauch themselves with a false worship even of their own God.

It was a very subtle temptation which thus came upon these young rulers, particularly if the king meant hereby to do national reverence to the Jehovah-power. Was it not, in some sense, an act of homage to the God whom they served? Was it not a wonderful concession of an idolatrous empire to the God of heaven? Had not the image been copied from the vision which that God himself had shown? Was not that gold the divine symbol of the king and government which it became them as good subjects to obey? Had not the king been very good and generous toward them? They were envied strangers at best, and why should they be so singular in such a small particular, and run the risk of being accused to their master and burnt in the furnace? Living, they might be of great service to their captive brethren, but provoking the wrath of their sovereign, they would only be forfeiting their own lives and entailing greater hardships upon those with whom they most sympathized. Why, then, hazard such interests by disobedience to their gracious king? Might they not, at any rate, direct their thoughts to the true God in heaven even while bowing down to this image upon earth? And over against such specious suggestions there was nothing but the simple command, *"Thou shall not bow down thyself to them."* But it was the command of God, who is above all kings, and no argument or earthly price or subtle glosses could induce them to disregard it. Let their enemies accuse them if they would; let the king upbraid them as ingrates, traitors, rebels, or even as enemies of their own God; let him strip them of their offices, disgrace them, imprison them or roast them in his ovens, — their minds were made up; their resolution was inflexible; *they would obey God rather than man,* though they should be burnt to ashes before the glass had run another hour. Therefore they kept their feet unflinchingly, though all Babylon fell prostrate in adoration.

Heroes were they, and models for all young men and all others when matters of conscience and faithfulness to God and truth are at stake. A true man in a case of clear duty will never sell himself for any price. He cannot be bought for gold or place or favor. No bribes can allure him, no sophistries can impose on him, no fires or furnaces can turn him. His soul is welded to unchanging Omnipotence, and nothing can break down his integrity. Had the religious character of these youths been made of the fragile stuff which so readily passes for piety in our day, we never should have read their names in this holy Book. But they had a faith which had substance in it, and it fashioned them into illustrious models for their day and for all after time.

Where Daniel was on this occasion we are not told. Perhaps he was sick, as he sometimes was, and could not be present. Perhaps he had duties assigned him in some other part of the empire from which he could not be spared.

Perhaps his presidency of the learned orders excused him, as only the officers of state were summoned for this occasion. Had he been present, we may be sure that he would have taken his stand precisely as did his three noble friends. He could not consistently have done otherwise.

But the eyes of self-seeking and jealous-hearted men are apt to find other employment than that of devotion, even while in the act and attitude of professed worshippers. And it often happens that those who make the loudest pretensions are the most sinister and heartless. "Certain Chaldeans — those very men who fain would be considered the most devoted — were watching these Hebrew youths, and under cloak of superior devotion pressed forward to make charges of irreverence and impiety against them. No honest-minded man is ever safe with these over-devoted people.

Nebuchadnezzar was particularly enraged when he learned that Shadrach, Meshach and Abednego had failed to obey his orders — not only because he had so highly favored and exalted them, but because from them, least of all, had he expected a refusal to join in a ceremony meant to be in honor of their God. That any in the realm should dare to disregard his imperial decree so publicly and in his very presence was indignity unpardonable; but that it should come from such a quarter caused his royal fury to rise very high. He summoned them before him. He indicated his displeasure. He laid his stern commands upon them with his own lips. He was about to repeat the ceremony for the special purpose of testing their obedience. He gave his imperial word that he would burn them up in a furnace of fire that very hour if they should dare to refuse the act of homage he enjoined admonishing them that even God himself should not be able to deliver them from his vengeance.

But their calm and unflinching answer was, "O Nebuchadnezzar, we are not careful to answer thee in this matter. If it be so, our God whom we serve is able to deliver us from the burning fiery furnace, and He will deliver us out of thine hand, O king. But if not, be it known unto thee, O king, that we will not serve thy gods, nor worship the golden image which thou hast set up."

The die was cast. The king's fury was full. The furnace was fired to its utmost heat, and Shadrach, Meshach and Abednego were bound hand and foot and cast into it. So intense were the flames that the very officers who cast them in were scorched to death.

The inspired writer of the Epistle to the Hebrews tells of some in ancient times who, "through faith, quenched the violence of fire." And here was an instance of it. The cords that bound these men were at once burnt off, but nothing else about them would burn. The king looked, and there they were, loose, and moving in the midst of the fire, with no hurt whatever upon them! Nay, more; only three were cast in, and, behold! a fourth was with them, and He so illustrious in form and mien that He appeared to the king *like a son of the gods.* The monarch's rage instantly turned to amazement. He cried out with wonder. He could not believe his own eyes, but, rushing "to the mouth of the furnace," he called to the men: "Shadrach, Meshach, and Abednego, ye servants of the most high God, come forth, and come hither." And out of the midst of the fire they came. Around them gathered "the princes, governors, and captains, and the king's counsellors," and they all looked and wondered, and saw and were convinced that not a blister or scar of burning was on the bodies of these heroic men, "nor was a hair of their heads singed, neither were their coats changed, nor had the smell of fire passed upon them."

A great and notable miracle of Israel's God was that day wrought in Babylon, and all the officers and nobles and princes of the empire were made the witnesses and heralds of it.

Skeptical criticism has railed out against all this, as showing too much of the wonderful to be believed. But with the Almighty one thing is no harder than another. He can make a blazing sun in the heavens with as much ease as make a daisy in the meadow. Some have urged that it was unfitting the Deity to show such wonders here. But who can decide what is and what is not becoming to a Being whose thoughts no man can fathom? And when we consider that millions of His chosen people were then in servitude in that empire; that the great object of their being there was to purge them of their idolatries; that no ordinary ministries for this purpose existed; that here was a great and mighty people that knew not God destitute of any effectual means of being made acquainted with His superior majesty and power; and that here was an assembly of all their heads and chiefs, who would thus be made to see His signs and to become the attestators and heralds of the miracle to all parts of the mighty realm, — there certainly would seem to be reason enough that here and now, if anywhere or ever, the greatest wonders of the God of heaven should be enacted. Who can say that there was not ample occasion for just such a display of the eternal omnipotence? And see also the effect. It so turned out that the white-heated fires, which would not act on the bodies of these men of God, served to send forth a glorious light into all the earth. The king lifted up his hands and cried, "Blessed be the God of Shadrach, Meshach, and Abednego, who hath sent His angel, and delivered His servants that trusted in Him!" A decree went forth from the throne to "every people, nation, and language," reciting the wonder, proclaiming the majesty of Jehovah, and forbidding, on pain of death, the speaking of "anything amiss against the God of Shadrach, Meshach, and Abednego." And these men were thenceforward promoted and honored by the empire as the living witnesses of the living God.

Many are the lessons which this record teaches. On the whole front of it there flames in letters of blazing gold that there is an almighty, living and independent God, unbound by Nature's laws and unlimited to natural forces, whose word is written in His Book, whose eye is upon His confiding servants, and who will never leave nor forsake them that put their trust in Him!

From the inmost spirit of it there comes the proclamation that if any kings or dignitaries or commands of Church or State go against Jehovah's laws, or demand obedience against His word, or undertake to keep conscience for the human soul, no true man of God dare obey them, nor shall he be the loser for his fidelity, no matter what penalties he may incur!

Around it, and on all sides of it, there sounds the admonition to every right-meaning young man, however prosperous he may be, to prepare for fiery times. The world is under an erring rule — a rule which often makes the greatest blunders when it means the best. Envious and malicious eyes are watching you, and eager to show their superior devotion by accusing you and bringing you into trouble. The way of faithfulness often lies through the fiery furnace, heated sevenfold to consume you. Therefore prepare for fiery times, and think it not strange when they come.

And in the whole make-up of it there stands memorialized for ever that *the only true expediency is inflexible principle.* It matters not for immediate consequences. God will make all right in the end to them that stand fast to truth and duty. They are, after all, the true heroes, and shall not fail of their rewards.

"The earth may drink their gore; their limbs
May sodden in the sun; their heads
Be hung on castle-walls and city-gates;
But still their spirit walks abroad;
Their names are in the Book of God;
Their honor is for ever!"

Lecture Sixth - The Great Man Humbled; or, the King's Insanity

Daniel 4: 1-37.

WE have seen that the God of heaven was pleased to select Nebuchadnezzar as the organ of a remarkable revelation touching the history and end of worldly empire. We need not wonder, therefore, that he should also be the writer of one of the chapters in the sacred volume.

The long passage which I have read, and upon the consideration of which we now enter, is entirely from his pen. If he did not write it with his own hand, he dictated it and gave it forth as his waiting and proclamation. It is also one of the most remarkable sections in this Book. It is the only complete state paper which has come down to us from those early times. It gives an account of the experience of a very great king, the official confession of his offence in unduly exalting himself, a narration of the warning that was given him before it occurred, of the singular punishment and humiliation which came upon him for it, and of the manner of his recovery and restoration. It is the royal sermon of an illustrious monarch, given forth from his throne to teach his subjects the majesty and dominion of the Lord God Almighty, and His claims to the reverence, fear, worship and obedience of all men.

It was not the first decree of this remarkable sovereign touching the honor of Jehovah, but it is the most ample and the most significant. The time to which it relates was doubtless long subsequent to the occurrences narrated in the preceding chapter. Nebuchadnezzar reigned about forty-three years, and the intimations of the record are that he was at this period well through with the many enormous public works which marked his administration, and the remains of which are still to be found. (See verses 22, 30.) The document itself seems to have been transcribed by Daniel from the archives of the empire, and from thence inserted bodily into this collection of sacred wonders. There are four leading particulars in it to which I invite your attention:

I. *The hinges prophetic forewarning;*

II. *His offence;*

III. *His punishment;*

IV. *His recovery and restoration.*

And may God help as to contemplate the same to our profit and edification!

I.

The ancients had a very intense respect for omens and tokens. The disposition to observe such things is one of the deepest feelings of human nature, and is one of the proofs that a strong religious vein is inserted in the very constitution of man. The most gigantic and inveterate superstitions have grown up upon it, and nothing has ever been able entirely to eradicate it. And whilst most of these systems are basely idolatrous, mischievous and degrading, and are therefore to be held in abhorrence by every good man, the fact still remains that God does thus betimes interfere for the government and guidance of men, the withdrawing of them from danger and sin, and the direction of them in cases which are unreached by other means. The divine Word is the Christian's great and infallible guide. To this he must at all times look, and to this he must ever contentedly and obediently conform. It is through this that God's hand is lifted up to direct us in the way of right, safety and peace. It also becomes a great sin and distrust of God to be on the lookout for any other light or to commit ourselves to any other directory. And yet the fact cannot be suppressed that special presentiments and foretokens are continually occurring in human experience, proving the existence of a special providence, and that there are occasions in which the hand of an ever-gracious Jehovah does show itself in extraordinary methods. Especially in great danger or impending calamity there is often some mysterious foreshadowing of it to put people on their guard and to divert them from peril. So it was in Nebuchadnezzar's case.

The king had another startling dream. It came this time quite independently of his own thoughts, and apart from any ascertainable earthly cause or connections. His own account of it is: "I, Nebuchadnezzar, was at rest in my house, and flourishing in my palace." He had been successful in his wars and in all his administrations. His enemies had all been effectually subdued, and everything was quiet and prosperous in his empire. He had succeeded in making Babylon one of the wonders of the world. Everything to which he had laid his hand had turned out favorably. There remained nothing more to be desired to satisfy his largest ambition as a man or to add to his glory as a great and wise king. And while he was thus at rest in his house and flourishing in his palace this dream came to him. He 'saw, and behold a tree in the midst of the earth, and the height thereof was very great. The tree grew, and was strong, and the height thereof reached unto heaven, and the sight thereof to the end of all the earth; the leaves thereof were fair, and the fruit thereof much, and it was meat for all: the beasts of the field had shadow under it, and the fowls of the heaven dwelt in the boughs thereof, and all flesh fed of it." From among the mysterious heavenly agencies there appeared one who "cried aloud, and said, Hew down the tree, and cut off his branches, shake off his leaves, and scatter his fruit: let the beasts get away from under it, and the fowls from his branches: nevertheless leave the stump of his roots in the earth, even with a band of iron and brass, in the tender grass of the field; and let it be wet with the dew of heaven, and let his portion be with the beasts in the grass of the earth: let his heart be changed from man's, and let a beast's heart be given unto him; and let seven times pass over him." And it was further added by the mysterious speaker that this was "the decree of the watchers, and the demand by the word of the holy ones, to the intent that the living may know that the Most High ruleth in the kingdom of men, and giveth it to whomsoever he will."

Though the king was utterly at a loss to understand the meaning of this dream, it is plain, from the very terms of it, that it was meant to give him a serious admonition and threat against pride and self-glorification, declaring all possessions, power and greatness to be God's gifts, distributed according to His will, and ever to be gratefully acknowledged as proceeding only from His sovereign goodness — indicating at the same time the speedy humiliation of those who give themselves the glory for what they have, achieve or enjoy. So also was it interpreted by the prophet, who told the king that this vision related to him, that it was a divine forewarning of calamities to come upon him, and that the only possible way of escaping them was to be admonished by it to humble himself before God, to break off his sins by righteousness, and his iniquities by showing mercy to the poor. (See verse 27.)

Some have wondered that he should send again for "the magicians, the astrologers, the Chaldeans, and the soothsayers" after their miserable failure on a former similar occasion. But it must be remembered that Daniel was now for a long time the appointed head and master of these orders (ii. 4; iv. 9; v. 11), and that in summoning them the king necessarily included him, and most likely had him specially in mind. You will also notice that he came in this instance without any personal summons. The reason of his coming was the same decree which had brought the others. But he sent them first, and himself remained in the background until they had tried their skill and proved their incompetency. The king says of all these "wise men of Babylon" that he "told the dream before them, but they did not make known the interpretation thereof." If they ventured to say anything, they utterly failed to satisfy him. "But at the last," says the king, "Daniel came in before me, Belteshazzar by name, in whom is the spirit of the holy gods, and before him I told the dream." A wonderful testimony to the feeling-ness, the courtesy and the courtly faithfulness of the prophet is also given by the king. Having related the dream to him, the king says, "Daniel was astonished for one hour, and his thoughts troubled him;" neither did he say a word till encouragingly entreated by the king not to hesitate, but to tell out the whole interpretation without fear or alarm. Whereupon the faithful prophet answered: "My lord, the dream be to them that hate thee, and the interpretation thereof to thine enemies;" and then proceeded to expound the sore personal calamities which God had thus pre-intimated, exhorting the king to such duties as would most contribute to ward off the threatened disaster.

Nebuchadnezzar was thus fully forewarned. God, by means of the dream and the honest interpretation and comments of the prophet, had foreshown him what would be the result of indulging in too proud a spirit over his greatness, or of a failure to acknowledge and adore the Lord Almighty as the sublime Governor of the nations and the Source, Giver and Sustainer of all that any man possesses.

II.

We would suppose that such a sacred and impressive forewarning and admonition could not fail of the most salutary effect. But there is nothing more treacherous and deceitful than poor depraved human nature. Nebuchadnezzar doubtless intended to profit to the full from the counsel he had received. He had the utmost confidence in the wisdom and inspiration of the prophet. He had every reason to accept the whole presentation as a veritable message from God. Nor was it in the composition of this monarch's character to make light of so evident a communication from the Deity, whose signs and wonders he had beheld. But it is hard for rich and great men, in the midst of their glories, powers, flatteries and cares, to be true and faithful to all that they know, feel and confess of their duty and of what is right and proper. The Saviour and His apostles have remarked upon the great difficulty of such to enter the kingdom of heaven. And Nebuchadnezzar was not an exception. If ever man had reason to take honor to himself and to be proud of his achievements, it was this king; and if ever such a man was kept from this sin in such a case, it could only be by the most marvellous power of divine grace.

I have alluded to some of Nebuchadnezzar's great achievements. There never was a more successful conqueror. There never was a sublimer earthly king. There never was a more magnificent empire than that which he consolidated and established. There never was a more absolute human lord of this world than he. Even to this day the whole territory of Babylon, north, south, east and west, tells of him, and attests the grandeur of his reign beyond that of any one other man that has lived. Babylon was a distinguished city before his day. Ninus and Semiramis are said to have done much to make it illustrious. But the Babylon of Nebuchadnezzar was tenfold more what he found it than the Rome of Augustus Caesar was more than the preceding Rome of the Republic, or than the Paris of the Napoleons was more than the Paris of the First Revolution. The old Babylon occupied but one side of the river; Nebuchadnezzar re-formed it on that side, and extended it to equal greatness on the other, connecting the two with splendid bridges, lining the river with walls and gates, and surrounding the whole with tremendous enclosures, such as perhaps never existed anywhere but there. He built a second palace, a very wonder of architecture, the grounds of which were ornamented with those famous artificial mountains and hanging gardens constructed in imitation of the Median hills which his Median wife so missed in the flat country around Babylon. But this was only a fraction of his works. Explorers report the ruins of Babylonia as spread over two hundred square miles, and that nine-tenths of the bricks found all over this space are stamped with Nebuchadnezzar's name. Sir Henry Rawlinson writes: "I have examined the bricks in situ belonging, perhaps, to one hundred different towns and cities in the neighborhood of Bagdad, and I never found any other legend than that of Nebuchadnezzar, son of Nabopolassar, king of Babylon." Another of these indefatigable antiquarians, the Rawlinsons, writes: "It is scarcely too much to say that but for Nebuchadnezzar the Babylonians would have had no place in history. At any rate, their actual place is owing almost entirely to this prince, who to the military talents of an able general added a grandeur of artistic conception and a skill in construction which place him on a par with the greatest builders of antiquity."

Now, with all on his hands and engaging his thoughts and energies which this would imply, it is not remarkable that his attention should be drawn away from his dream and its moral monitions, or that his heart should be very greatly elated over his magnificent achievements. Where is the public man among us who could be entrusted with such glory without having his head completely turned and his self-consequence lifted higher than the stars?

Full a year had now passed since the king had the dream, and received the interpretation and admonition of the prophet. He was walking upon the high places of his palace, the enclosure of whose walls was six miles square, ornamented with battlements and towers. All around and beneath him lay the city with its grand avenues and one hundred mighty gates. He looked and admired, and said, *Is not this great Babylon, that I have built for the house of the kingdom by the might of my power, and for the honor of my majesty?*

As men ordinarily reckon and speak, there would not seem to be much out of the way in such a remark. It was, above all men, *his work*. Babylon was a great and glorious city, and it had come to be what it was chiefly through him. As we hear men refer to their works and doings, we would expect any of them to express themselves after the same style. I know of none who would not speak in the same way, and with much the same emotions, under the same circumstances. But this only shows, not that Nebuchadnezzar was innocent, but that humanity all over is very perverted and wrong. It will leave God out of everything creditable wherever it can. It will parade its own puny self, powers and achievements whenever occasion presents. It loves to contemplate what it has done. If in anything it favorably differs from one or another or from the general mass of men, it inwardly gloats over it and rejoices itself in its superiority, not remembering Who it is that maketh it to differ, and whose alone is the credit and honor for it all. And Nebuchadnezzar fell into the common offensive and criminal mistake which so deeply inheres in all unsanctified humanity. Taking a survey of his magnificent honors and achievements, he refers them exultingly to himself — to his own genius, strength and wisdom — and leaves out that eternal Providence without which he was no more than the meanest beggar or the dirtiest dog in all his kingdom. He had himself confessed that, of a truth, Jehovah is God of gods and Lord of kings. He had heard the heavenly "watcher" say, and Daniel repeat, that it was his duty, as that of all men, to know and realize that it is the Alost High that ruleth in the kingdom of men and giveth it to whomsoever He will. But in the moment of transport over what had been accomplished through his instrumentality he forgot all this, and set everything down to his own credit. He knew better, as all men know better when they do such things, but when he looked on the glory of the city he had so exalted and adorned, his pride and vain-glory got the mastery over all his better knowledge and the prophetic warnings, and his soul was lifted up in exultation over his own wisdom and might. The gracious God above, from whom, apart from any worth or deservings of his, he had all that distinguished him from any other member of the race, was completely thrown out of his reckoning. And thus he lent his soul and speech to a miserable atheistic pride, which seems to have been this man's besetting sin — the besetting sin of all human greatness and success — which reached its culmination as he thus walked and spoke amid the towers and battlements of his glorious palace.

III.

But our God is a jealous God, and His glory will He not give to another. They that walk in pride He also is able to abase, as Nebuchadnezzar soon found out to his sorrow. The "watcher" had said, Hew down the towering tree to its stump; let the heart of him whom it represents be unmanned, let the soul so brutish have his portion with the beasts, till seven times pass over him!

Twelve months of trial and opportunity for reform were given. God is slow in the execution of His threatenings, and very long-suffering to usward. But when wickedness has come to the full His visitations are apt to be terrifically sudden. And so it was in this instance. "While the word" — the God-ignoring word — "was in the king's mouth there fell a voice from heaven: O King Nebuchadnezzar, to ihe it is spoken, the kingdom is departed from thee; and they shall drive thee from men, and thy dwelling shall be with the beasts of the field; they shall make thee to eat grass as oxen, and seven times shall pass over thee, until thou know that the Most High ruleth in the kingdom of men, and giveth it to whomsoever He will. And the same hour was the thing fulfilled upon Nebuchadnezzar."

Precisely what this punishment was we may not be able to tell, but by consulting the records of medical science we may still come to some reasonably accurate idea of it. That it was a species of insanity would seem to be implied. With reference to his recovery the king says, *"mine understanding returned unto me;"* which cannot well mean anything else than that he had been in some sense and degree demented.

Mania and lunacy take on very many, and often very curious, forms. Among others is a certain melancholic alienation, in which the subjects fancy themselves animals, and set themselves to act and live as the particular creatures they imagine themselves to be. Cases are on record from very early times, and are still of common occurrence, in which persons take on the belief that they are wolves, dogs, lions, cats, cocks and the like, reproducing in themselves the habits of these creatures. An alienation of this sort seems to be referred to by Virgil in his sixth *Eclogue,* in which persons are represented as lowing like cattle, looking for their horns, fearing to be yoked, and ranging the pathless woods as veritable bovine creatures.

The expressions with regard to Nebuchadnezzar — that his heart was made like the beast's, that a beast's heart was given him, that his dwelling was with the wild asses, that he did eat grass as oxen — would seem to identify his affliction with this form of mental disease. The rest of the description would also accord entirely with such an affection. And, although its occurrence is rare, we must not lose sight of the fact that it was brought upon the king by the foretold and special judgment of God, who was at no loss to fill out every particular in the account. With this fact given, it does not rest on us to show that the affection was wholly natural, or that in the ordinary course of things one suffering thus for seven years might still be curable. The affliction was meant to be extraordinary, and the falling of it within a category of common affections, though with peculiar features of its own, serves the double purpose of showing that it was not at all unlikely on the one hand, and that it was not a mere natural disorder on the other.

The affliction likewise ran in direct contrast with the offence of which it was the punishment. The king's self-congratulation was, in principle, an ungodding of the Deity, and he was visited with a dehumanizing of the man. He put himself and his own agency above the Lord of kings or into His place, and God put him in the brute's place, and even into a sub-brutish humiliation. He had unduly glorified his own genius, and God turned that genius into the low instinct of an ox that eateth grass, as helpless and as base as if he had never been a man at all. And the description throughout exhibits one of the most melancholy and horrible afflictions that could well come upon a human being, to say nothing of so sublime a potentate as Nebuchadnezzar.

Think of that king, the sovereign of the earth, the grandest genius of his age, who had written his name in conquests and constructions the fame of which still echoes and resounds through all the world — think of him as he that day walked the ramparts of his palace, the most honored and successful man that lived, the golden head of the golden empire in its golden age — think of him as he looked forth to the rising of the sun and to the setting thereof, and numbered all the nations on whom its rays fell as his own subjects and tributaries — and then come hither to these wild morasses. Behold here among the cattle the figure of a man, who for these many long years has avoided all human habitations. See him feeding on the young grass with the oxen, herding with them, lowing like them and esteeming himself one of them. Observe his nails coiled around his toes and fingers like eagles' claws. Mark his nakedness, his matted hair and beard, the feathery and swine-like bristles that hang from his body. Note his dull expression, his avoidance of the presence of man, his refusal to hear or answer anything that any human being may say to him. Look at his revolting beastlike mien and beastlike habits and mimicries of all beastlike ways. Contemplate the obstinacy with which he resists being housed, how thoroughly enchanted he is with his beastly condition and associations, and how profound is his persuasion that he is a beast, and that everything human had better keep far from him. Is this a man? Will you call it a king? Does it look to you like a mighty conqueror, before whom the nations stand in awe? Would you suppose it the builder of great Babylon and author of those riches and wonders? Can such an object be the possessor of a sceptre which sways dominion over all the earth? Would it ever enter your thoughts that this is the sublime and matchless golden head of all human empire? Can it be the great Nebuchadnezzar? Ah me! it is even so, and this is the punishment which the Almighty hath sent upon him for ignoring his Maker and taking to himself honor which belongs alone to Jehovah. Verily, "it is a fearful thing to fall into the hands of the living God."

IV.

"Seven years" was this terrible humiliation of the vain-glorious king to last. Whether such an affection is ordinarily curable after so long a standing we need not inquire. It came as a special judgment of God, and its duration was determined in advance by the same power which brought it upon him. It is enough to know that the man recovered, returned to his throne, and lived to tell his subjects and to record for all time the facts in the case.

Whether the king retained his inner consciousness during this great calamity we cannot fully determine. The medical records refer to cases of corresponding affection in which neither consciousness nor memory was seriously impaired, though the patients persisted in maintaining that now they were beasts, and wondered that any should not so regard them. Dr. Browne, the eminent commissioner of the Board of Lunacy for Scotland, gives it as his opinion, made up from an experience of thirty years in the treatment of mental alienations, that "the idea of personal identity is but rarely enfeebled, and that it is never lost." He says: "All the angels, devils, dukes, lords, kings, gods many,' that I have had under my care remained what they were before they became angels, dukes, etc., in a sense, and even nominally." This author says: "I have seen a man declaring himself to be the Saviour sign himself *James Thomson,* and attend worship regularly, as if the notion of divinity had never entered into his head." And in reference to the very case now before us he says: "I think it probable that Nebuchadnezzar retained a perfect consciousness that he was Nebuchadnezzar during the whole course of his degradation." But whether he retained it all the while or not, he did have it as he drew near the termination of his malady. His affliction struck him while a voice from heaven was speaking, and as his reason returned he found himself looking up. He says: "At the end of the days I Nebuchadnezzar lifted up mine eyes unto heaven.' He knew then that he was a grievous sufferer, and looked imploringly for mercy and help whence alone they could come. It was a look of reverence for the God of heaven, and a look of prayer for pity. But it was an availing look. He says with joy and gratitude, "Mine understanding returned unto me, and I blessed the Most High, and I praised and honored Him that liveth for ever, whose dominion is an everlasting dominion, and His kingdom from generation to generation; who doeth according to His will in the army of heaven, and among the inhabitants of the earth, and none can stay His hand, or say unto Him, What doest Thou?

He had endured a most signal judgment, but it had upon him the intended' effect. It humbled his pride. It brought him to the most devout personal recognition of the true God. It set him to work to do all in his power to honor and glorify Jehovah. It took away from his heart all shame or hesitation in confessing his sin, and the justice of the punishment he had suffered on account of it. It made him a penitent adorer and royal missionary of the true God. Not a great golden statue now, but his own imperial station, his recovered reason, his softened heart, his royal pen, himself and all his power and faculties as a king, were dedicated to that infinite One whose majesty he had offended, whose judgment he had suffered, and whom all men should fear, worship, and obey. He transmuted his throne into a pulpit and his state papers into sermons, that his erring subjects might learn the wonders of Omnipotence, be led to honor the high God, and have peace multiplied unto them through His name. He had "learned that the heavens do rule;" and now his royal desire was that all people, nations and languages that dwell in all the earth might learn the same, without coming to it through such sorrows as he had felt. He had through deep waters reached the better shore, and he now sung his psalm of royal praise to the "King of heaven, all whose works are truth, and His ways judgment." He had come to a pious appreciation of "the signs and wonders that the high God had wrought toward him;" and, touched with that beneficent missionary-fire which always attends a true experience of grace, he now would have all men reverence and adore that same almighty Being who is able to humble all the children of pride.

Men have debated whether his was a full and genuine conversion or not. To me it seems as if everything that could be expected under the circumstances was actually wrought. There breathes through the whole document so quiet, candid, earnest and beautiful a spirit that I know not how to explain it without referring it to a thorough transformation of his entire character, which only the converting grace of God could work. The offensive pride of the heathen autocrat gave place to that penitent humility which frankly confesses its sin and blesses the Hand that chastised it. The man of war now prays upon all men the blessings of peace. The hand which held the sword, and wielded it with such terrible effect, is now stretched forth in benediction. The lion, so fierce and ravenous, is tamed into a lamb. The harsh enactor of decrees to cut men to pieces and to burn them in furnaces of fire now exhorts and admonishes them as a very prophet of God. If his language and speech are not yet completely purged of their heathen accent, and do not in all respects conform to that of the inspired teachers of Israel, we can still distinctly trace in it the soul of a true worshipper and servant of the Most High. Nor do I know by what authority any one can deny him place in the great congregation of them that know God and share in His redeeming grace.

This chapter gives us the last that we hear of this illustrious monarch. After this grand proclamation the veil is drawn, and all is hidden till the great day of final reckoning. And I take it as not a little significant that the last view of him which the sacred record gives exhibits him in the noble posture of official exhortation to all people to fear the high God, whose signs are so great and whose wonders are so mighty, exultingly praising, extolling and honoring the King of heaven. It tells of a great soul won to God and salvation.

That after so deep, long and total a disability he found his imperial authority still reserved to him must likewise be referred to the special providence and merciful goodness of God, the while foreseeing what a salutary change the sorrowful affliction would work. We may justly attribute it, in good part, to that generosity and sound statesmanship which led the king to put Daniel and the three other Hebrews at the head of things. Faithful to their God, they would not be unfaithful to their king, nor allow advantage to be taken of his melancholy sufferings to set up another in his place. These men knew that the trouble was only for a definite time, and that then the king would be recovered to his right mind in a still higher sense than it was ever before possessed. And, so far as their high authority and influence would go, they would reserve the kingdom for him, as the Chaldeans had done when his father died. Accordingly, he had this testimony to give, that when the days of his affliction were accomplished his counsellors and lords sought unto him, and he was established in his kingdom, and excellent majesty was added unto him. God's discipline, acknowledged and accepted, is always God's favor secured.

Let every one therefore behold, consider and learn wisdom. Who is it to whom no prophetic warnings from the God of heaven have come, admonishing of impending calamity and of the need to break off sin by righteousness and iniquity by showing mercy? Look, then, at Nebuchadnezzar, and be moved to immediate attention to these necessary duties. You may be at rest in your possessions and put far off the evil day, but the vision of approaching ill has shown itself and the word of the "watcher" has been spoken. Even while you are promising yourself obedience the hidden causes are at work to disappoint your hopes and blast all your fancied tranquility. Above all things, beware of a proud and self-glorifying spirit. You plead to enjoy yourself a little, but while you are surveying your comfortable estate, and flattering yourself with your achievements, and blessing yourself for what your hands have wrought or genius won, the stroke is making ready in the sky, and the hour of fearful humiliation is at hand. It seems to you no serious wrong to be a little appreciative of your talents, your learning, your honors, your beauty, your accomplishments — to look admiringly upon the lands you have acquired, the houses you have built, the reputation you have made, the fortune you have won — to indulge a little self-complacency over what you have made of your life and opportunities; but while the feeling of self-laudation is forming in your secret heart, who knows what judgments are ready to break forth and crush all your glorying into the dust? That beauty in which you pride yourself so much — that dignity, intelligence, reason and power of self-direction — that mastery of the means of honor, fame, influence and enjoyment — those fond possessions which distinguish you so highly from the common masses, — all may be wilted and gone before the completion of another hour! It is only by the unmerited favor of God that they are preserved unto you for a single day, and yet you would ignore and neglect Him to indulge your vanity!

"Oh why should mortal man be proud?"

Let his attainments be what they may, he holds them by a tenure as frail as the spider's web, which may be broken any moment.

"His brightest visions just appear,
    Then vanish, and no more are found:
  The stateliest pile his pride can rear
    A breath may level with the ground."

One slight touch from the hand of God made all Nebuchadnezzar's greatness as nothing to him, and imposed a degradation so melancholy and so deep that we can hardly think of it without tears of profoundest commiseration. Nor is there any guarantee for any one against the like calamity. There's no humiliation like that of insanity, and yet no vigor of intellect, no clearness of mind, no height of intelligence, no place in life, no birth, no blood, no virtue, no influence, even of religion itself, can secure a mortal man against it. And if we even should by God's goodness escape it, all the sublimities of mere earthly fortune and achievement must nevertheless soon be to us as if they never had been. We tarry here but a little while, and then death comes and ends all.

"Oh why should the spirit of mortal be proud?
 Like a swift-fleeting meteor, a fast-flying cloud,
 A flash of the lightning, a break of the wave,
 He passeth from life to his rest in the grave!

"The leaves of the oak and the willow shall fade,
 Be scattered around and together be laid;
 And the young and the old, and the low and the high,
 Shall moulder to dust, and together shall lie!

"The hand of the king that the sceptre hath borne,
 The brow of the priest that the mitre hath worn,
 The eye of the sage, and the heart of the brave.
 Are hidden and lost in the depths of the grave!

"And we are the same that our fathers have been;
 We see the same sights our fathers have seen;
 We drink the same stream, and view the same sun,
 And run the same course our fathers have run.

"They loved, but the story we cannot unfold;
 They scorned, but the heart of the haughty is cold;
 They grieved, but no wail from their slumber may come;
 They joyed, but the tongue of their gladness is dumb!

"'Tis the wink of an eye, 'tis the draught of a breath,
 From the blossom of health to the paleness of death —
 From the gilded saloon to the bier and the shroud; —
 Oh why should the spirit of mortal be proud?"

Lecture Seventh - The Doom of Sacrilege; or, Belshazzar's Feast

Daniel 5: 1-31.

THIS chapter introduces us to a new personage in Babylonian affairs, though one almost unknown to history except in connection with the scenes which are here narrated. Nebuchadnezzar is referred to as his "father," but he was the son of Nebuchadnezzar only in the second generation, as Jesus was the "son of David" in a still remoter generation. There is no word in Hebrew or Chaldaic for grandfather or grandson.

From certain cylindrical records found in 1854 in the ruins of Um Ghier (the Ur of the Chaldees, whence Abraham came), it appears that Belshazzar was the son and co-regent of Nabonnedus, who was the probable husband of one of Nebuchadnezzar's daughters, and who, through conspiracy, had succeeded in becoming the king of Babylon. When Nebuchadnezzar died, his only son, Evil-Merodach, took the throne; but he reigned only two years, when he was murdered and supplanted by his brother-in-law, Neriglissar, who reigned four years. After him his son, a mere boy, was made king. He held his place for only nine months, when he fell a victim to the conspiracy of Nabonnedus, who, together with his own son, Belshazzar, whom he made co-regent with himself, were the last kings of Babylon.

It was while this father and son were on the throne that the Medo-Persian invasion occurred. Nabonnedus, at the head of the army, went forth against Cyrus, but was worsted in an engagement with him. Taking refuge in the Borsippa temple, he was there surrounded by the Medo-Persian army, and held until he surrendered; whereupon he was honorably retired to Carmania, where he died.

When the father thus went out with the army, Belshazzar the son was left in charge of affairs in Babylon, where the scenes narrated in this chapter were enacted, and he and the Babylonian dominion came to a sudden end together.

This Belshazzar was a young, dissolute and unworthy prince. A recent writer says of him that "he was addicted to the lowest vices of self-indulgence, and felt no restraint whatever in the gratification of his desires. With all this there was combined an arrogance of the haughtiest kind, which would brook no interference with his designs, and would submit to no expostulation in the interests of morality. The severe lesson read by Jehovah' to his grandfather in that mysterious malady was entirely lost on him, and he went on to greater and greater excesses, as if to show that he had no regard whatever either for God or man." Daniel shows nothing of that sympathy or liking for him which he felt for Nebuchadnezzar.

Even the heathen historian Xenophon pronounces him an "impious" man, and instances his passionate cruelty in slaying one of his nobles for anticipating him in striking clown the game in a hunt, and in mutilating a courtier at a banquet because one of the women said he was handsome.

The attitude in which he appears in the matter now before us is quite in keeping with just such a character. With his father a captive, the armies scattered, and himself a prisoner within the besieged walls of Babylon, not knowing what hour he and his empire might fall, only the most infatuated and reckless of sovereigns would have thought of venturing upon such demonstrations as marked the last night of his life and empire. A proud sensualist, however, is always impervious to serious reflection so long as opportunity remains for the gratification of his passions or the indulgence of his selfish gayety.

We read that "Belshazzar the king made a great feast to a thousand of his lords." There has been much learned surmising as to the nature of this "feast." Some think it was meant to be an expression of a vain-glorious contempt for Cyrus and his besieging army. Some think it was the celebration of some repulse of the invaders. Others think it was an anniversary occasion, meant to commemorate the king's birth or coronation, or some victory on which he prided himself, or the founding of the kingdom. Others think it was a stated religious festival in honor of the gods, perhaps of the kind of the Jewish Purim or the Roman Saturnalia. I doubt if it was either of these. Belshazzar was hardly serious, devoted or patriotic enough to warrant the supposition of anything historical, traditional or commemorative in the business. The record says *he made it*. It was most likely the suggestion and outbirth of his own arbitrary, reckless and vain-glorious sensuality, looking only to that sort of display, enjoyment, revelling and defiance of all care or fear in which his debased soul most delighted. Daniel says he made it *"to his lords,"* leaving us to infer that it was rather in royal compliment to them than to the honor of the gods. Drinking to the gods was the usual concomitant of heathen banquets. Cyrus was quite as likely to hear of it whether it was a religious or state festival, or a mere prank of the pleasure-loving king. Belshazzar certainly laid himself out to make "a *great* feast,' which would naturally be very loud in its preparations as well as in its actual observance. At any rate, it was made an occasion of general license and carousing from the lordly court down through all classes. Gobryas in the camp of Cyrus, when the command for making the furtive assault was given, said, "I should not be surprised if the doors of the palace are now open, *for* the *whole city seems to-night to be given up to revelry."* (*Xenophon.*) Cyrus had received intelligence of a grand royal frolic to be held in Babylon. He anticipated that the night would be spent in revelling and drunkenness. And the facts prove that he was not mistaken in his calculations.

Such excesses, at such a time, betray the utmost recklessness and infatuation. It can be explained only on the old maxim, "Whom the gods mean to destroy, they first make mad." Such a king deserved to be dethroned, and such folly well merited the calamities which it invited and facilitated. The sin was not so much in the festival, for festivals, holidays and banquets are not necessarily wicked, though apt to degenerate into all sorts of excesses. The grand banquet is here brought into the foreground, not as the one lone and particular offence for which these sore judgments came, but in illustration of the character and spirit of the man. It was merely the crown or topping-out of a vast pyramid of rottenness, which alone, at such a time, could have brought forth and sustained these proceedings. It was simply the last stone in the edifice of Babylonian degeneracy — the last touch in the dark picture of Babylon's gigantic licentiousness, infatuation and towering impiety.

To say the least, it was a most ill-timed and inopportune festiveness. What if the walls of the city were great and high and its gates strong? What if it had provisions to last it for twenty years? With the army vanquished, the royal father a prisoner in the invader's hands, and the whole army of the Medo-Persian conqueror investing the place on all sides with persistent determination to reduce it to subjection, this was no time to be showing off such pranks of royal voluptuousness. Such mighty thunderings surely called for something different from this proud glee and merrymaking. No man with a grain of proper sense or right feeling left would have thrown open the doors and led the way to such a carousal amid such a state of things. It shows every becoming sensibility gone, a besottedness of mind and heart that leaves no place for the virtues of patriotism and rulership, and a licentious depravity and extravagance betokening the worst moral lunacy.

But the extraordinary excesses of the thing added tenfold to its heartless offensiveness. It was idiocy loading itself with intensest crimes. The "great feast" turned out to be a scene of mere bacchanalian orgies, in which the king himself led off. It was not the custom of kings to eat and drink before their subjects; but here all restraints were thrown aside. The dignity of the monarch was all sunk in the loose hilarity of the occasion. Drinking wine was a chief part of the performance, and Belshazzar familiarly joined the thousand of his lordly guests to do royal justice to it. He "drank wine before the thousand," and drank till he felt it, and continued to drink till it became his counsellor and put all sorts of wild thoughts into his head. "Whilst he tasted of the wine," the treacherous spirit of it began to work, and he bethought him to add still more to the glory of the occasion, himself, his company and his gods, and so made a decree which completed the abomination and sealed the fate of Babylon.

In the treasure-house of one of his gods were deposited the holy vessels which once did service in the temple of Jehovah at Jerusalem. They had all been consecrated to the Lord Almighty, who never is without respect to what has been dedicated to His name. Nebuchadnezzar had seized them when he took Jerusalem, and brought them hither and placed them where they were, but always treated them as sacred, and never had allowed them to be used for any purpose whatever. But what cared the wine-heated Belshazzar for the reverence of his grandfather or for what was devoted to Jehovah? He would show at once his independence, his contempt for the God of Israel, and his triumph over all the considerations which had influenced other men, by fetching out those golden bowls and making them do honor to his drunken revels. He therefore commanded to bring the golden and silver vessels which his father Nebuchadnezzar had taken out of the temple which was in Jerusalem, that the king and his princes," and all the women whom he had immodestly brought out to his infamous banquet, "might drink therein." It was of no use to remonstrate with such a libertine, if any had been so disposed; therefore the golden vessels were brought, and he and his lords and his women "drank in them." If any compunctions were felt on the subject, they had to be stifled and suppressed in the presence of His Imperial Majesty. So "they drank wine, and praised the gods of gold, and of silver, of brass, of iron, of wood, and of stone." Not only their ill-timed merriment, their trampling on the customary proprieties, and their drunkenness, but even their foolhardy and blasphemous insult to the most high God, is veiled over and cloaked up with a pretence of devotion!

This was as far as it was possible for human daring and infatuation to go. It was more than the powers of Heaven could quietly endure. The divine resentment broke forth on the spot. *"In the same hour* came forth fingers of a man's hand, and wrote over against the candlestick upon the plaster of the wall of the king's palace." The moment of doom had been reached, and here was the miraculous writing of the sentence. There was no legerdemain, no deception, about it. 'The king saw the part of the hand that wrote." His own eyes followed it as it traced the mystic letters where no hand of mortal could reach to do it. He beheld the black characters it left frowning down upon him from the palace wall. He saw the consternation of men and heard the shrieks of women. He could not read the letters nor decipher their meaning, but his conscience took alarm, and he could not treat it with indifference. All his courage, daring and proud bravado quite broke down. "The king's countenance was changed, and his thoughts troubled him, so that the joints of his loins were loosed, and his knees smote one against another."

Alas, alas for the dignity and bravery of those who think it mean, little and cowardly to fear God! They may think it manly to set at naught the scruples of a tender conscience and all dread of Jehovah's judgments, but their superior stateliness is the first to give way when the trying moment comes. Nor is there a more craven cowardice or dastard pusillanimity than that which underlies the noisy courage of men who defy God and glory in trampling moral restraints beneath their feet. Show me a man who thinks it great and heroic to despise the bonds of piety and the inculcations of religion, and I will show you a miserable poltroon at heart. The audacious and defiant King Belshazzar is horror-stricken and unmanned in the midst of all his gallant valor before a handwriting on the wall, not a single syllable of which he can read!

Off for "the astrologers, the Chaldeans, and the Soothsayers"! is now the cry of the cringing and horrified monarch. "Bring them quick, that they may read this writing for me, and show me the interpretation thereof! The highest honors of the kingdom to the man who will tell me what it means! He shall be clothed with royal purple. He shall wear a necklace of gold. He shall be the third ruler in the kingdom. He shall be next to me, as I am next to my father V Poor dastard soul! Why did he not consult wisdom before casting himself so recklessly upon this moment of alarm? The cry of *"Solon! Solon! Solon!"* comes too late when once the judgments for setting him at naught have been kindled. The astrologers appeared and gazed in mute astonishment, but the writing they could not read, "nor make known to the king the interpretation thereof.' The horror was only intensified by their presence and failure. "Then was King Belshazzar *greatly* troubled, and his countenance was changed in him, and his lords were astonied." What was to be done? An age of alarmed bewilderment was crowded into a single hour!

The queen-mother was in the palace. She had taken no part in the banquet. Her royal husband was a prisoner in Borsippa, and she was the daughter of Nebuchadnezzar. She had most likely advised against this whole demonstration. She knew what her father had experienced in his lifetime, and to what sort of doctrines he had been converted before he died. She had respect for his memory, for the convictions he had so fully pronounced, for the God he had learned to fear and honor, and for the noble men whom he was pleased to favor for their holy services to him; and she could look with no favor upon this ill-timed and impious behavior of her licentious sou. I am the more led to this from the fact that when troubles come upon the wicked they generally betake themselves to those whose warnings and good counsels they have despised. The coarse blasphemer, when taken down in his impieties, is most likely to send for the very minister whom he most hated and cursed before. And so Belshazzar now betakes himself to that queen-mother whose kindly admonitions he had haughtily cast to the winds!

And though the man was now beyond the reach of redemption, this woman does by far the best for him of all his lords and counsellors and wise men. There is a trueness, a readiness, a self-command and a fertility of resources in a genuine woman of which all kings and all men do well to avail them- selves whether in shadow or in sunshine. No sooner did the queen-mother learn what had happened than her thoughts ran back to the days of her fa- ther, and to the holy prophet who had served him so well. Taking in at once the whole situation, her mind was made up as to the next thing to be done. A splendid contrast did she present over against those astounded, pale and nonplussed lords and that agitated and trembling king! With what a steady composure she stepped into that banquet-hall, a little while ago resounding with the noisiest of gayeties, but now all subdued and silenced with terror and dread! Behold the queenly majesty with which she seeks to recover those blanched imbeciles to their senses! If woman is apt to be agitated with trifles, yet when some great crisis comes she has more calm magnanimity than a thousand lords — more sense and self-possession than they all. From her finer-strung nature she may feel it the more afterward and suffer the more severely under the rebound, but while the dread crisis is upon her the other sex sinks greatly by comparison.

The first thing this queenly woman said was a word of expostulation with the king for being so unmanned by his terror and perplexity. She set herself with motherly speech to recompose his shattered dignity and to bring him once more to himself. She knew of one who could read the writing for him, for in him was the light, understanding and wisdom of the holy gods. He had proven himself a matchless revealer of secrets, interpreter of dreams and solver of doubts to her illustrious father, and she was sure his prophetic power was adequate for this case also. Therefore she said: *"Let Daniel be called, and he will shew the interpretation."*

This time the mother's voice was heeded, and it was not many minutes un- til Daniel stood before the alarmed king. Though hitherto manifestly treated with indifference, he did not forget his allegiance and duty to his sovereign — even Belshazzar. Though neglected himself, he still did not neglect the king's business (viii. 27), and when he was called he promptly answered. He could do the miserable sensualist no good, but he still might interpret for him the sentence of outraged Omnipotence, and why it was pronounced.

In broken sentences Belshazzar recounted what had happened, pointed to the frowning letters on the Avail, and promised a glorious reward to the noble prophet if he would read the writing and interpret what it meant. The grand fee Daniel at once declined, but agreed to read the writing and to tell the whole meaning of it. And stranger was it than all fiction that such a banquet, conducted with such noisy defiance of Jehovah, should end up with a sermon to which all those lords, and even that presumptuous king, were the willing and eager listeners.

A splendid sermon also was it. With what grand and affecting reminiscences of Nebuchadnezzar did it begin! In what sharp contrast did it sketch the effeminacy and impiety of Belshazzar! With what directness did it point out the inexcusable and defiant wickednesses of its chief hearer! With what solemn and unflinching faithfulness did it tell the sentence God had written, and make known the doom which it was now too late to escape! It almost takes one's breath to hear the massive utterances roll from that holy preacher's lips. The solemnity of the scene almost overwhelms us.

Transfer yourself into that royal banquet-hall, and listen. There stands the tall and reverend prophet. Nothing of the obsequious courtier is upon him now. He has not a word of sympathy for the king in his guilty alarm. His voice, his brow, his words, his composed manner and solemnity, are all in deep accord with the Spirit which had traced those letters and with the awful sentence which was in them. He saw that the end of the impious contemner of the Almighty had come. He knew that he was about to utter the last words the royal sinner should ever hear in this world. And he spoke exactly as became the occasion. Fixing his eyes upon the pale and trembling criminal, now ripe for destruction, he measuredly said:

"O thou king! The most high God gave Nebuchadnezzar thy father a kingdom, and majesty, and glory, and honor: and for the majesty that he gave Him, all people, nations, and languages trembled and feared before him: whom he would he *slew;* and *whom* he would he kept *alive;* and *whom* he would he set up; and whom he *would* he put down. But when his heart was lifted up, and his mind hardened to deal proudly, he was made to come down from his kingly throne, and they took his glory from him: and he was driven from the sons of men; and his heart was made like the beasts, and his dwelling was with the wild asses: they fed him with grass like oxen, and his body was wet with the dew of heaven; till he knew that the most high God ruled in the kingdom of men, and that He appointeth over it whomsoever He will. And thou his son, O Belshazzar, hast not humbled thine heart, though thou knewest all this; but hast lifted up thyself against the Lord of heaven; and they have brought the vessels of *His* house before thee, and thou, and thy lords, thy wives, and thy concubines, have drunk wine *in them;* and thou hast praised the gods of silver, and gold, of brass, iron, wood, and stone, which see not, nor hear, nor know: and the God in whose hand thy breath is, and whose are all thy ways, hast thou not glorified: therefore was the end of this hand sent from Him, and this writing was written. And this is the writing that was written: *Mene, mene, tekel, Upharsin.* This is the interpretation of the thing: *Mene;* God hath numbered thy kingdom, and finished it. *Tekel;* thou art weighed in the balances, and art found wanting. *Peres;* thy kingdom is divided, and given to the Medes and Persians."

There was nothing more to be said. From such a sentence there was neither escape nor appeal. How the doomed king took it we are not informed, save that he commanded to have his promise to Daniel fulfilled. But *"in that night was Belshazzar the king of the Chaldeans slain."*

"The shroud, his robe of state;
   His canopy, the stone;
  The Mede was at his gate!
   The Persian on his throne!"

Friends and brethren: It is for our learning and admonition that these things have been written. They call up to us afresh the solemn truth, which none should ever forget, that there is a great invisible Power, high over all gods and kings, who carefully observes and justly weighs all the actions of men. An all-seeing Eye was on Nebuchadnezzar in his pride, and a great humiliation was sent upon him till he was made to know and confess that the Most High ruleth; and that same all-seeing Eye was on Belshazzar, who failed to profit by the awful judgment, but lifted himself up against the Lord, defied His providence, wilfully profaned the sacred vessels of His worship, praised the gods of silver, gold, brass, iron, wood and stone, which can neither see, nor hear, nor know, and despised the almighty Being from whom he had his life and breath. Such impiety and wickedness could not pass unpunished. Sin has a voice that is heard in heaven. It may be thought nothing of by men, but God notes it in His book, and takes account of every item of aggravation in it.

The Scriptures everywhere assure us that "the Lord is a God of knowledge, and by Him actions are weighed." Solomon writes: "All the ways of a man are clean in his own eyes; but the Lord weigheth the spirit." He puts every Belshazzar and every other in His balances, weighs every soul, marks every folly, and records every good and every deficiency. Every opportunity misimproved, every admonition disregarded, every ungrateful feeling indulged, every impulse of pride entertained, every instance of power abused or talents squandered, every word and act of profanity, every neglect and slight of Jehovah's messengers, every effort to get away from duty, every attempt to drown serious thoughts by sensual excesses, every sending away of God's servants to wait for a more convenient season, every contempt for the Bible and for those who believe and follow it, every thought and passion, or idle word that men speak, — all of them, singly and together, are surveyed and weighed, and written down in heaven against the day of final account. And did the children of pleasure, pride, selfishness and unbelief but see the reality, they would likewise behold a writing from a mystic hand frowning from the walls that witness their impieties, and containing a sentence of impending judgment. It is a startling thing to contemplate, but it is true; and the sooner our modern Belshazzars, sensualists, materialists, pantheists and atheists learn to know it, the better for them and all else.

Very clear and pointed also are the indications here given of what things weigh the heaviest against a man in these heavenly balances.

Belshazzar had miserably neglected and abused his office and place as a king. Political positions are not intended for the glory and gratification of those who occupy them, but for solemn and faithful service to the community which upholds them. God is strictest in His reckonings with those in power. An official personage is responsible beyond a common individual. People are apt to take it just the contrary, but in God's account sin takes its intensity according to office and place. A parent is responsible beyond a child; a minister, beyond his hearers; a judge or ruler, beyond an ordinary subject. Wherever there is power there is increase of accountability according to that power. And the wickedness of Belshazzar was the wickeder and all the more severely punished because he was a king. Office is a serious thing. It cannot be entered and handled as men please with impunity. Over its portals stands the inscription, *"Let him who enters here beware, for a jealous God is within."* Sins of office are the blackest of all sins. Abuses of power and place are the most offensive of all abuses. And Jehovah's most signal judgments are those with which He avenges himself upon unfaithful rulers and ungodly office-holders.

Particularly offensive to God is sensuality, licentiousness, revelling and drunkenness. It is the special defilement which He hates. It is a filthiness of the flesh and of the spirit which He most intensely abhors, and to which He has affixed His sorest penalties. This living for gayety and pleasure — this everlasting pampering of the flesh and its lusts — this steeping of the soul in the slough of mere carnal enjoyment and debauchery — this deifying of our likes and passions, and making everything bend and contribute to their gratification, — is just what marked the character of Belshazzar's life, the result of which is before us.

Still another item of his guilt was his total disregard of God's providential warnings. This is particularly charged upon him by the prophet as the head and front of his offending. Jehovah had shown His resentment of all vainglorious pride and exaltation of self over against Omnipotence in the tremendous humiliation He had sent upon Nebuchadnezzar. Belshazzar knew all this. It was fully written out in the archives of the empire, and published officially by the repentant king to every portion of the realm. It was too conspicuous, evident and publicly emphasized not to have -come to Belshazzar's notice or not to have been to him an ample admonition against the sort of life he was leading. But he disregarded and despised it. Without Nebuchadnezzar's sense or majesty, he was prouder and more defiant than his illustrious grandfather had ever been. With the example before him of the terrible heinousness and certain fearful punishment of such self-lifting up, he deliberately went into it regardless of consequences. He was adequately warned, but he profited not by it. God means that we should learn from history and take to heart the lessons of His providence. His word and acts are written, that we may note them and direct our way by them. And when people shut their eyes to all that He has shown, set at naught His counsels and refuse to take the instructions He gives, it is all reckoned up in His books as so much the more against them. These sermons unheeded and these admonitions despised will prove to be bottled thunders, to increase the dismay in the day of judgment.

But the crowning guilt of this dissolute monarch was his wilful and besotted profanation of the vessels of God's house. There was no need for them at the feast. There was no reason or excuse for invading their long and reverent retirement to bring them forth for any such use. It was nothing but a piece of base, defiant and wilful sacrilege. Hence the special mention of it as the intensest element in Belshazzar's guilt, and that which barbed the arrows of the summary judgment which befell him. And well would it be for men in our day if they had nothing of this sin to answer for. In external form, of course, there is no chance now for just such a profanation, but Belshazzar's sin is not confined to Belshazzar's circumstances. When the precious things of God's holy Church are seized and appropriated to gild and glorify a party or a sect or to satisfy the narrow whims of some modern Diotrephes, what is it but a desecration of holy things? When Baptism, a profession of religion, or the sacred Supper of our Lord is used as a passport to citizenship, a qualification for secular office, a means of gratifying friends, securing favors or gaining credit and standing in society, what is it but a misappropriation of holy vessels to an unholy use? When the Christian pulpit and the honors and sanctities of the holy office are laid hold of for mere personal display, the securement of notoriety, the building up of a reputation or the putting forth of doctrines contrary to the Gospel, what is it else than a profanation of what is sacred to the Lord? When people come to the sanctuary, bow before its altar, join in its holy services, mingle with those who worship there, and wear the livery and mien of Christians just to cloak their secret ill-doings, to pass for virtuous that they may the better accomplish their selfish ends, what is it but a prostitution of the things of God to a base unholiness? When the facts and expressions of God's Word, its pure and glorious truths, its sublime and awful doctrines, are taken to point a pun, to edge a jest, to sharpen a sarcasm, to excite a laugh, to raise a sneer, what is it but Belshazzar over again profanely taking hold of the sacred vessels to add to the zest of an impious carousal? It has also been remarked that something of the same is done when the sublime descriptions of the judgment to come, or the momentous history of our Saviour's Passion, or the grand visions of the Apocalypse are taken for musical exhibitions, using the holiest of words to intensify artistic performances, add to the emotions, deepen the effect and please the hearers, to secure applause to mere musicians. And still more does this spirit of sacrilege exist where the heart that was made for God is turned into a throne of Mammon, lust and greed; where the affections meant to cluster around Jehovah are all transferred and fastened on the things of earth; where the talents the Almighty has lent are all employed in the service of self and the devil; where these souls, which were fashioned to live and shine in the beautiful home of heaven, are made the filthy reservoirs of degrading passion and uncleanness.

We fault Belshazzar for his profanations, but in these things his sin still lives.

Seeing, then, how it went with this man, is there not reason for us to be a little anxious about how we stand in the celestial records? He was a heathen prince, and had not half our light and opportunities; we are the children of Christian lands and homes, reared under the sound of church-going bells, and familiar with all sacred knowledge from our infancy. He had but one great example to influence and direct him; we have thousands of them, and the ministries of many ages and divers dispensations. The vessels he profaned had been won in battle, and had become the property of the crown, which a heathen monarch might suppose himself entitled to use as he saw fit; the sacred things we have we know to be the Lord's, and we know, too, how jealous He is of their rightful use and His rightful honor. And if Belshazzar met a doom so sudden and awful for his profanity, what have many around and among us to expect? If he was so deficient when weighed in the just balances of God, how will it be with those who drive on with guilty pride and ungodliness over a preached Gospel, over a crucified Saviour, and in defiance of all the holy lessons and warning admonitions with which their way is strewn? If the pagan in his pagan surroundings could not escape, how will it be -with pagans who are such in spite of all the better light and hallowing influences of a complete revelation and a pure Christianity? If *Mene, mene, tekel, Upharsin,* was written against the heathen Belshazzar, what, suppose ye, stands written to-day against those who so well know their duty, but do it not?

O my friends, there is something peculiarly alarming in these inquiries. A world of ominous suggestion presents itself. I seem to be looking on scenes of judgment in which the wheels of God's almightiness thunder and crash through throngs of shrieking souls, the nurslings of unnumbered mercies, for whom there is no more help or hope! Among them are many whom I know, whose fathers, mothers and friends I know, to whom I have often preached and with whom I have often pleaded. I wonder, *Is this to be reality?* Ah, dear hearers, that is for you to decide. As things now stand with many, it is on the way to become reality. And when I see how light some make of it, how dull and dead many are to the whole subject, with what haughty indifference one and another turns from it as the veriest trifle, I wonder still more how can it otherwise than become reality, perhaps with all the suddenness of Belshazzar's end! God be thanked that it is not reality yet! Judgment still lingers. How much longer it will delay for the persevering sinner God only knows. Now, therefore, while yet the sun of mercy shines, let no one who hears me turn a heedless ear or trifle any further with the precious interests of his endangered soul.

Lecture Eighth - The Medo-Persian Prime Minister; or, the Faith of Daniel Tested

Daniel 6: 1-28.

THE chapter upon which we now enter very clearly attests the change in the government of Babylon declared in the verses preceding. It was common for the Chaldeans to administer capital punishment by burning. To the Persians, who were worshippers of fire, this was regarded as something of an abomination, and hence they destroyed their condemned criminals by casting them to savage beasts. The lion's den, in place of the burning fiery furnace, thus points to an entire revolution in the laws and administration of the empire.

The same is indicated in the division of the kingdom into principalities, and the assignment of a particular head or prince to each, whilst over these, again, were three presidents, one of whom was the chief over the other two, and stood in relation to the throne as prime minister or grand vizier. We thus find ourselves in the presence of quite another government from that which was administered by the exalted Nebuchadnezzar, and which perished with his infamous grandson Belshazzar.

You will remember that it was said in the conclusion of the preceding chapter that "Darius the Median took the kingdom, being about threescore and two years old." Critics, historians and antiquarians are much at sea in their attempts to identify this king. There are three different theories on the subject, and it does not seem to be possible, in the present state of our knowledge, to determine which is certainly the true one. Fortunately, it is not necessary to settle this question in order to understand what is here meant to be taught us. All the facts and lessons remain precisely the same whether we can tell who this Darius the Median was, or not. The strongest probabilities are that he was the same who is known as Astyages, in whose court Cyrus the conqueror was reared. He was, at any rate, the embodiment and representative of the Medo-Persian dominion over Babylon after it was conquered by Cyrus.

Coming into power in Babylon upon the fall of Nabonnedus and Belshazzar, lie would necessarily have his attention very particularly directed to Daniel, not only from his connection with the court for such a long succession of years, but chiefly on account of his interpretation of the mysterious writing on the wall, his prediction of Belshazzar's fall, and his remarkable wisdom in connection with the reign of the great Nebuchadnezzar. Very naturally, he would desire to avail himself of the services and talents of so wise, experienced and faultless a man. Coming in contact with him, as he thus would. Darius could not be otherwise than impressed with the extraordinary character of his talents and his eminent fitness to be selected as his chief helper in the organization and administration of his newly-enlarged kingdom.

Though Darius himself seems to have been a somewhat weak, impulsive and vacillating man, yet he had had a long experience in rulership, and was not deficient in discernment and wisdom in selecting trustworthy and competent men to whom to assign responsible trusts. Even weak and bad men like to have good and faithful servants, and prefer those with better principles than their own. It is a homage which they pay to virtue, even though they do not follow it. No matter how depraved people may be, they would always rather have servants whom they can trust than such as are as base as themselves. And whatever may have been the deficiencies of this Darius, he had the shrewdness to find out the best and most competent man in Babylon to serve him as his prime minister. He made Daniel the chief of the three presidents over all the other princes and principalities into which the realm was divided under the Medo-Persian rule. Such a man, in such a position, administering affairs with rigid exactness and impartiality, strictly honest himself and tolerating no dishonesties or falsities in others, and ever growing in the esteem of his king and in favor with the people, could not, in the nature of things, escape the envy and malice of those who suffered by comparison, and who found him in the way of their selfish ambitions. It is part of the disease that is upon depraved humanity to be dissatisfied and unamiable toward the excellences and honors of others. It is loath to bear anything above itself. It is the nature of the devil to be the accuser of the good and of those who are favored for their worth; and all his children have the same family trait. They are pained, mortified, chagrined and full of spiteful resentment at the superior excellence or prosperity of those above them. It is their delight to humiliate those who happen to be more favored than themselves. If compelled to give credit in one direction, they are exceedingly ingenious in finding some point at which to take it back. Admitting that Job is a just and upright man, they always have a "but" as to the motives in the case, by which to make it appear a mere sordidness after all.

"Be thou as chaste as ice, as pure as snow,
Thou shalt not escape calumny,"

And this is particularly true in affairs of public office. It seems to inhere in politicians and aspirants to hate and persecute every man in official place who honestly tries to do his duty and seeks to carry ethics into public administrations. Few men go into these arenas but with sinister and selfish aims, and if one in power will not share their plans for self-aggrandizement, flatter their pride, shut his eyes to their dishonesties and let his conscience go, he is sure to be assailed, to have charges trumped up against him, to have snares and traps set for him, and subtle plans laid to embarrass, disgrace or displace him. The greatest personal enemies readily make common cause to get rid of a man who has the principle and nerve to stand firm against their self-seeking, their oppressions, their robberies and their wicked ambitions. Though they may have been loudest in trying to put him into place, they will curse and defame him if they are not made sharers in his successes or cannot use him for their ignoble ends.

And so it was in this case. Daniel was an honorable and true man. His record marked him as the proper person for the place assigned him. He did his business on the highest principles of justice and virtue. He was faultless as a man and as an officer of state. The king suffered no damage under his administration. His excellent spirit commended him more and more to his sovereign the more he knew of him. "And the king thought to set him over the whole realm." This was unendurable to these Medo-Persian officials. It did not suit their ideas. It was in the way of their low aims. It was an embargo on their bribery and peculation, the particular vices in Oriental, if not also in Occidental, administrators of authority. It augured a pure court and honest transactions, which is never agreeable to underlings in power. Hence the conspiracy on the part of these presidents and princes to displace and destroy Daniel. No matter for the method, the end was to get him out of the way; and that end was deemed of sufficient importance to justify the means. They had the advantage of numbers. What one or two could not accomplish a general combination might effect. And so they went to work with all their malignant ingenuity to break down and destroy the noblest man and the purest officer that ever held authority in Babylon. They set themselves to watch and study him. With cold blood they subjected every feature and every act to the keenest microscopic scrutiny of hate. They brought to bear upon him all "that fierce light that beats upon a throne and blackens every blot." They thought of his advancing age — whether they might not sustain a charge that he had got beyond the time of life in which to perform such heavy duties with efficiency. They thought of his foreign birth and Jewish blood and former slavery — whether they might not develop a disabling prejudice from that quarter. They thought of his being with the Babylonians, and not with the Medo-Persians, in those wars and campaigns which gave them the kingdom — whether they might not on this ground vacate his right to such high authority among the conquerors. They dogged his steps, thinking to overtake him in some indiscretion whereby to blacken his character to his destruction. Had there been the least appearance of a flaw, they would have found it. Had there been the remotest semblance of a fault, they were fully made up to bring it out. And never, perhaps, was a man on earth subjected to a scrutiny so intense, backed with such a pressure of determination for his overthrow, as that to which Daniel was put by these envious and unprincipled presidents and princes of the Medo-Persian government. Few, indeed, are the public men who could stand the test of such a crucible.

But see what the true fear of God will do for a man! "As the mountains are round about Jerusalem, so the Lord encampeth round about them that fear Him.' With all the determination of these malignants to ruin Daniel, they could find no fault in him. Piety was rooted in him, and it wrought for him a pureness, dignity and integrity of life and character on which the most envious tongues could obtain no hold. They could sustain no charges against him as a man or against his administration. His hands were not stained with bribery nor his heart with the wages of unrighteousness. With patience and impartiality he inquired into all complaints, determined all causes and redressed all wrongs. He dispensed his patronage with justice and equality. His counsels to his sovereign were so wise that only prosperity came from them to the crown. His policy always proved itself sound and good. His management of the revenues was unimpeachable, his accounts correct, his receipts and disbursements transparently honest. He had no favoritism to indulge, no selfish ends to secure, no dishonest ways or equivocal proceedings to account for. His devotion to his God made him true in all his life and faithful to all his trusts. He cheated nobody, he oppressed nobody, and he never compromised himself with evil or connived at unrighteousness. And so pure and exalted was he in his principles and administrations that even the black-hearted conspirators, in all their anxiety to humiliate him, "could find none occasion for fault, forasmuch as he was faithful, neither was there any error or fault in him." Against their will they were obliged to admit and conclude, "We shall not find any occasion against this Daniel, except we find it against him concerning the law of his God." And scarcely has there ever been an eulogium passed upon any public man so justly founded, so completely attested and so absolutely perfect as that which these unprincipled Medo-Persian presidents and princes thus pronounced. It was hate itself doing reverence to the object of its bitterest dislike. It puts the character of Daniel high above all question or reproach. And thus in the midst of a heathen people, at the head of a cabinet of dishonest, envious and plotting officials, and surrounded with all the temptations which the indulgence of a confiding sovereign threw in his way, he went through the ordeal, as his three friends had gone through the fires of Nebuchadnezzar's furnace, without the singeing of a hair or so much as the smell of burning on his clothes. Nor was the miracle much less in his case than in theirs. Yet such is the protecting and exalting wisdom of honesty, and the glorious shield which a true and practical righteousness gives.

Having thus satisfied themselves of the impeccable integrity of Daniel, both as a man and as a competent officer, the eyes of these plotters should have been opened to their unreasonableness in wishing to overthrow him. Convinced of his fitness, worth and purity, we would naturally look for some symptoms of shame and remorse for the injustice they had done, and some signs of relenting and reparation. Plato was of opinion that if perfect truth and virtue were to come from heaven and manifest their real glory among men, all would at once bow down and worship them. But he did not understand the depths of human depravity. Perfect truth and virtue did come from heaven in the person of Jesus Christ, and stood before the eyes of men for years and years in untainted beauty and glory; but the children of this world, rulers and mobs, cried, "Away with Him!" and crucified Him. And when the devil of selfishness, envy and malice takes possession of the heart, no charms of virtue, no beauties of goodness, no adornments of innocence, no excellences of merit are sufficient to cast him out or to break his dominion. The more invincible the arguments of Stephen became, and the more his face shone with the brightness of angelic purity, the more his wicked persecutors stopped their ears, rushed for his life and hurried his martyrdom. And so it was in the instance before us. The more convinced these men were of Daniel's unimpeachableness, the more desperate they became in their determination to destroy him. There was one tiling, however, upon which they were persuaded they might securely count. They saw how true and inflexible he was in his religious principles, and if they could only devise a scheme in which he would be compelled to relinquish his religious fidelity or die, they were perfectly satisfied that their desires would be accomplished. To this they therefore set themselves with consummate eagerness, dissimulation and hypocrisy. Glance for a moment at the cunning baseness of their proceeding.

It was necessary, in order to displace Daniel, that they should somehow enlist the authority of the king in the matter. They were convinced that any attempt to impeach the prime minister must fail and react upon themselves. They determined, therefore, to leave all mention of Daniel entirely outside of their proceedings, and to feign a worshipful devotion to the king, as if profoundly concerned for the majesty of his person and the exhibition of his divine greatness. It was not uncommon for Oriental monarchs to have the worship of their subjects as representatives of Deity, indwelt and possessed by the celestial powers. The monuments and the histories attest that it was regarded as one of the noblest of civil duties to honor and worship the king as a god. And the movement of these conspirators now was to prove how much they were devoted to the sublimest honor of their sovereign, and to induce him to unite with them in establishing some royal decree which should memorialize his divine dignity and bring to him the sacred reverence which belonged to his person. The holding of the laws of the Medes and Persians to be unalterable was founded on the assumption that the king is something of a deity, and can make no mistakes. And this divinity of their king these men professed to be most anxious to bring forward and to have impressed upon all the subjects of the realm.

Nor could they see a more reasonable and practical way for it than for the king to sign and issue a decree "that whosoever shall ask a petition of any god or man" — put up any prayer or act of worship — "for thirty days," save of himself alone, should "be cast into the den of lions;" that is, publicly executed. This was, therefore, the flattering proposition which they laid before Darius. With many eloquent protestations of their own devotion, and of the sacred propriety of having every subject in the kingdom thus to honor him on pain of death, did they urge the matter. Nor need we wonder at the enormous wickedness of it when we remember that even in our own day a general council of the highest officials in what claims to be the one only Church of the living God united in solemnly pronouncing a feeble old man in Rome possessed of divine infallibility! And if the pope of Rome is pleased to accept and appropriate such absurd honors in the name of the sublimest truth given for human enlightenment, we need not be surprised that these proposals of Medo-Persia's "presidents, princes, counsellors, and captains" proved acceptable to the vain-glorious heathen monarch who then occupied the Medo-Persian throne. At all events, the sacred history tells us that these disguised murderers succeeded, and induced, the flattered and easy king; to establish the decree and sign the writing which they dictated, "that it might not be changed," but stand firm as the divine-regal act "which, according to the laws of the Medes and Persians, altereth not."

Such was the subtle scheme, and such was the success of it. Ostensibly, it was for the honor and alleged rightful glory of the king; in reality, it was for the murder of the man who stood next to him, and who had in him more of the divine than all the kings, presidents and princes of Media and Persia put together. It had a heathen lie for its basis; it was a huge hypocrisy in its suggestion; and it was nothing but a scheme of cold-blooded murder to destroy the greatest, best and purest man in the kingdom. Well may we stand amazed that rational men could be so malignant, so treacherous, so regardless of every obligation of truth, so sacrilegiously hypocritical for the accomplishment of an end so base. But so it was, and to such depths will men descend when once they throw off allegiance to right and conscience. O ye triflers with conviction and better knowledge! be admonished of the gigantic wickedness that lies in yielding to your dislikes and passions against the claims of righteousness and virtue! To sacrifice reason to envy and malice, to let go right for selfishness, to overstep the bounds of justice for one's own gain, though it should be only for once or in small matters, is a most perilous experiment. No man can tell in what monstrous iniquity it may end or what overwhelming confusion it may bring. Let us see, then, what came of this nefarious business.

Darius had the poor honor of being hypocritically flattered as a god. These envious and plotting presidents had the gratification of seeing the high authority of the throne now pledged for the success of their murderous wishes. And there appeared no more hope for the holy Daniel but to demit his duties to Jehovah, or die. What was to be done? He knew the feeling that was against him. He was not unaware of the proceedings which had been instituted. To complain against these men would be to indict nearly all the officials of the realm and to dash himself to destruction against the combination of numbers. To remonstrate with the king against the decree would seem like taking sides against a popular sentiment of the nation, present him in the attitude of a revolutionist trying to set aside one of the proudest traditions and most sacred political doctrines of the Medes and Persians, and make him seem to be a disloyal opposer of the king's acknowledged honor and dignity. To abandon his position and flee the country would show a cowardly spirit, and had but little promise of success. Indeed, he was so hedged up on all sides that nothing seemed left for him, as a true servant of Jehovah, but to compose himself to his fate, go on with his accustomed devotions and meekly trust the result to God. Therefore, when Daniel knew that the writing was signed, he went into his house; and his windows being open in his chamber toward Jerusalem, he kneeled upon his knees three times a day, and prayed, and gave thanks before his God, *as he did aforetime.*" He knew that honorable escape from these bloody conspirators was impossible without a miracle. The lions den and death from the ferocity of the savage beasts seemed to be his inevitable fate. But he also knew in Whom he believed. If it was best that God should save him from such an end, he was sure that not all the fierceness of bloody men or devouring lions could harm him; and if God should deem it best that so his earthly life should terminate, why should he wish to have it otherwise? He knew that God was with him, and that in any event no loss could come to him from it. He could look back upon a life of untarnished devotion, and had always had with him the evidences of Jehovah's favor, and why should he be alarmed or disconcerted now at what man might do unto him? And though the lions should presently crunch his bones, why should he disgrace the last remnant of his stay on earth by any cowardly abridgment of his pious habits or his wonted prayers? Therefore, with a quiet self-possession which makes him even more illustrious in the face of death than in the duties of life, he does not demit a jot of what he did aforetime, nor take a single precaution to screen himself from the malignant observation of his watching foes. Great indeed is the power of living faith. It can make adversity as though it were not. It enabled the first Christians to despise bonds, stripes, imprisonments and death. It lifted Paul so high above this world's calamities that he even gloried in tribulations. It made Poly carp look upon the flames that were to consume him as a chariot of God to waft him to eternal glory. It kept Daniel as serene as the stars of heaven, though another day should give his body to feed the wild beasts in their den. And of all things within human reach, there is nothing that can so bless, enrich, compose and ennoble its possessor as the genuine fear of the Almighty.

Great was the king's sorrow when he found who was struck by his insane decree. But vainly did he now reproach himself for his wicked folly. Fain would he have recalled the document, but he had suffered himself to be cajoled into a commitment beyond his power to undo. He had played the fool. He had unwittingly put his signature to the death-warrant of the truest man and most valuable officer in his empire. He had become the abettor of plotting murderers. He had bound himself to become the executioner of the very individual whom he was thinking to set over the whole realm. He had permitted himself to be flattered into a measure which was now about to put out of the world the most faithful friend he had on earth. And well might he be "sore displeased with himself, and set his heart on Daniel to deliver him," and labor in his remorseful distress to prevent the sad consequences of his indiscretion. But it was all of no avail. People who will not think and consider when they act must expect to suffer for their mistakes.

Under the Medo-Persian laws Daniel could not be delivered. The treacherous princes became clamorous for the execution of the decree. It was clear that their envied prime minister had prayed to his God contrary to the prohibition. It was clear what consequences were annexed to such disobedience. And the very men who a little while ago were so zealous for the king's divinity now did not hesitate to intimate disaster to him if he should fail to fulfil what he had signed. Sycophants and flatterers are always tyrants in their hearts. They will oppress when they get the power. And the poor king, out of a self-consistency which we find it hard to respect, gave the command, "and they brought Daniel, and cast him into the den of lions." And, to make all sure, "a stone was brought, and laid upon the mouth of the den; and the king sealed it with his own signet, and with the signet of his lords, that the purpose might not be changed concerning Daniel."

This was supposed to be the end of the noble president — sad end of a man so great, so faithful and so good! Those who hated him rejoiced over their murderous success, and now considered their fortunes made. But "the triumphing of the wicked is short, and the joy of the hypocrite but for a moment." God had not forsaken His servant, and a Higher than Darius had decreed that he should not thus perish before his enemies. Jehovah holdeth in His hand the devices of men and the savageness of beasts. He can bring to naught the machinations of princes and shut the mouths of lions. And in this case He did both. Not a lion in the den moved to hurt the venerable prophet. As the fire would not burn Shadrach, Meshach and Abednego, so the beasts would not attack the faithful Daniel. When the king came calling to him in the morning, he loyally answered, and told what a miracle God had wrought for his preservation. Gladder for Daniel's safety than Daniel for himself was the troubled king when he heard these tidings. With joyous haste he hurried to have his noble servant taken up from that horrible prison and the infamous conspirators put in. So Daniel was taken up out of the den. And they brought those men which had accused Daniel, and they cast them into the den of lions, their children and their wives. And the lions brake their bones in pieces or ever they came at the bottom of the den.' Verily, the wicked shall fall into their own pit, but the upright shall have good things in possession. Haman hangs on the very gallows which his vaulting pride prepared for faithful Mordecai. "So this Daniel prospered in the reign of Darius, and in the reign of Cyrus the Persian."

See, then, from this, and learn to take it deep to heart, that there is a righteous and merciful God at the helm of things, however crooked or unevenly they may seem to go. This world is not an orphan orb. Its histories are not matters of mere chance. The good may suffer and the wicked may prosper for a time, and God may often seem to have abandoned His servants, but He maketh the wrath of man to praise Him, and the remainder of wrath will He restrain. His ever-watchful eye is on all that transpires, and nothing can occur without His fore-calculation and His wise and gracious pre-determination of what shall come of it. His throne is established in the heavens, and His kingdom ruleth over all. Even the heathen Darius was convinced of this from what he saw in Daniel's deliverance, and he who had signed a decree involving his own deification now made and published another, that in every dominion of his kingdom men should tremble and fear before the God of Daniel, seeing that He is the living God, steadfast for ever. His kingdom indestructible, His dominion eternal, Who delivereth and rescueth, and worketh signs and wonders in heaven and in earth. And why should we ever think or feel as if this God were dead, or as if it were a vain thing to trust in His goodness or to hope for His mercy? Though our soul be among lions and we lie among them that are set on fire, even the sons of men whose teeth are spears and arrows, and their tongue a sharp sword, yet will He send from heaven and save us from the reproaches of them that would swallow us up.

"Judge not the Lord by feeble sense,
    But trust Him for His grace;
  Behind a frowning providence
    He hides a smiling face.

"His purposes will ripen fast,
    Unfolding every hour;
  The *bud* may have a bitter taste,
    But sweet will be the *flower.*"

This is a mixed world, where good and evil are in continual conflict, and where the administration is not always according to the right, because not yet final. Excellence and virtue do not exempt from earthly ills and adversities. Nay, the greater the saintship and fidelity, the greater the trials are apt to be. The tree that bears the best fruit is always the most assailed, shaken and stoned. The loftiest mountains are most familiar with storms and thunderbolts. The prophets before us were reviled, persecuted, falsely accused and evil-entreated because they were loyal to their Lord. The most perfect Man the world ever saw, and the greatest benefactor it ever had, was defamed, accused, condemned and crucified. It must needs be that some suffer for truth and righteousness, or the whole world would go to destruction. The salvation of the race is by the shedding of innocent blood — by the sacrifice of the bodily peace, fortunes, comforts and lives of the righteous. It is part of God's redemption-plan. And therefore we are not to think it strange when trial comes, as if God had vacated His throne or abandoned His rule over things. We are not to conclude that we are saints because we suffer, but neither are we to give up as forsaken of our heavenly Father because our way lies through deep and stormy seas and howling wildernesses. Daniel must endure his conspiring foes, and may be so compassed by them as to see no outcome but through horrible death.

See, then, also from his case, and let it be firmly rooted in the soul, how we may best conduct ourselves with reference to all these things. From early youth Daniel gave himself to God, and was very strict not to defile himself with anything questionable or contrary to God's law. Here was the first and grand planting for a true and successful life. There is nothing like an early rooting and grounding in the truth and in the fear and love of God. This was the spring of Daniel's greatness. This was his shield and buckler in the midst of his adverse surroundings. This steadied him for one of the sublimest careers that ever was run by mortal man. Nor can a young man or woman possibly do a better or a wiser thing for the successful running of the race of life, wherever or whatever it may be, than to give the heart to God, to live and die cleaving always and above all to His Word and laws. This gives fixedness, shape and purpose to the being. This fashions character into solidity, worth and beauty. This supplies a base and groundwork on which to repose and compose one's self, whatever storms life may develop.

In pursuance of his early principles, Daniel was very diligent in his devotions. He had his oratory for prayer, with its window ever looking to Jerusalem. He had no temple to which to betake himself, but he made a temple of his own house, and his upper room was his holy of holies. Three times a day he went into it with the incense of praise and prayer to the Lord God of his fathers. Not all the cares of state, nor all the perturbations of the affairs of empire, nor all the subtle plottings and malignant watchings of his foes, could induce him to demit this constant habit of his life. He kept himself in communion with heavenly greatness, and it served to make him great and to fill him with the spirit of the holy Powers. The manner, form or precise number of times a day in which he performed his devotions was not the material thing, but he kept open communications with Heaven; and this was the secret of his strength and the nurturing force in all his great qualities. Nor can any man make of himself and of his life what he should without systematic earnestness in his prayers.

But the crowning feature in Daniel was that he dared to obey God rather than man, and would not abate a tittle of his religious habits, though knowing that he must pay the forfeit with his life unless saved by miracle. He lived up to his principles. Those who watched and studied him the closest, incited with all the energy of hate, gave up, confessing it impossible to find whereof to accuse him, and built their final plot on their confidence in his unflinching fidelity to his God even though he should die for it. Nor were they mistaken. He treated the infamous decree as if it were not. No king or parliament has any right thus to interfere with private conscience. The edict was itself an act of treason to the sovereign Maker and Lord of all things. It was an attempt to legislate a divorce between the creature and the Creator, without consent of either. It was therefore no disloyalty, but a higher loyalty, to disregard and disobey it. So Daniel went on with his prayers precisely as he had done aforetime, and could not be turned from them in the slightest particular. He went to the same place; he went just as often; he went at the same hours of the day; he knelt by his open window toward Jerusalem the same as ever; he prayed just as loud and as long as before the decree existed; and he was as calm and undisturbed about it as if the decree had never been. Here was the man of principle and faith, and here is our example for a successful life and a proper death. There was no bravado or defiance. There was no ostentatious putting of self forward for applause. There was no indecent haste or low ambition to appear a martyr. But here was the dignity of a meek and honest faith, living only for God, and made up to die, if it must be, just as the life was shaped, unruffled with regrets or fears and peaceful in the keeping of a faithful God.

"Oh for a faith that will not shrink,
    Though press'd by many a foe;
That will not tremble on the brink
    Of poverty or woe;
That will not murmur or complain
    Beneath the chastening rod,
But in the hour of grief and pain
    Can lean upon its God!
Lord, give us such a faith as this,
    And then, whate'er may come,
We'll taste e'en here the hallow'd bliss
    Of our eternal home!"

Lecture Ninth - This World's Governments; or, the Vision of the Four Beasts

Daniel 7: 1-28.

THE Book of Daniel is made up of two main sections — the historical part and the prophetical part. The first part, over which we have thus far travelled in these Lectures, consists of a succession of scenes relating to the more personal history of the prophet and those with whom he had to do; whilst the second part, which begins with the chapter now before us, consists of a collection of his own prophetic visions, beheld at different periods of his life and explained by the heavenly Powers. Prophetic visions are described in the preceding chapters also, but they were not Daniel's visions, though he was called to interpret them. So there are also some personal particulars given in the chapters remaining, but only to indicate the time and circumstances under which the visions were given and explained. The topics from this onward are all prophetic.

In point of time the chapter on which we now enter takes us back again to the reign of Belshazzar, king of Babylon. It was in the first year of that monarch's regency that Daniel had this vision. It came to him in the night-time, for it was a period of great darkness and sorrow to God's people. It came to him in the shape of a dream, a vision of his head upon his bed, for the more this world is shut out of our thoughts and attention the more sacred influences from another flow in upon us. He also carefully wrote it all down at the time.

What Daniel saw was "the sea," perhaps the Mediterranean Sea, at least some "great sea." It was not in calm, but in heaving commotion. The winds of heaven were fiercely rushing upon it in contrary directions, tossing it with tempests and driving it hither and thither. And as he looked, four great beasts came up out of it. They did not all come at once, but in succession, one at a time. The first was like a Lion with eagle's wings. There is no such animal in Nature, but this was the appearance to the prophet. Following the career of this beast, he saw its wings plucked and the feathers all torn away. It then was lifted up from going on its four feet, and stood erect on two feet, as a man, and for its beast-heart it was made to possess a man's heart. After this winged lion came up another beast, heavy and ponderous, after the style of a Bear, but stronger and higher on one side than the other. It had three ribs of some mutilated creature between its teeth, whilst command was given to it to "arise and devour much flesh." After this bear came a third beast, more monstrous than those which preceded it. Its general form was that of a Leopard, or panther, but it had four heads, and on its back were four winos, like the wino-s of some strong fowl. Great power was likewise given to it. After this four-headed and four-winged leopard came a fourth and still more terrible beast. The prophet gives it no name, and seems to have been at a loss to what to liken it; but he describes it as "dreadful and terrible, and strong exceedingly." It had great iron teeth and claws of brass and ten horns, and it devoured and brake in pieces, and what was left it stamped down with its ponderous feet. It was diverse from all the beasts that were before it; and in the course of time there sprang up still another horn among the ten, and plucked up three of them from their roots, absorbing them wholly in itself. It was small at first, but soon became stout and imperious, the front and leader of all the remaining horns. It had eyes like the eyes of a man (or great sagacity), and a mouth speaking great arrogance, defiance and blasphemy. Of all the beasts and horns, this beast and its last defiant horn most struck and affected the prophet. It was upon this that his chief interest and anxiety centred.

But while, gazing upon these manifestations from the agitated sea, and contemplating the several careers of these monsters, another scene opened upon him. Whilst the last beast was operating in its eleventh horn, Daniel saw thrones set in the upper spaces, as if brought near to the earth, and amid these thrones the Eternal One seated in all the solemn majesty of His infinite Godhead. He had upon Him the long flowing robe of authority and empire, as white as the snow in purity and splendor; and the hair of His head was as fair as the unsullied fleece. He seemed to sit in a throne of fire, resting on wheels of living flame. The lightnings poured forth from before Him in incessant streams. Thousand thousands of heavenly ministrants were with Him, and ten thousand times ten thousand made up His awful suite. There was no mistaking the character of these presentations. It was the grand inquest of eternity now set for the awarding of doom and destiny upon these beasts, especially the last, blasphemous, eleventh horn. Daniel recognized it as the sitting of the judgment, and beheld the books opened. He therefore watched with intense interest to see what would be done with a power which had shown such consummate and defiant blasphemy. Nor was he kept long in suspense or doubt. The monster was slain and its body given to the devouring fire. As for the other beasts, their dominion was taken away, and only their reft existences lingered on to the time appointed.

But still another scene passed before the prophet as part of this same vision. He saw one like the Son of man coming in the clouds of heaven, and invested by the Eternal Father with dominion and glory and a kingdom, that all people, nations and languages should serve Him, and that He might reign for ever and ever.

Such is the description of what the prophet beheld. It was. all so mysterious and awful that he was immensely affected by it, and troubled in spirit as to what it meant. In his dream he inquired of one of the celestial beings whom he saw about the throne, who also told in the vision what it signified — to wit, that the four beasts denoted four khigs, dominions or empires; that the fourth beast was to be "the fourth kingdom upon earth;" that out of it should arise ten contemporaneous kings; and that after these should come up still another, who would be the most defiant of them all, speak great words against the Most High, wear out the people of God, and seek to change the whole order of earthly things, wielding a power which nothing but the day of judgment would destroy, when the sovereignty should be given to the holy people of God in a new, abiding and heavenly administration.

From this explanation of the angel it is clear that the vision was intended to be a symbolic synopsis of political history and world-power from the first rise of empire among men to the day of judgment, and what is then to take its place. It accordingly compasses precisely the same ground covered by the dream of Nebuchadnezzar, given and explained in the second chapter. The four metals in the great image which Nebuchadnezzar saw denote the same powers as the four beasts which Daniel beheld, except that the one beheld them as a world-ruler, from without, and as would most naturally strike a politician, whilst the other beheld them as a spiritual prophet, from within, as they really are in the light of truth and holiness. What the king from his worldly standpoint beheld as a splendid colossal human figure, Daniel as a man of God beholds as a succession of beastly monsters, savage, cruel, despotic and unhuman. But in both instances the thing set forth is one and the same world-power, in its fourfold development and varied phenomena from the commencement of secular empire to its final termination, when the sublime and eternal rule of Heaven shall be set up in its place, to change no more.

There has been little or no question among interpreters that the first beast stands for the Babylonian empire, the sun of which was about to set when Daniel saw this vision. It here appears as the noblest of beasts, with the addition of the wings of the noblest of birds, just as it appeared to its most illustrious head as the noblest of metals shaped according to the noblest part of man. The Scriptures elsewhere liken Nebuchadnezzar to a lion and his armies to eagles (Jer. iv. 7, 13; Ezek. xvii. 3, 12), and the characteristic marks of his empire were great savage strength, magnificence and irresistible conquest. It was a lion with eagle's wings. But its aggressions soon flagged, its eagle-wings were plucked and its career of conquest stopped. By the lessons which God taught its most distinguished king it was lifted up from the crouching attitude of a beast of prey, and made to stand erect as a man, whilst the weaker and gentler heart of a man was given to it. By the experiences to which Nebuchadnezzar was subjected its wild and savage spirit became humanized. Thus every feature of the description answers to the facts recorded concerning this power.

Nor is there any difficulty in tracing 'the correspondence between the second beast and the Medo-Persian dominion, which conquered Babylon and succeeded it in the sovereignty of the world. The burly brute answers to the heavy chest of Nebuchadnezzar's image. The two sides, one higher and stronger than the other, fit to the dual composition of this empire. The three torn ribs in this beast's mouth also correspond. They answer to Lydia, Babylon and Egypt, which the Medo-Persian empire seized and held. The bidding of it to devour much flesh was likewise fulfilled in the great waste of human life which characterized the ponderous aggressions of this power, which never had the speed and agility of a winged lion, but always moved with the huge heaviness and massive strength of the awkward animal here made to represent it. The Medo-Persian armies, even on moderate expeditions, ranged from a third to a full million of men. Darius marched through the desolate regions of Scythia with seven hundred thousand men, exclusive of a fleet of six hundred ships carrying a naval force of one hundred and twenty thousand more. Xerxes came against Greece with two millions and a half of fighting men. Artaxerxes brought an army against his brother, Cyrus the Younger, numbering nine hundred thousand, with a contingent of three hundred thousand which did not come up in time. Never, by any dominion, were such heavy masses of men brought together to such wholesale slaughter and destruction as by this Medo-Persian power, thus fulfilling every lineament of the prophetic picture drawn before that empire had yet come into existence.

The third beast was therefore the symbol of the next "great" power which succeeded the Medo-Persian, which was none other than the Macedonian empire as extended and established by the conquests of Alexander. The leopard is not one of the noblest or greatest of animals, but belongs more to the lion order than to that of the bear. It is of a fierce and cruel nature, noted in the Scriptures for its fleetness, its insidious and watchful lying in wait for its prey, and its very sudden bounding upon the objects of its attacks. But this particular leopard had the further assistance of four wings, greatly intensifying the idea of celerity and quickness. All this is pre-eminently true of the conquests of Alexander. It is written of him that the was impetuous and fierce in his warlike expeditions as a panther after his prey, and came on his enemies with that speed as if he flew with a double pair of wings." He began his wars at the age of twenty years, and at thirty-two the world had been subdued to his authority. Nations were his playthings, thrones were his toys. And in a most emphatic and special sense dominion was *given* to him. With comparatively insignificant means he reached the most momentous results. Read his history and you cannot but wonder that such mighty empire should have been acquired as he acquired it. But he did not live to enjoy it or to put it into fixed and settled shape. Nor did he have a regular successor to organize it. It fell to his four principal generals, who ruled and administered it from four different centres, whence this winged leopard is represented with four heads. It was the same dominion, but exercised from four points under four sovereigns — Lysimachus for Thrace and Bithynia, Seleucus for Syria and the East, Ptolemy Soter for Egypt, and Cassander for Macedonia — till all was intimately swallowed up in the conquests of Rome. Though Alexander was not yet born, nor his father before him, when Daniel wrote, we here have an exact foreshowing of him and his dominion.

The fourth beast, however, is the one that most arrested the attention of the prophet, and whose career and end he was most concerned to understand. That it was meant to represent an empire, dominion or rule in the world, the same as the three other beasts, we are assured by the angel who gave Daniel the interpretation, saying, "These great beasts, which are four, are four kings" — dynasties or empires — and "the fourth beast shall be the fourth kingdom upon earth." But though the descriptions in this case would seem to be the most extended, definite and particular in the whole account, and already measurably determined by the preceding identifications, it is just here that the greatest diversity has arisen among expositors of these visions, and, as I take it, with the least reason for it.

Taking this beast, as explained by the angel, as a particular form of political world-power, several points present themselves which, to my mind, inevitably and certainly fix the identification. First, it is completely successive to the three preceding forms of the great political administrations upon earth. Second, it is a great universal dominion, and no mere section or fragment of coexistent governments. And third, it continues, substantially, in one form or another, to the end of time — to the coming of the Son of man as the appointed King and Judge of the world. In other words, it is the only great world-power from the termination of the four-headed Macedonian empire to the end of all mere earthly political rule. Who, then, that but glances at the way the Macedonian dominion ended, and at the political history of mankind from that on to the present, can be at a loss to find the only great imperial dominion or rule answering to this prophetic outline? There is no history of man apart from it. There "is no possibility of tracing the general current of human affairs from the fall of the Macedonian empire till now without having it before us as the mightiest, the most conspicuous, the most long-lived and the most decisively marked of all political powers which ever controlled our world, and thus far exactly filling out the picture which was shown to Daniel more than two dozen centuries ago.

The fourth great dominion upon the earth, that which swallowed up the empire which Alexander founded, and took its place, and which has perpetuated its laws and method of rule in all the governments since that time, is most manifestly and unquestionably the great Roman empire, which rose from out the agitated sea of the world, and added territory after territory to its iron sway till it became in reality the government of the whole earth. When we read of the fourth beast, that it was "diverse from all the beasts that were before it," that it had teeth of iron and claws of brass, that it was "dreadful and terrible, and strong exceedingly," that it "devoured and brake in pieces, and stamped the residue with its feet," — we have a complete summation of what all history has recorded concerning the Roman dominion. Crushing power was its chief characteristic. Permanent subjugation and organization on common principles of law were its distinguishing attributes, in which it was diverse from all preceding empires. Unlike the great powers before it, it utilized and brought under every diversity of form for the building up of one eternal authority and dominion. It did not sweep over the world like a tornado, ravaging, extorting submission and receiving tribute, without moulding things to itself; but it relentlessly consolidated all its materials into a settled and abiding order of common law which still holds its place in living force after the lapse of more than two thousand years. All the governments on earth are still essentially Roman, and in their laws and codes Roman empire still holds the sway of the world, and must as long as human governments exist. This fourth beast cannot, therefore, stand for anything other than the Roman dominion and rule.

As to the ten horns that grow out of this beast, they may perhaps be somewhat identifiable in the past by making the peculiar and blasphemous eleventh horn represent the papacy; but the nature of the presentations will not admit of being confined to what has already transpired. This beast was not born with its ten horns, any more than with its eleventh, which came up subsequent to the ten. They were all developed as the beast fulfilled its historical career. Nor can it be clearly shown that just so many divisions of the Roman dominion have occurred, either contemporaneously or successively, in the past. Neither does the papacy with any fulness and particularity answer to what is said of the eleventh horn. The general type may be the same, but the details will not all apply, nor any of them in strict accuracy. The eleventh horn is atheistic; the papacy never has been. The eleventh horn persecutes and wears out the people of God, who are given into its power for a definite period terminating only with the beast's own existence at the great day of judgment; but not the half of Christendom is within the reach of the pope, nor has the Eastern Church ever been, whilst his temporal authority has ceased, and with it his power to persecute; and still the day of judgment has not come. The papacy also came into being *before* the disseverance of the Roman empire into the several governments which some take to be the ten horns; but according to Daniel's vision the eleventh horn came up *after* the ten. Literally taken, the blasphemous and persecuting dominion of the last horn continues but three and a half years; but the papacy has existed more than twelve hundred years, and more than the twelve hundred and sixty years which some read into "a time, times, and half a time." So, again, the ten-fold partition of the Roman beast, subsequent to which the blaspheming horn exercises his transient dominion, is just before the destruction which sweeps away the whole animal for ever — that is, just before the Lord comes to judge the world; but the past divisions which men count for these ten horns have long since disappeared, and no such ten kingdoms can now be enumerated. Besides, those kingdoms all belonged to the western half of the Roman empire, and did not take in its great eastern part at all. These ten horns also answer to the ten toes of the great image, but these certainly were not all on one foot.

From these and other equally cogent reasons I am compelled to refer this part of the vision to the future, and to take it as a prophecy of the political condition and rule of the world immediately preceding the day of judgment. The great Roman beast must yet somehow put itself forth in just ten king-doms, covering the whole territory of the ancient empire, if not the whole world; and in the time of these horns there is to come up an eleventh horn, small at first, but growing in might and arrogance, which shall pluck up three of these ten kingdoms by the roots, and enact a scene of blasphemy, of defi-ance of everything divine, and of persecution and oppression to the people of God such as has never been from the beginning of the world till then. The Scriptures everywhere speak of this power, and also all the Church Fathers from the days of the apostle John onward. They were accustomed to call it the great Antichrist of the last days, who should pervert and lay waste every-thing in the world, and press his awful domination for three and a half years, till suddenly overwhelmed by the revelation of Jesus Christ in the great day of judgment.

Such, then, is the outline of this world's political history as here foreshown to the prophet while the first of all the great empires was yet standing. As far as time has unfolded the facts we see how true and accurate that foreshow-ing was, proving to us that it could have come only from Him who knows the end of all things from the beginning, and making It infallibly certain that what else of the vision yet remains will likewise be fulfilled to the very letter. And pre-eminent among these prophetic indications is the great Judgment which Is to end man's dominion and set up in its place the beneficent and everlasting rule of the Prince of Peace. One verse is assigned to each of the first three kingdoms, one verse contains the explanation of them, but all the rest of the vision and explanation is occupied with this great crisis. Very sub-lime and impressive also is the picture which the prophet beheld.

On earth is the last beastly horn of apostate man's dominion, full of the in-tensest Intellectual subtlety and acuteness, with the loudest and most arro-gant of assumptions. It is a man energized with all the power of the devil, and with his confederate kings defiantly setting himself over against the Al-mighty, destroying the saints of the Most High and ordaining new worship and laws for the world, whilst everything for an allotted time is given into his hand.

Heaven, however, is not indifferent. The prophet sees the eternal Powers in action — the Throne of God, and the Ancient of Days upon His everlasting seat, surrounded by thousands of thousands of heavenly beings, who delight to do His pleasure and all ready to execute His will. He sees the judgment set, the books opened, the records of man's deeds and misdeeds laid bare, the just and irrevocable sentence passed and the blasphemous monster given to the devouring fires. It is the same scene to which Paul refers where he speaks of the fiery destruction of that Wicked One, "whose coming is after the working of Satan with all power and signs and lying wonders, and with all deceivableness of unrighteousness." 2 Thess. ii. 8-10. It is the same scene which John describes in the account of the battle of the great day of God Almighty, when the beast was taken, and with him the false prophet that wrought miracles before him, and were both cast alive into a lake of fire burning with brimstone." Rev. xix. It is the same scene to which the Psalmist alludes, where he says, "The kings of the earth set themselves, and the rulers take counsel together, against the Lord, and against His Anointed, saying. Let us break their bands asunder, and cast away their cords from us." But "He that sitteth in the heavens shall laugh: the Lord shall have them in derision. Then shall He speak unto them in His wrath, and vex them in His sore displeasure...He will break them with a rod of iron; He will dash them in pieces like a potter's vessel." Ps. ii.

For purposes which to us are at present inscrutable, God allows evil to live and operate in our world, and to go forward with its schemes of unwisdom and infamy to the highest possible culmination of iniquity. Bat it is not because He is powerless against it, or because He is indifferent to the affairs of men, or because He does not hold evil-doers to the strictest accountability. From the beginning He made known how it would be, what savage monsters would oppress, desolate and destroy the earth, and into what defiant, blasphemous and bloody domination the boasted progress of this world should develop, that mankind may see and experience what must come from the throwing off of His beneficent rule, and what horrors are involved in the following of their supposed better wisdom and ideas of liberty. But, at the same time. He has foreshown what estimate he puts upon it, and what awful catastrophes await the enactors and abettors of such wickedness.

Men think to build up the world upon their own philosophies and atheistic fancies and conceits, but when all comes to all, it is the instalment of Hell in the dominion of the earth, and the dashing of everything to utter destruction against the invincible sovereignty of indignant Heaven., God can afford to wait and let all be acted out to the full. He is patient because He is eternal. But He is not asleep; neither has He abandoned His prerogatives, forgotten His threatenings or lost His Omnipotence. The account of all is in His books. His abhorrence of the iniquitous trampling of His truth and honor is not abated because it is for the time restrained. His blasting thunders are ready for their work when the appointed time arrives to let them loose. Perdition's fires are kindled, and the furnace of His consuming wrath is heating hotter and hotter every day against the nearing moment when its devouring flames shall seize the bloody prey for which they have been clamoring with ever-increasing violence for all these ages. And the great and terrible day of the Lord surely cometh, when His fury shall be poured out like fire, and the wicked shall be as stubble, and the world and all that is therein shall be consumed before Him. (See 2 Pet. iii.)

But the foreshowing is not all disaster. The prophet at the same time saw One like the Son of man — like man, but not a mere man — man, but much more than man — coming in the clouds of heaven, and receiving from the Ancient of Days dominion, glory and a kingdom, that all nations and languages should serve Him and share with Him in the blessedness of a divine and indestructible sovereignty over the whole earth. What Nebuchadnezzar saw as the Stone cut out of the mountain without hands is here identified to the prophet as the God-man, Christ Jesus, the King of glory and the Captain of salvation, supernally anointed and ordained as the only rightful Lord of the world which He hath ransomed with His blood.

You remember how constantly the Saviour spoke of himself as the Son of man in connection with every work looking to the completion of human redemption. It identifies Him as that promised "Seed of the woman "which was to bruise the serpent's head. It recognizes His human nature and the summing up of humanity in Him as its representative, fulness and completion. It singles Him out as the Head of the race for salvation, as Adam was the head of the race as to nature and disaster. It presents Him in the character of the King Messiah.

Equally familiar are you with the evangelic phrases, "kingdom of heaven," "kingdom of God — "the kingdom" of which Christ is the King. It is usually and not improperly understood as the reign and rule of God through Christ which is set up by the Spirit in the hearts of believers. But that is its hidden form, its interior beginning only. It is yet to be amplified and manifested outwardly in the transformation, glorification and eternal regency with Christ of all who are Christ's. It is the sum of all grace and good to man, as the Son of man is the sum and embodiment of all redeeming and glorifying agencies. There is nothing more precious in all the Word and promises of God than is set before us in these familiar terms. And, what is the more singular, they come to us from Babylon, from the visions and pen of an official of the Babylonian empire. The use made of them in the New Testament and in common Christian theology and discourse sets an honor and distinction upon Daniel and his prophecies of which few are conscious, and impacts his prophetic spirit with the very heart and soul of all evangelical ideas and consolations.

The coming of this Son of man here spoken of was not His coining when he first appeared as the Babe of Bethlehem and the meek Man of Nazareth. Neither was it His investiture at His resurrection and ascension, as some have taught. For the ten horns of the fourth beast did not then exist, and the destruction of the blasphemous, persecuting horn that arises after the ten is still future, as the day of judgment is still future. And it is only when the judgment sits, and the fourth beast is finally slain and given to the eternal fires, that the Son of man obtains this kingdom and enters upon His reign with His saints. The great judgment sits first, and He gets His kingdom and takes this rule afterward, or as the result and consequence of what the great judgment brings. Neither has the Son of man ever yet come *in the clouds of heaven,* as here beheld, and as everywhere foretold and promised by himself and by all the inspired apostles and evangelists.

There is, then, to be a future coming of the Son of man which can be nothing short of a literal and personal apocalypse. Men may question and cavil and explain, and shrug their shoulders, and spit out ugly epithets, when we preach to them and forewarn them that this same Jesus who died on Calvary and ascended from Mount Olivet shall presently so come again in the clouds of heaven as the disciples saw Him go up into heaven. But it is the very heart and soul of Christian hope, the pole-star of our Christian faith, the great burden of the inspired messages of all God's holy prophets since the world began. According to these Scriptures, it is only "scoffers, walking after their own lusts" — "filthy dreamers, feeding themselves without fear" — "clouds without water, carried about of winds" — "raging waves of the sea, foaming out their own shame" — "wandering stars, to whom is reserved the blackness of darkness for ever" — who taunt us and say, *"Where is the promise of His coming? for since the fathers fell asleep, all things continue as they were from the beginning of the creation."* (See Jude and 2 Pet. iii.) Yes, "Yet a little while, and He that shall come will come, and will not tarry." Heb. x. 36. And "when they shall say. Peace and safety; then sudden destruction cometh upon them, as travail upon a woman with child; and they shall not escape." 1 Thess. v. 3.

Nor is the kingdom here foreshown a mere spiritual and invisible kingdom, with no outward and tangible reality, and which can as well coexist with the dominion of the beasts as not. According to this vision, it does not come, or is only in process of coming, till the beast-kingdoms, to their very last, are utterly swept away and destroyed. It is distinctly presented as coming into their place, and as exercising the same dominion for peace and blessedness which had been for so long perverted to every savage brutality, devil-rule and destruction. It is specifically said to be the dominion and kingdom over all peoples, nations and languages — "the kingdom, and dominion, and the greatness of the kingdom [or sovereignty] *under the whole heaven"* — the kingdom which "all dominion shall serve and obey" — the only government which shall then be upon earth. It must therefore be a literal kingdom as truly as those empires which it displaces and supersedes. John had a vision of its final realization, and he heard the great voices in heaven celebrating it as the very government and regency of the world that now is wrested from its perverters and put into the hands of our Lord and His Christ, to administer it as

His empire for ever and ever. And whosoever conceives or teaches concerning it in any way so as to cut out of it the idea of a literal and real dominion of the earth, such as we may suppose that Adam would now possess and exercise if he had never sinned nor died, as I read God's word, browbeats some of the plainest texts of Holy Scripture, abridges the ordination and prerogatives of the Son of man, dwarfs and disables the Biblical idea of redemption, and stultifies a great element of the faith and hope of God's people in all the ages of time and in heaven itself.

And in connection with that coming and kingdom great and glorious things are also here foreshown as the portion of the saints. Though in humility, depression, disability, and more or less persecution and distress through all the long and weary ages of the beast-rule, "when the wicked are cut off they shall see it." When the final and eternal kingdom or dominion of the Son of man is once set up they are also to share in all its prerogatives and blessedness; for what in the fourteenth verse is said to be given to the Son of man only, in the twenty-seventh verse is said to be "given to the people of the saints of the Most High." Jesus is one with his people. They share with Him in all His virtues, works and honors as their Head, Saviour and Representative. They are sons of God through his Sonship, justified and upheld by His righteousness, and joint-heirs with Him to all that He inherits and receives as the Son of man. If He has an everlasting status of acceptance and honor with God, His people share it with Him. If He is invested with the rule of "the world to come/' with dominion and glory and a kingdom, that all people, nations and languages of the future eternal generations should serve Him, those who lia-ve borne the cross with Him, and held fast to the confession of His name amid the apostasies and infidelities of the world that now is, shall in like manner share the "kingdom and dominion and the greatness of the kingdom under the whole heaven." Our calling is to be kings and co-regents with our glorious Lord in the eternal principalities. "Do ye not know that the saints shall judge the world?...Know ye not that we shall judge angels?" 1 Cor. vi. Hath not the Lord himself declared, "Verily, ye which have followed me, in the regeneration [the general regenesis of things] when the Son of man shall sit in the throne of His glory, ye also shall sit upon twelve thrones, judging the twelve tribes of Israel"? Matt. xix. 28. Hath He not caused it to be written from heaven, "He which overcometh and keepeth my works unto the end, to him will I give power over the nations, and he shall rule them" — "To him that overcometh will I grant to sit with me on my throne"? Rev. ii. 26, 27; iii. 21. Is it not one of the sublimest songs which the saints in glory sing as they look forward and wait for the final consummation: "Thou hast redeemed us to God by Thy blood, and made us unto our God kings and priests, *and we shall reign on the earth"?* Rev. v.; ix. 10.

Oh, my brethren, the Church does not half understand the exceeding great and precious promises which God has given and guaranteed to the true and faithful followers of Jesus, though they shine out like purest diamonds in all the utterances and records of His holy prophets. We are not called to serve

God in vain. We are not asked to stem the tide and endure the hardships of this adverse world without an abundant compensation for all when once the battle is over. Not only eternal life is ours, but thrones and crowns and kingdoms, of which all earthly empire is but the poor and perishable shadow. Let us not, therefore, grow weary and faint under the burdens that are now upon us. They will soon be lifted off, and give place to a kingship supernal and without end.

Lecture Tenth - The World-Powers and Israel; or, The Ram, He-goat and Little Horn

Daniel 8: 1-27.

WE here come to the consideration of Daniel's second vision, which occurred two years subsequent to the one described in the preceding chapter. The armies of Cyrus were at the time investing Babylon, and as Daniel was in Babylon when the city was captured, the probabilities are that it was there he had this vision. The statement that he was "at Shushan in the palace, which is in the province of Elam, by the river of Ulai,' only designates the locality in which the vision placed him — where he seemed to be in what he saw, where he was in spirit — without determining where he was in body. So John in the apocalyptic visions seemed to be at different places — now on earth, now in heaven, now on an exceeding high mountain — whilst corporeally all the time in the isle called Patmos. A vision or a dream may make us seem to be in very different places from those in which we really are; and so "in a vision"

Daniel was "at Shushan," though in reality most likely in Babylon. The reason why the vision was located in the Shushan palace was that that was to be the royal seat of the power with which this vision begins and the starting-point of the events contained in this prophecy.

A glance at the particulars in this vision is enough to satisfy us that we here have again to do with some of the same powers brought to view in the preceding chapter as well as in Nebuchadnezzar's dream. And if any should be disposed to think strange of this repeated travelling over the same ground, they need only recur to the existence of four Gospels, all devoted to the one subject of Christ's earthly life, or turn to the number of times Isaiah describes the Assyrian invasion, or note how repetitive are the prophecies touching the destruction of Babylon, Tyre, Egypt, Moab and other cities, nations and powers. It is part of the plan upon which revelation is formed to give "line upon line and precept upon precept," that everything may be fully brought out and the most deeply impressed. There is a wonderful force in repetition, and particularly in the effective inculcation of important truth. A thing needs to be held before the mind, and looked at again and again, and viewed from varied points of observation and with regard to different qualities and relations, in order to be thoroughly seen, understood and impressed upon the soul. We are so constituted, and usually so slow to take in, that one look will not suffice. We must gaze and gaze, and ever come back to look again; and even then we are prone to overlook, and fail to see.

But what, at first glance, we might be disposed to regard as mere repetitions are not such in reality. A return to the same subject, besides serving to emphasize that subject, nearly always develops some new circumstances, or puts it in some new attitude or relation, or connects with it some special purpose, association, duty, threatening or promise. And when the subject is a prophecy, there is always something connected with the repetition to adapt it to some altered position, end or intent. For this reason I am always suspicious of what are called *harmonies,* or attempts to combine in one single account what is given by the Spirit in separate accounts. People think to strengthen the record by these harmonies, but for the most part they only weaken and mar it. It is like taking a number of photographs of a thing from various points and distances, and then trying to make one picture out of them all by fitting together the several parts of each. It is an absurdity. God never meant it so, and man can never succeed in it. What we need is each picture by itself, from its own standpoint and with its own individuality. And though we have three several visions covering the same general objects, and each of them deals in part with precisely the same things, it still is impossible to understand them rightly or to get a full impression of them without viewing each by itself entire, and apart from the weaving in of one with the other, as I find attempted by some. Nor is there any difficulty in accounting for the differences of these several visions.

Nebuchadnezzar's dream gives a general outline of the political history of the world as viewed by a world-ruler and estimated from external presentations. Hence the splendid human figure, by the side of which the kingdom of God appears in humility as "a stone." Daniel's first vision gives a somewhat more particular outline of the same world-power, but as viewed by a spiritual prophet and estimated with reference to moral properties. Hence ferocious wild beasts take the place of excellent metals, whilst the kingdom of God appears in its real worth and dignity as the crown of humanity, or the Son of man coming from heaven with the sublimest investiture from the eternal Throne. Nebuchadnezzar's dream contains no particular reference to that eleventh horn in which the iniquities of the rule of man finally culminate and call forth the great judgment. The picture is simply that of the world-power in general, through its various phases to the end, viewed from a worldly standpoint. In Daniel's vision this eleventh horn is the chief thing, since it is the consummation of that savage beastliness inherent in the rule of apostate man which it is the intent of this vision to exhibit. Hence also that great session of the divine judgment whence the final destruction of this beast-power proceeds, for which there was no place or occasion in that outward view of things presented to Nebuchadnezzar. And so the vision now before us, though it travels for the third time over the same general track, has its own particular standpoint by which it is conditioned.

In the two preceding visions we behold the pictures of the powers of the world as a whole, without regard to any distinction between Jew and Gentile. It is human dominion in its broadest view, in the entirety of its history — first as outwardly considered, and then as spiritually considered, and finally superseded by the kingdom of God. Hence, also, the language in which these revelations, up to the chapter now before us, are recorded, which is the common world-language used at the time, and not Hebrew; whilst the vision now in hand is given in the language of the Jews, as all that follows in this Book. What Daniel is here shown of these world-power manifestations he sees and hears not only as a spiritual man of God, but more particularly as a Jewish prophet, and as mainly concerning the Jewish people. Hence the dominion of Babylon is loft out entirely, for it was now on the eve of its downfall, and nothing more was to come of it to the Jews. Hence, also, nothing is said of the fourth beast, except as it might be considered included in the third, and nothing of the ten kingdoms, except as represented or included in the little horn in its final stage. Accordingly, also, we here read of the spiritual hierarchy or host, and their prince — of the daily sacrifices, the sanctuary and the pleasant or holy land — of which nothing appears in the preceding visions. It is still the same world-power in its various forms which constitutes the subject of the vision, but with the emphasis now on what particularly concerns the Jewish people, and with all else touched but lightly or not at all. It is therefore a distinct vision to itself, and is to be interpreted only in its own proper relations and intent.

What Nebuchadnezzar saw as the silver breast and arms of the great image, and what Daniel in the preceding vision beheld under the image of a clumsy Bear, here appears under the figure of a solitary Ram, with two horns. The change of the symbol lies in the reference of the vision to the Jewish people. Medo-Persia, viewed in relation to Israel, was not a devouring wild beast, but, for the most part, a friendly power, which religiously approximated toward the Shemitic race and the theocracy. It was this power which restored the Jews after the seventy years of captivity in Babylon, and helped them in many ways in the rebuilding of their temple and the restoration of their worship. Many Jews long afterward continued to reside among the Medo-Persians, filled high places in the government and exerted great influence, as we see from the Book of Esther. Viewed as a world-power in general, this dominion was a ferocious and all-eating Bear, but in its relation to Israel it was a much more domestic and harmless animal.

The solitariness of this Ram denoted the unity of this kingdom, while the two horns had reference to the two nations of which it was made up and in which its chief power resided. Media was an independent kingdom long before Persia was anything but a province, but when Cyrus came to the throne the Persian part of the kingdom became much the greater of the two. This was foreshown in the vision, in that the horn which sprang up last became much higher than the other.

Daniel beheld this Ram *"pushing"* — thrusting violently with its head — denoting military aggressions. These are specified as being toward the west, toward the north and toward the south from Shushan. The east is not mentioned, as the Persians made no important or lasting conquests in that direction. To the westward, however, they conquered Babylon, Syria and Asia Minor; to the northward, Armenia and the Caspian countries; and to the southward, Egypt, Libya, etc. The history thus agrees exactly with the vision.

So, again, what Nebuchadnezzar saw as the brazen abdomen and thighs of the great image, and Daniel beheld in his first vision as the four-winged and four-headed Leopard, here appears in the form of a Goat. There can be no question that this Goat represents the Graeco-Macedonian empire, and its conspicuous horn Alexander the Great. The interpreting angel says, in so many words, "The rough Goat is the king (or dominion) of Grecia, and the great horn between his eyes is the first king." Even the escutcheon of this empire bore this figure. As a world-power in general it had all the savage qualities of a Leopard, but in relation to the Jews it was a mild and fostering power rather than a beast of prey, and hence is here symbolized as a Goat. Josephus relates that when Alexander was on his Eastern expeditions he came into Palestine with all the pride of a victorious conqueror, and was about to turn his armies loose upon Jerusalem, but that a remarkable dream on his part, and another on the part of the Jewish high priest, served to bring about a friendly conference, which resulted most favorably to the Jewish people. When the great conqueror met the high priest and saw upon his golden mitre the great name of Jehovah, he bowed down before it and gave the high priest his right hand. Having come into Jerusalem, he had sacrifices offered for him, whilst the priests brought to him this very Book of Daniel and pointed out to him the very chapter before us, in which the holy prophet had recorded the coming of a Greek conqueror who should vanquish and destroy the Persian dominion. Accepting the prophecy as referring to himself — as it really did — he was so pleased and assured with regard to his plans that he engaged to favor the Jews in anything they might ask. They therefore prayed him that they might be permitted to enjoy their own laws and institutes as established by their fathers, and not be required to pay tribute in sabbatic years. This he willingly granted, engaging that the same should hold for all the Jewish people who might be found remaining in Babylon and Media in case his expedition should prove successful. Such a power, with such a bearing toward the Jews, could not be consistently symbolized by a ferocious beast of prey, at least not in that particular relation. Hence the change of figure here from a Panther to a Goat.

The prophet beheld this Goat coming from the west, for it was to the far west from Persia that the Macedonian power originated. It came with marvellous velocity and determination, seeming to be supernaturally helped. It struck the Medo-Persian Ram, shattered both his horns, trod him down and took his dominion. It required more than a single battle to accomplish this, bat it was accomplished, as history tells.

But in the midst of the greatest power and triumph of this Goat, its great horn was broken — not in battle, as the horns of the Ram were broken, but by the early and unexpected death of Alexander. Giving himself to unbridled excesses over his victories, he was seized with fever, and died at Babylon in the thirty-third year of his age, about three hundred and twenty-three years before the birth of Christ. His empire, however, still stood. The great horn dropped off, but in place of it came up four other horns. The throne was nominally left to his son, but that son never came to it. The military chieftains whom he had placed over the conquered countries wrangled and fought with each other for years, until finally, at the fall of Antigonus, the dominion settled into four monarchies, answering to the four heads of the Leopard and the four horns of this Goat.

Out of one of these four sections of the Macedonian empire the prophet beheld the springing up of "a little horn" — a sprig of one of the four — which waxed great toward the south, the east and the pleasant or holy land, even to the host of heaven — the hierarchy of the temple — some of whom it cast down and stamped upon, magnifying itself even to the Prince of the host (God himself), abolishing the daily sacrifice, wasting the sacred dwelling-place, polluting the temple, setting up a multitude of its own over against the heavenly order, and enacting the most blasphemous and murderous scenes against Jehovah, His truth and His people.

Expositors in general interpret this of the infamous Antiochus Epiphanes. Jews and Christians for nearly seventeen centuries have been taking it in this application, at least in its germinant and precursive fulfilment. Nor have they done so without reason. Antiochus Epiphanes certainly answers more fully to the prophetic delineation than any king or power that has yet existed since Daniel wrote. He came up out of one of the four divisions of the empire of Alexander, from the stock of Syrian kings, and toward the latter time of that empire, when it already began to come under the growing power of Rome. He came up from a very small beginning, from being a hostage at Rome, with no prospect of ever becoming a great king. He got the kingdom by deceits and flatteries. His conquests and depredations were all in the directions noted in the vision. And especially his treatment of the Jews, his profanations of the temple, his bloody tyranny against the faithful worshippers of Jehovah, and his blasphemous audacity over against God himself, well accord with what is said of this horn. The writings of Josephus and the Books of the Maccabees tell the story of his doings, which one cannot read without being touched at the miseries he inflicted; all of which wonderfully accords with the prophetic outline.

Time would fail me here to present the merest sketch of those infamous transactions. Suffice it to say that this vile man conceived the idea of establishing throughout his kingdom, inclusive of Palestine, the worship of Jupiter Olympus, identifying himself with that god, and intent on making his own worship universal. With infatuated zeal and stubbornness he tried to extirpate every other worship, and particularly the worship of Jehovah at Jerusalem. Among the Jews themselves he found many faithless ones ready to enter into his plans and to help on his idolatrous designs. He bought up these traitors, sold out the high priesthood to the highest bidders, ejected one and another from it for a price, and rifled the temple again and again of all the gold, silver and treasures in any way connected with it, dealing out slaughter and death to those who dared to remonstrate. With the most shameful perfidy and deceit he got possession of Jerusalem, fell upon its inhabitants, destroyed the lives of multitudes in cold blood, robbed and destroyed the houses, carried off women and children into slavery, made a military stronghold of the city, put the worst of men into it to watch for and slay every earnest believer in the God of Abraham who might come thither to do homage to Jehovah, polluted the sanctuary on all sides with innocent blood, prohibited circumcision on pain of death, abolished the temple services and kept it vacated till the weeds grew up in the passage-ways of God's house, set the image of his own idol on the Almighty's altar, offered swine's flesh in sacrifice in special defiance of the God of Israel, and forced all Jews who would remain faithful to the religion of their fathers to hide themselves in the mountains and desolate places in order to save their lives. Thus did he practise and prosper, and destroy the holy people, slaughtering them by thousands in times of peace and under professions of peace, magnifying himself against the God of Israel, calling to his aid every treacherous craft, casting down the rightful priests, burning the sacred books, determined to abolish both the Law and the prophets and to submerge the Jews and their religion in the vilest heathen abominations.

The *time* which the angel gave as marking the duration of the treading down of the sanctuary by this horn likewise accords with the history touching Antiochus. The whole vision of the displacement of the daily sacrifice is called "the vision of the evening and the morning;" and when it was asked, "How long shall be the vision?" the answer came, specially confirmed as true, "Unto two thousand and three hundred" — not *"days,"* as our version says, but —*"evening (and) morning;* then shall the sanctuary be cleansed." The allusion is not to the evening and morning making up the day, but to the sacrifice interrupted, which was offered each morning and each evening; and twenty-three hundred times of these offerings was to be the measure of the interruption, each evening being counted as one, and each morning as one. This would make the angel's answer cover eleven hundred and fifty days, or three years and a portion of a year. And so, according to the records in the Book of Maccabees, it was just three years from the day that the first idolatrous sacrifice was made upon the altar of God under Antiochus until the first regular offerings were again restored; whilst the king's letters forbidding the regular sacrifices were proclaimed in Jerusalem several months before the sacrifice to Jupiter on Jehovah's altar. Or, if we take the twenty-three hundred "evening and morning" as so many *"days"* — that is, a little more than six years — we again have the length of the time from the first denudation of the temple by Antiochus to the righting of it again under the Maccabean heroes.

The miserable end of this proud and bloody blasphemer also answers well to the end assigned to this little horn. The angel said, "He shall be broken without hand," indicating his destruction by some supernatural power; and after this sort was the end of Antiochus Epiphanes. Marching into Persia and robbing the temple at Elymais, he was driven away by popular tumult. Receiving tidings about the same time of the defeat of his army in Palestine, and of the restoration of the temple services there, he ravingly declared his purpose to exterminate the Jewish race. Whereupon he was suddenly smitten with a terrible disease, like that which befell Herod, and amid un measurable agonies of body and mind he horribly ended his life under what he himself and all beholders regarded as a manifest judgment of God for his blasphemous iniquities. Poly bins says of him that lie "fell into a madness and died" — the madness of inconsolable bodily anguish and mental remorse. Tluis, without violence from the hand of man, he miserably perished; and this stage of the desolating horn was at an end. Josephus declares unhesitatlngly that these events happened in fulfilment of this eighth chapter of the Book of Daniel. And from a review of the whole history it seems to be abundantly manifest that there was in the career of Antiochus Epiphanes at least a preliminary or precursive fulfilment of this horn.

But we are not therefore to conclude that the whole meaning, or even the chief emphasis, of this vision has been exhausted, and is now to be viewed as belonging only to the past. The profound remark of Lord Bacon ever comes up, that "there is a latitude which is agreeable and familiar to divine prophecies, being of the nature of their Author, with whom a thousand years are as one day, and therefore they are not fulfilled punctually at once, but have springing germinant accomplishments throughout many ages, though the height or fulness of them may refer to some one age." And so we may trace a general identification of this little horn in Antiochus Epiphanes, and perhaps also in some other Antichristian powers since his day, whilst "the height or fulness" of the matter may still await fulfilment. History is ever repeating itself, and especially those histories which are singled out for special description and fore-announcement in the word of God. And there are accumulated items specifically given in this chapter seemingly on purpose to prevent the conclusion that the vision in its final fulfilment belongs to any period other than that immediately preceding the great day of judgment. Gabriel was commissioned to tell Daniel, and to make him understand, that *at the time of the end shall be the vision.* He also distinguishes between a former part and a latter part in the fulfilment, and refers the latter part to the time appointed for the end. He says that the vision extends to a remote period, and is "for many days." He says that the particular rising up of the king of fierce countenance is to occur "in the latter time" of the great world powers, which are contemplated as in some sort still in being up to the day of judgment. The time for the full realization of the vision is also said to be "when the transgressors are come to the full" — at the final consummation of all rebellion and wickedness — which is everywhere referred to the great judgment-period, when our God shall come and shall not keep silence. The character and doings of this horn likewise correspond with Paul's Man of Sin, and with the great Beast of the Apocalypse, which are unmistakably in being at the time of the revelation of Jesus Christ to judge the world. Hence, as Luther tells us, "these chapters of Daniel, as all expositors unanimously declare, refer to Antiochus and to the Antichrist of the last times, in which we are now living." (*Walch,* vol. vi. col. 1458.) Christ himself said of the Jews who rejected Him that another should come, not in the name of the Father, but in his own name, and that him they won Id receive. And it is pre-eminently this devilish pseudo-Saviour of the last evil days of this world, around whom the Christ-rejecting Jews will rally, and in whom all the abomination and devil-rule of the earth will finally head up, whom we are to see in this little horn which waxes so great. When that which now hinders shall be taken out of the way, when the true and waiting people of God have been caught up into the clouds to meet the Lord in the air, then shall be the apocalypse of that *Wicked One* whose coming is after the working of Satan, with all power and signs and lying wonders, with all deceivableness of unrighteousness, captivating all that have not the love of the truth. And nothing short of that last and mighty scourge of the world, whom the Lord will blast and destroy with the glory of His own epiphany, will satisfy the portraiture of this infamous horn as given in these visions. Even the Jews of Jerome's time, as he tells us, still looked upon this prophecy as yet to have a further fulfilment in another king yet to arise and do after the style of Antiochus, in whom the wickedness of earth shall have its final consummation, and whose end shall be in the great day of God Almighty. "This," said Jerome, "is also our understanding concerning the Antichrist whose shadow has thus been projected before."

In this view of the matter the instruction and warning which come to the Church of our day from the contents and past fulfilments of this chapter are exceedingly important. As Antiochus Epiphanes and his doings and successes met the prophetic description for that time, we may the better see and understand by his history how it will be in the last days. People sometimes wonder who the final Antichrist is, and how he shall come. Christian antiquity, with one voice, answers: "He is Antiochus Epiphanes reproduced, ill larger proportions and intensified energy, immediately before the great day of God Almighty." And by observing after what manner and for what reasons the calamitous inflictions of that Graeco-Syrian king fell upon the Jews of old, we may see and know how the final Antichrist will come.

Certainly, the miseries which proceeded from Antiochus came not alone of his wickedness and power. The source and seat of all were in the apostasies and sins of the Jewish people themselves, and particularly of their priests and rulers. Too easily were they beguiled and won over by the smooth flatteries and soft speeches of this deceiver. Too readily were they moved by his gracious professions and profuse liberality. And then they, in their turn, sought honor, popularity and preferment from him by base concessions, compromises and bribes. One of the main features of the evil case was their secularization of the Church of God. They set up Gentile gymnasiums in Jerusalem, where the Hebrew youths might be trained in Hellenic ways. They mimicked Greek fashions in everything, and endeavored to assimilate the manners of the people of God to heathen usages. Foreign travel, commerce, Greek philosophy, literature, religion and the arts filtered in new and strange influences, to which place was approvingly given over against the institutes of Jehovah. Many of the Jews denied their own circumcision. Three high priests — one Jesus, who by means of bribery supplanted his elder brother in the priesthood, and one Onias, who in turn supplanted Jesus — Grecised their own names, and chose to be called Jason and Menelaus; whilst the successor of the latter, Joachim, Hellenized himself into Alcimus, and in every way sought to disparage the zeal and thwart the efforts of that heroic champion of God and his country, Judas Maccabaeus, and attempted to betray him to his heathen enemies. In a word, liberality and reform made up the spirit of the times, and everything was fostered and encouraged which tended to make Jerusalem a Greek city — an Athens, an Alexandria or an Antioch — till all that was distinctive in the Jewish Church was weakened down to a mere matter of empty forms and names. Many of the priests renounced their belief in the religion of their forefathers, and apostatized from the faith of Moses and the prophets, and thus became the easy and pliant tools of enthroned and persecuting infidelity. God was forsaken, and He withdrew His grace and protection, took away the spiritual privileges which were so underrated and scorned, and turned the whole nation over to their heathen enemies. They first profaned the sanctuary, and He forsook it. They faithlessly heathenized Jerusalem, and he abandoned it. The holy of holies was no longer in truth the shrine of the living God, who had once revealed himself there on the mercy-seat, and He ceased to defend and protect it. And the temple itself, built on the spot where Abraham's faith so nobly triumphed, and where David met the angel of God, became a temple of Olympian Jove. The high priest himself sent a deputation to the Tyrian games in honor of Hercules. In place of the sacred processions of palm-bearers and singers of hosannas, who once chanted the holy melodies in the streets of Zion at the feast of tabernacles, were the bearers of ivy-tufted thyrsi, who sang lyrical dithyrambs in honor of Dionysus. And for the waters drawn forth in golden urns from the well of Siloam were the libations from the sacrifices of unclean animals, immolated on Jehovah's altar, on which was reared the image of Jupiter Olympus! The abomination of desolation had come, but the cowardice, the ambition, the covetousness, the mutual jealousy, the treachery and the apostasy of the anointed priests gave occasion for it all.

To little purpose also do we read the Book of Daniel not to find in all this a most solemn warning to the Church of our times, and for all the days yet to come, to beware of the fascinating flatteries and secularizing expedients and compliances which, in the self-idolizing spirit of spurious charity, specious liberality and heartless skepticism, would tempt her to forget her divine origin and heavenly destiny. There is a spirit abroad which would have the Church rescind her sacred charter, cancel her authentic commission and assimilate herself to a mere political or conventional institution. Men call it a liberalizing spirit, a spirit of improvement, which would change our Christian schools and colleges into mere secular gymnasiums and scientific museums or artistic studios and literary athenaeums; but it is a spirit which is prone to treat the Holy Scriptures as mere human lucubrations of worthy men before the ages of better light, rationalize away all the definite doctrines of the authorized creed into mere scholastic or philosophical theorems, dissolve the sacraments into picturesque symbolisms and visionary shadows without life or power, and dismantle the ministry and services of the Church as if they never had a solid right to be regarded as the appointment of very God for conveying and imparting to lost man the regenerating, sanctifying and only restorative gifts of Jehovah's grace. It is the spirit of Antichrist. And more and more will this spirit strengthen till it has effectually done its work. Paul specifically tells us that in the latter days men will not endure sound doctrine, but after their own lusts shall heap to themselves teachers who will minister to these alienated fancies. Creed, catechisms and all distinctive formularies of faith, as well as all proper claims of Church and sacraments, they will proscribe and trample under foot. Many whose sworn business it is to defend these things at all costs will be the leaders in betraying them. More and more will men throw off the restraints of true piety and religion, and become lovers of their own selves, boasters, proud, blasphemers, unthankful, unholy, without natural affection, false accusers, incontinent, fierce, despisers of those that are good; having a form of godliness, but denying the power thereof. Jesus himself says, "When the Son of man cometh, shall He find faith on the earth?" And thus, by the sins, compromises, apostasies and general heathenizing and secularizing of sacred things on the part of the guardians of the faith, the final and full-blown Antiochus shall come as the just judgment of the Lord Almighty upon those who thus paved his way and threw open the doors. (See Wordsworth's *Preface to Daniel.*)

Oh, my friends, many of the so-called churches and the leaders of the prevailing religious sentiment of our day are sowing for a harvest of miseries of which they but little dream. By the light of holy prophecy, and by the necessities that hold between causes and their effects, I see it coming on all sides like an overwhelming flood. By the emptiness of faith and life, which persist in covering themselves with the holy name of Christianity and religion, myriads who would be honest with themselves are stumbling and falling, and filling up the ranks of downright infidelity and atheism; and by the promises of peace and universal brotherhood on the lips of those who think they are leading the vanguard of the Lord's host, myriads on myriads more are being deceived and betrayed to bitter disappointments and helpless miseries in this world, if not to eternal discomfiture in the world to come. In how many instances do we find the very high priests of God's temple sacrificing its holiest treasures to win the favors of the treacherous and insatiable horn of the world's power, selling themselves and their most sacred trusts for the emoluments of the great destroyer! In how many instances do we find them cajoled into the taking of his side and the espousing of his cause over against the Mattathiases and Eleazars and Maccabseuses who would recall the bewitched multitude to their proper senses and rally them around the old and everlasting standards! And how can it be otherwise but that the devil-inspired world which they have courted, and to which they thus give over the heritage of God, shall eventually assert and enforce its right to command, even to the seating of itself in the temple of God, the magnifying of itself over all gods, and the dictation of infamies for its own worship as the only God, under whom no true saints can live except as they remain secreted in the desolate mountains and wildernesses of the earth, till the Lord's indignation is satisfied, iniquity is perfected and the day of God Almighty breaks in with its riving thunders!

Daniel, you will observe, was greatly affected by these visions and the explanations made of them; as he well might be. He fainted, and was sick for days. Some take this as a sort of special visitation upon the prophet, that he might not be unduly exalted through the abundance of his revelations; but there is no ground whatever for such a thought. It was an unprecedented scene of calamity to his people, his country and his religion that he thus beheld; and this it was that affected him. It was not God's interference to keep him humble, but the exhibit of the terrible things to happen to what was dearest to his heart. It was his cogitations that troubled him, changed his countenance and prostrated his enemies. From this Bishop Newton draws what he considers "a conclusive argument that the calamities under Antiochus could not possibly be the main end and ultimate scope of this prophecy." It likewise serves to show how wide is the difference between the way in which the holy men of old regarded sacred prophecy and the manner in which it is treated by the great mass of professed believers in our day. Nothing so interested the prophets as the foreshowing of things to come. Peter tells us that they "inquired and searched diligently, searching what, or what manner of time the Spirit which was in them did signify, when it testified beforehand the sufferings of Christ, and the glory that should follow." Daniel's whole soul was almost drawn out of him by the intensity of his interest, study, fasting and prayers with regard to what was here foreshown. But what is the temper of our modern theologians on the subject? The common idea is that a man is a little beside himself and departs from proper soberness if he ventures to give any serious attention to unfulfilled prophecy. Though God has been at the pains to tell us much about what is yet to come, many would warn us away from it as dangerous ground, and tell us that we unwarrantably intrude into the secrets of the Almighty if we undertake to read it or entertain any definite expectations with regard to it. The popular doctrine is that prophecy is not meant to be understood until after it is fulfilled — that to found any faith upon it is fanaticism — that none but crazed brains ever bother themselves about it one way or another. According to these sober people, the prophets were the silliest of men to concern themselves about what they were commissioned to foretell, and Daniel was a particular fool to let his soul be troubled concerning these zoologic visions of things in the distant ages. But this is just the difference between the true and acknowledged servants of God and those who claim to be their brethren, successors and representatives in our day. By the Fathers whatever the Holy Ghost made known concerning the future was treasured and studied as the most precious of communications, dwelt upon with the most special interest and heeded as the guiding light of God amid this world's abounding darkness. But with most of our modern teachers to ignore and avoid what is written about the future is the higher wisdom and the better piety. And if perchance they are pushed into the subject, the sum of their teaching is that it may perhaps mean this, or perhaps that, or perhaps nothing that we can at present decipher. And thus a vast and vitally interesting part of God's revelation is emasculated and practically turned into a useless encumbrance of the sacred pages. Jehovah says, *"Write the vision, and make it plain upon tables, that he may run that readeth it,"* even though it be a vision which is yet for an appointed time unknown to us. But men have become wiser than their Maker, and know better what becomes a sober theologian and a right preacher; and we must shut the Book and close our mouths about it, or consent to be accounted mad! Alas, alas for the reigning religion of our day!

Brethren, if we would be like the holy prophets. and prove ourselves their followers, we must have an eye, an ear and a heart for their sacred word concerning what must shortly come to pass. Every utterance of the Lord is precious, and especially every word which tells what we are to look for and expect. And as you value your safety in these ominous and perplexing times, and would be ready for what is about to come upon the earth, beware how you ignore or neglect what God has caused to be written for our learning, lest, being in darkness, the great day should overtake you as a thief!

Lecture Eleventh - The Chosen People's Fortunes; or, the Seventy Weeks

Daniel 9: 1-27.

THIS chapter, more than any other in the Book of Daniel, lays open to us the inner life of the prophet. It shows that he who was so illustrious in his wisdom and public relations was no less noted for his deep spirituality and earnest private devotions, whilst it suggests that the former were largely the result of the latter. True faith and living piety help to make wise and great.

Close personal communion with God and habitual leaning upon Him are the source of man's greatest dignity and grandest successes. Nor could Daniel have been the man that he was, so honored a premier, so wise a prophet or so beloved a favorite of Heaven, but for his having been so earnest a believer and so devout a suppliant. And if we would learn something of the manner and substance of those prayers which he offered three times a day at his window looking toward Jerusalem, we here have a specimen of them written and put in form by himself, just as it poured forth again and again from his saintly lips. Nor can I but think that if the government officials of our day would learn to indite and use such words as the daily outpouring of their deepest hearts, they would learn a patriotism of which, unfortunately, they know too little, though they talk so much, and our political affairs would cease to be the shame and scandal of the country and the mortifying grief of all right-minded citizens which they now are. Certainly, better public servant than Daniel, as tested by three different administrations, and fully admitted even by those who hated him most, never filled an office of state. He was vise, faithful and absolutely faultless. And the secret source of it was that no engagements of empire, no plots or accusations of men, no subtle attempts to draw him off, could ever serve to keep him from his prayers and duties to his God. And here in this chapter we are enabled to come near that open window and to listen to the very words of his intensest prayers. A writer on the subject has said, "I know not that there is in the Bible a sublimer litany than that which is contained in this chapter, or clauses more appropriate as channels of a Christian's prayers than these earnest, beautiful, yet simple petitions." Happy they who are kindled by the same spirit to a like unction!

It is worth observing, too, by what exercises and circumstances this particular intensity of devotion and pious earnestness was inflamed and fed. It appears from the first verses that Daniel was a student of prophecy, of unfulfilled prophecy, and especially of the numbers and dates contained in the sacred predictions. It seems that he was very anxious to find out about "the times and the seasons" to which the prophetic word had alluded, and wished to decipher all about the days and the years in which God's foreshowings were to be accomplished. Many consider such studies and anxieties the most barren and dangerous to which we can give ourselves. It is a common idea that we are not only not called upon, but not even authorized, to pry into unfulfilled prophecies, and especially unfulfilled prophetic dates. The assertions are even put forth in the name of Christianity that it is damaging to true piety and destructive of all right Christian activity and devotion to examine and talk about such things. But the holy Daniel was of a different mind and spirit. He studied the writings of the prophets. He searched into what was foretold to come to pass, and particularly "the number of the years whereof the word of the Lord" had spoken. But, so far from working harm to his piety, or of unfitting him for the practical duties of life, he here writes it down as the special source and spring of the intensest of all his devout activities — the very thing which aroused him to the sublimest exhibition of living soul-religion —

which in no manner unfitted him for due attention to "the king's business." There is indeed much reason to suspect that one of the real causes of the superficiality and leanness of modern piety is that the professed people of God no longer understand or believe what the prophets have written, and refuse to study or hear about things to come as God has revealed them for our learning. Let them study what Daniel studied, and learn the whole plan of the divine administrations as Jehovah has sketched it to us in His word, and we shall soon see and realize more of Daniel's spirit, wisdom and unction. He caught it largely from books of unfulfilled prophecies, and we must go to the same source, and in the same way, if we would be really toned up to that sublimity of earnestness and hold-taking on God which this chapter records. The more definite our apprehensions of what God has foretold, and the more sure we are of the certain fulfilment of the same, the more contrite, importunate and confident will be our supplications that He may make haste and accomplish all His blessed purpose.

There is abundant material in this prayer of Daniel on which to dwell with interest and profit. The manner of it was deliberate, reverent, humble and self-chastening. He did not rush into the matter as the unthinking horse into the battle. He set his face unto the Lord, pre-arranged the -subject, substance and form of his supplications, and fasted in sackcloth and ashes, that he might fittingly come before that God under whose chastisements he and his countrymen were then suffering for their sins. And thus Ave need to humble ourselves under the mighty hand of God.

The character and attributes which this piece of devotion ascribes to Deity, are also very impressive and sublime. The grandeur and awfulness of Eternal Majesty are blended with unsearchable goodness and faithfulness, presenting to our contemplation "the great and dreadful God, keeping covenant and mercy to them that love Him and keep His commandments," whose almighty hand is in all the administrations on earth and in heaven, and all whose ways are righteousness and truth.

The same is vastly occupied with confession of sin as the cause of Israel's miseries. The expressions on this point are the most explicit, unreserved and contrite. With deepest sorrow of soul the prophet rehearses the whole length and breadth of the dark catalogue of Israel's offending. Nothing is left out, nothing is extenuated, nothing is held back, nothing is excused; for so long as people apologize for their sins, or fail to acknowledge them with genuine contrition and sorrow, they cannot be forgiven. It was not a mere outcry under the miseries which sin had brought, but an unreserved confession of its inherent evilness and ill-desert, and a thorough acquiescence in the righteousness of God in the punishments which He visits upon it.

The great subject of this prayer was not simply that affliction might be removed, but that the house and ordinances of God might be restored and a true spiritual recovery wrought; for it avails but little to be released from particular punishments of sin if the inner cause of them be not healed.

So the plea upon which this prayer rests is the truest and only availing one — not any merit of man, not any right or claim on the sinner's part, but alone and entirely the mercy of God and the honor of His great Name.

And there is also a pathos and importunity the most intense running through and through it. What an outpouring of all the feelings and energies of the prophet's being are in that *Kyrie Eleison* with which he concludes! —

"O Lord, hear!

"O Lord, forgive!

"O Lord, hearken and do!

"Defer not, for Thine own sake, O my God;

For Thy city and Thy people are called by Thy Name."

Such praying, confession and supplication could not fail to reach the gracious ear of an ever-merciful Jehovah. And while the prophet was yet speaking the angel Gabriel was sent on quick commission to assure Daniel that his devotions were accepted, and at the same time to disclose to him a full outline of all that was to come to his people in all the ages of time. And it is to this prophecy, the fullest, the most precious and the most important in all this series, that I now invite your particular attention.

That it is difficult the history of opinions concerning it abundantly shows. That it is of the most momentous import and intensest worth all agree. Nor can I help but think that most of the trouble in understanding it has originatednot so much from the prophecy itself as from the inadequate, one-sided or falsely-emphasised systems or pre-occupations which expositors have brought to it, and to which they have thought it must needs be made to conform. Volumes on volumes of the profoundest learning and minutest criticism have men devoted to it, and yet to this day the great body of the Christian world is still at sea with regard to a complete, straightforward and exhaustive understanding of what Gabriel was so specially commissioned of God to make understood. Perhaps if we were particular to hear Gabriel more, and the cumbrous disquisitions and rationalizing opinions of men less, we might come to a better apprehension of what was thus made known to Daniel. What, then, is to be ascertained from the divine revelation touching the so-called *"seventy weeks."*?

1. The first remark I have to make is, that they are not *"weeks"* at all, in the ordinary acceptation of that word. A "week," as we speak, is a period consisting of seven days, but Gabriel says nothing about *days*. What he speaks of is a period of *seventy sevens,* without saying whether they are sevens of days or years or thousands of years. But when we turn back to the beginning of the chapter and note what Daniel had been investigating, and observe to what this communication was to a degree the divine answer, we see exactly to what these sevens refer. The prophet had been studying the pre-intimations of the limit of the Babylonian captivity. From the sacred writings, as he tells us, he had ascertained "the number of *the years,"* and that the Lord "would accomplish *seventy years* in the desolations of Jerusalem." It was because of this knowledge that he set himself to this particular supplication, as God had directed in connection with these date-indications. And it was in answer to this prayer, and on the precise subject of Israel's fortunes, that Gabriel was sent to give this revelation of the so-called "seventy weeks." It was *time numbered by years,* and hence sevens of *years,* that was the thought and subject of discourse at the beginning of the whole matter; and it is therefore unwarrantable to think of anything else than *years* — sevens of years and seventy sevens of years — in this continuity of the same general topic. There is no prophetic putting of days for years, as some speak — no symbolism whatever — but a plain didactic continuation of the discourse about the dates and times in Israel's fortunes, in the same terms *understood* which at the beginning had been doubly *expressed.* Not *"weeks,"* therefore, or sevens of *days,* are we to understand here, but sevens of *years* — nothing more and nothing less.

2. These sevens of years are given in three distinct sections — the first a multiple of seven by seven; the second a multiple of seven by sixty-two; and the third a single seven, making a series consisting severally of forty-nine years, four hundred and thirty-four years, and seven years — in all *ten times seven sevens of years,* covering the entire period to which the accomplishment of all that is contained in this prophecy, from first to last, is embraced. Whether these sections of time are immediately continuous in each instance, so that where one ends the other promptly begins, is not specifically determined, and remains to be ascertained by other elements of the prediction. The first and second sections, the forty-nine years and the four hundred and thirty-four years, appear to be unmistakably continuous, as they together are meant to mark one specific and most important date. But this does not seem to be the case with the third section, as things are spoken of as occurring "after" the expiration of the four hundred and eighty-three years, which, in their nature, cannot be embraced in the final seven, but introduce what would seem to be a long hiatus, or intercalary period, between the second and third sections, the measure of which is not given, for reasons quite explainable from the subject and nature of the revelation itself.

3. What is to be accomplished in these seventy seven of years, as thus parcelled out by the angel, *relates exclusively to the fortunes of Israel as a nation and to their city and state.* This is specifically stated by Gabriel at the very beginning as the key to the right understanding of all that pertains to this particular prophecy. He says that these seventy sevens of years "are determined," divided out, severed from all other reckonings of time, and appropriated in the foreknowledge and counsel of God *"upon thy people and upon the holy city;"* that is, beyond mistake, upon the Israelitish race and their metropolis. This is a vital point, and must be taken with us in all that follows, or we misapply the prophecy. There is no authority on earth for shifting these statements, in any of their parts, to any people, city or events but those which concern the Jews and Jerusalem. However else the whole earth, or any portion of it outside of Abraham's descendants, may be reached, blessed or afflicted through what is here embraced, the entire matter is presented by Gabriel in this discourse in no other light or relation than that which pertains to the Abrahamic race, and to Jerusalem as their representative city. It is not the Jew and Jerusalem in one case, and Christians and the Church in another. It is the Jew and Jerusalem first, last and all the time, and nothing but the Jew and Jerusalem, and what pertains to them. If this be not true, then Gabriel did not tell the truth, for he speaks of these sections of the seventy sevens of years, and of the whole of them together, and of all that is connected with them, as being selected out and determined of God upon the blood-kin and people of the prophet, then in captivity, and upon their holy city, then in ruins, but presently to be rebuilt. Having settled this, we rule out a vast mass of ingenious comment, criticism and erudition as wholly irrelevant to the interpretation of this prophecy, and clear the way for a consistent understanding of it, which is otherwise hopelessly encumbered.

4. A general summary of what these seventy sevens are to see accomplished is the first thing explained by the angel. Ver. 24. If we ask for what these periods are thus divided out, we here get the answer: (1) *"To consummate transgression"* — finish it, bring it to its final stopping-point, after which there will be no more of it. (2) *"To make an end of sins"* — seal them up, shut them in prison, so as never to break forth again. (3) *"To cover iniquity"* — expiate it by adequate satisfaction, blot it out, liide it for ever. (4) *"To bring in everlasting righteousness"* — put man in normal relations with God, set human life into thorough accord with Jehovah's will and law, induce a condition of moral rectitude, which thenceforward shall never again be interrupted, but endure for all the ages. (5) *"To seal vision and prophet"* — authenticate and vindicate by fulfilment, make good and finish out in fact and deed, all that God hath spoken by the mouth of all His holy prophets since the world began. (6) *"To anoint"* — consecrate, put into place and effectiveness — *"a holiness of holinesses,"* which is the literal sense of the words in this last clause. It has been applied to the baptism or christing of Jesus, to the rededication of the temple and to various other things, one as impossible as the other if the actual wording and connection is adequately observed. It can refer to nothing less than the completed outcome of the redemptive administrations as a whole — the ultimate result and crown of grace and providence, of which all the prophets speak. Zechariah sings of this "holiness of holinesses" where he says, "In that day there shall be upon the bells [or bridles] of the horses, **Holiness unto the Lord;** and the pots in the Lord's house shall be like the bowls before the altar; yea, every pot in Jerusalem and in Judea shall be holiness unto the Lord of hosts." Zech. xiv. 20, 21; also Isa. xi. 4-9. It is not the consecration of a person, an altar or a house, but the consecration of the whole nation and of everything pertaining to them. Everything promised, prophesied or ever to be hoped for Israel is thus summed up in what these seventy sevens are to bring. It is said by the angel that they reach to "the consummation," and hence to the fulfilment of all Scripture and prophecy, otherwise called "the regeneration," "the restitution of all things."

5. Having given this sketch of final results, the angel proceeded to explain the particular periods and events as included and distributed in the various sections of these seventy sevens.

The great section, and that first announced, is the sixty-two sevens added on to seven sevens, or four hundred and eighty-three years, the reach of which was to be to *Messiah Prince.* As Christians, with the New Testament in our hands, we can have no difficulty in determining who is to be understood by this *Messiah Prince.* It is here for the first time in the Bible that we find the word *Messiah* put thus absolutely. It was applied to Cyrus in Isaiah to designate him as a chosen instrument of God for the deliverance of His people from their long captivity, but only in so far as he was a type of that greater Deliverer promised from the beginning and looked for by believers of every age. At the time Jesus appeared in our world the Israelitish people everywhere were speaking of that coming Deliverer as *Messias* or *Messiah,* meaning He who should come as the anointed and sent of God to accomplish eternal redemption in Israel. (See John iv. 25, 41; Matt. ii. 4; Luke ii. 26; iii. 15; John i. 20; iii. 28; vii. 26; x. 24.) And to that promised and expected Redeemer the reference here must needs be. That the promised Messiah was to be a King, a Ruler, one administering with royal authority and in regal office, was also implied, if not expressed, in all the predictions concerning Him. After the establishment of the Hebrew monarchy He was continually referred to as the Prince of the house of David. Hence He is here designated as *Messiah* **Prince,** and hence the New Testament everywhere ascribes kingship to Jesus of Nazareth as belonging to His Messiahship. And to Jesus as *Messiah King* these four hundred and eighty-three years were to reach.

To what point in the life of Christ, then, does the angel refer? Some say to" His birth; but Jesus was not then presented to the Jewish nation as their Prince or King, though called "king of the Jews" by the Magi. Some say the reference is to His baptism or His anointing by the Holy Ghost immediately after His baptism, or both; but not a word was then said to the people about His being *King,* but only of His being the Son and Prophet of God, to whom they should give audience. And for more than three years of His ministry, in all His authoritative teaching and miraculous healing, He did not once make the slightest pretensions to being a *king.* On the contrary, when the people would willingly have crowned Him, and insisted on making Him their king, He peremptorily refused to take any such place, honor or title. But the time came when He did make profession and claim to be the rightful King of the Jews, and so presented himself to the Jewish nation at one of the greatest of their national festivals at Jerusalem. It occurred but a few days prior to His Passion, and was one of the principal and most direct causes of His condemnation and crucifixion. For the first time in His career we behold Him *mounted as a king,* with multitudes doing honor to Him and hailing Him with hosannas as the Prince of the house of David. In the midst of the loud-sounding proclamations of Him as *the King,* He triumphantly rode into Jerusalem, entered the temple, cast out all them that sold and bought in the temple, over-

115

threw the tables of the money-changers and the seats of them that sold doves, and took to himself all the authority and majesty of the rightful King and Lord of the chosen people, their temple and their state. And when the officials came to Him, insinuating treasonableness in these pretensions, particularly in the outcries which hailed Him as the blessed *King*, the Davidic Prince, He promptly answered, *"If these should hold their peace, the stones would immediately cry out."* Luke xix. 40. He had to be presented to the nation as its rightful and anointed King; and this is when and how it was done. We make no mistake on this point. Ancient prophecy foretold that the Messiah King should come to Jerusalem sitting upon an ass, even a colt the foal of an ass; and inspiration under the New Testament narrates this very scene, and says, *"This was done that it might he fulfilled which was spoken by the prophet, saying. Tell ye the daughter of Sion, Behold, thy King; cometh unto thee."* Matt. xxi. It was here specially, emphatically and for the first time that Jesus presented himself to the Jewish people as their *Messiah* Prince; and only to this point in His earthly history can the words of the angel literally and fully apply, for not till then did He come as the Ruler, the King. We thus find the exact *terminating-point* of the angel's four hundred and eighty-three years.

If, now, we can find the *commencing-point* equally answering to the angel's description, we will have at once ample demonstration of the truth and inspiration of the Book of Daniel 'and of the Messiahship of Jesus of Nazareth. Let us see, then, whether we can identify such a point.

The communicating angel is very distinct and definite. He tells of a command, commission or edict "to restore and to build Jerusalem," from the going forth of which on to Messiah Prince were to be four hundred and eighty-three years. Legitimately taken, this could be none other than a command or commission from some one or other of the Medo-Persian kings under whom the Jews were restored. Three several such commissions with reference to the return of the Jews also appear upon the sacred record — one from Cyrus, to rebuild the temple (given in Ezra i.); one from Artaxerxes, in the seventh year of his reign, to Ezra, to reorganize the Jewish economy and worship (given in Ezra vii.); and one from the same Artaxerxes, in the twentieth year of his reign, to Nehemiah (given in Neh. ii.). Of these only the last-named was strictly for *the rebuilding of the city.* The first related to the temple only; the second related to the temple polity only; but this last related particularly to *the city,* its streets, walls and defences, as a residence and hold for the Jewish people and state. Of the three, the last was politically by far the most important. It is that which gave the Jews a place and standing again of their own, and hence, above all others, would be the natural date of Israel's renewed national existence. The angel's words respecting the character of the times in which the rebuilding of which he speaks was to occur also helps to identify most vividly this last commission as the one meant. The rebuilding was to be "in troublous times," amid great straits and adverse pressure. This was, above all, the case under the third commission, which was the one given to Nehemiah, and was opposed because of the fortified strength which it would again give to the Jews. We have only to read the Book of Nehemiah to see with what formidable difficulties and antagonisms he had to contend, and how the sword for defence had to be held in one hand while the trowel was in the other. I therefore fix upon this commission to Nehemiah by Artaxerxes, king of Persia, in the twentieth year of his reign, as the going forth of the commandment to which the angel referred as the starting-point for the four hundred and eighty-three years to Messiah Prince.

Now, as near as the ablest chronologists can come to certainty, our Saviour was born somewhere about four years earlier than our common era makes it. This places Christ's entry into Jerusalem as *King* in or close about the year 29 of our reckoning. Counting back, then, from A.D. 29 four hundred and eighty-three years, we come to the year 454 B.C., or close thereabout, for the time of "the going forth of the command to restore and to build Jerusalem." *And this,* according to Archbishop Ussher, Tregelles and others, *was the exact year noted as the twentieth of the reign of Artaxerxes, king of Persia!* Precise chronology is so involved and unsettled that it is not possible to reach absolute certainty as to any one date of so distant a past and in a region concerning which we have so little connected history. But this twentieth of Artaxerxes is determined with more harmony, and within a smaller limit of possible error, than any other similar date of that age and section. Hengstenberg, who has gone into the whole subject with an ability and thoroughness unsurpassed by any other man, agrees so nearly with Ussher and Tregelles as to differ from them only by a single year. Mahan, by another and quite independent process, comes out on almost the same date. And one of the ablest recent writers on the subject (Hengstenberg's *Christology,* iii. 223) states that the range of variations in all the current chronological calculations in relation to this period of time does not extend over a circle of ten years for the precise date of the twentieth of Artaxerxes, estimated at four hundred and eighty-three years back from Christ's triumphal entry into Jerusalem. So close an agreement as this does not exist with reference to any other equally remote Oriental date which has no astronomical connections on which to lean. And from all that man now knows, or can show to the contrary, we are fully warranted in saying that this communicating angel foretold exactly to the year and month the length of time to elapse between the going forth of a word from Artaxerxes to rebuild Jerusalem and the coming of Messiah Prince to that self-same city as the anointed King.

6. The angel then adds some further and most vital particulars following the termination of these threescore and two sevens, but without touching at all the final seven. Though Christ as Messiah Prince came to the Jewish people, they disallowed His claims, rejected Him, condemned Him and had Him crucified. "He came unto His own, but His own received Him not." And so the angel said, "After the threescore and two sevens, *Messiah shall be cut off"* — not in the middle of the last seven, as so many say, but simply *"after"* the termination of the sixty-two sevens, with no allusion to the last seven. How

long "after" was not said, but all agree that the cutting off is contemplated as close upon the completion of the four hundred and eighty-three years and Messiah's presentation of himself as the Prince. It occurred, in fact, within the next six days succeeding. And this cutting off of Christ was of the widest, deepest and intensest description. The elders of Israel condemned Him, and so cut Him off from the congregation of God's professed people. The Roman government gave Him up into the hands of His enemies, and so cut Him off from its protection. The soldiers crucified Him with consent of both Jewish and Gentile authority, and so cut Him off from the land of the living. The long-promised, the long-looked-for, the divinely -chosen Messiah Prince was dead, crucified, officially murdered; and the angel's word had another item most literally fulfilled, demonstrating the reality of inspiration and the presence of a foreknowledge which could come only from God.

There has been an endless amount of learned criticism to determine the grammatical construction of the little phrase added by the angel, which our English translators, as all agree, have improperly rendered, *"but not for himself."* And in that little phrase is really the turning-point in the angel's prediction, from which its only right interpretation subsequent to the cutting off of Messiah flows. But whilst no two critics precisely agree as to the grammar of the terse but very significant little words of the original, orthodox expositors are well enough at one on the general sense to be taken from them. True as the doctrine of Christ's vicarious sufferings is, all hands concede that it is not to be maintained from this passage. The reference is not at all to the character of Messiah's death, but to the result of His rejection and cutting off upon the relations and consequent fortunes of the Jewish nation. In whatever particular phraseology we translate, the inner meaning is that the cutting off of Messiah by those to whom He came as their King was the cutting of themselves off from the preferments and guardianship which would have been theirs had they accepted Him as their King. As a nation they rejected their Messiah Prince, and in that they chose and accepted rejection by Him as His nation. Killing their King, they ceased to be that King's people, and precipitated themselves to the same level with the Gentiles, burdened with the additional guilt and stain of having killed their own Messiah, Thus the angel said, "After the threescore and two sevens Messiah shall be cut off, *and it is not to Him"* — the nation so cutting Him off being no longer the nation to Him in that sense in which He was and proposed to be their Messiah Prince. In other words, the angel here told Daniel that immediately after the end of a given term of years his people would reject their Messiah Prince, and cause Him to be slain, and that by consequence they would cease to be that Messiah's people, and cut themselves off from being a nation to Him whom, by their cutting of Him off, they had made to be no king to them. And we are all the more sure that this is the angel's meaning from what he further adds concerning the spoliation and destruction to befall the Jewish nation as the consequence of their cutting off of their proper Prince. As God's chosen people they thus forfeited all their superior privileges; and so the angel said that their city and temple should be destroyed, that dreadful invasion and desolation should overflow and overwhelm them, that their punishment should last till within seven years of "the consummation," or great day of judgment, and that even then the latter half of those final seven years should bring a reenactment upon them of the scenes which their fathers experienced under Titus and Vespasian.

How accurately all this has been fulfilled up to this present we know. Jerusalem fell amid horrors and fearful desolations. Through full one thousand eight hundred years have the holy city and temple now been in ruins, helplessly trodden down of the Gentiles, and its people scattered to the ends of the earth, with God's judgments cleaving to them with a tenacity unexampled.

7. But with all this following the termination of the threescore and two sevens and the cutting off of Messiah, there still remains a final section of the seventy to which nothing thus far has been referred. The angel therefore proceeds (ver. 27) to tell us concerning that last seven. You will notice that he makes it terminate at *"the consummation,"* when the great Desolater receives his doom. This cannot be anything short of the final close of this present world, the great day of judgment, which issues in "the restitution of all things." These last seven years must therefore be counted backward from that notable time, as the others are counted forward from the going forth of the command to rebuild Jerusalem. It is hence impossible to reckon them continuously from the termination of the threescore and two, for that period ended more than eighteen hundred years ago, and "the consummation" has not yet come. As the day of judgment is still future, so these final seven years, which terminate at the judgment, must likewise be future, as the Christian Fathers with great unanimity held, and as many of the soundest of the more recent expositors now see and confess.

The things which specially mark this final seven of the apportioned seventy years, as stated by the angel, are the presence and doings of the final Antichrist, or *the prince* elsewhere abundantly prophesied of, who is here described as the last embodiment of that power by which Jerusalem and the temple were destroyed after the cutting off of Messiah. The seven years begin with the establishment of a covenant between this prince and many of the Jewish people, which he violates after the first half of the period, and then goes forward with his fell work during the last three and a half years to his sudden and everlasting perdition at their end.

It is thus included in the Aery texture of this foreshowing of the angel that the Jewish people will be largely regathered again from their present dispersion to their ancient land, with their temple rebuilt and their worship restored. It is said of this prince of the destroyers that "in the midst of the seven he shall cause the sacrifice and the oblation to cease," that for the remaining half he will perpetrate the most infamous profanities and blasphemies, and set up "the abomination of desolation," which the Saviour speaks of, in Matt, xxiv., as "in the holy place." All this presupposes some regathering of

Israel, the existence of their temple, and something of a Jewish renationalization. This return will be in the same anti-Christian Judaism which has characterized this people since Messiah was crucified, if not in still intensified infidelity; for they come back and take their place again under compact with a power which is to prove itself the most blasphemous and tyrannical that has ever existed. They will have a prince, but that prince will be the Antichrist. According to the angel's words, another Caesar is to arise — a pseudo-Christ and an Antichrist at the same time. He will come, not in his own power, but In that of the devil. Him, according to the Saviour's saying, the Jews as a people will receive, and will covenant with him as their proper Messiah Prince over against Jesus, whom their fathers hanged on a tree.

But sadly will they rue their misplaced confidence. He whom they accept as their greatest friend and helper will prove their fiercest oppressor and destroyer. He will be to them the second Antiochus, who will rob and plunder them, again prohibit their sacrifices except as rendered to an idol he will set up, again pollute their temple, again drag off many into captivity or drive them into the wilderness, and fill the whole land with bloody desolations which only the great day of God Almighty will serve to interrupt and remove.

Such, in brief, are the contents of this most important chapter. About the last of the seventy years of the Babylonian servitude Daniel was engaged in the study of the sacred prophecies concerning events to come. Through these investigations he was brought to the conclusion that the time for Israel's deliverance was at hand. To fulfil the conditions on which God had promised again to undertake the cause of His people, then in suffering for their sins, he set his face unto the Lord in penitential supplications, which must ever stand as one of the intensest and sublimest specimens of penitential devotion. In answer to his prayers God sent the angel Gabriel to assure him that his prayer was heard, and to explain to him the whole future history of his people. In seven sevens of years from the going forth of a royal word to build and restore Jerusalem the restoration was to be complete. In threescore and two sevens more Messiah Prince, the subject of promise, hope and prayer for thousands on thousands of years, was to present himself, and immediately thereafter He was to be rejected and cut off by the elect nation whose King He proposed to be, who thus cut themselves off from Him, and subjected themselves to a deeper, vaster and a thirty-fold more lasting desolation of their city and temple than their former sins and apostasies had entailed.

After this sore experience, indefinitely lengthened out, another count of a single and isolated seven is named as apportioned in the divine counsels upon the prophet's people and their city, the termination of which is specifically located at "the consummation" and the great judgment upon the prince of the destroyers. For the first half of these last seven years the prophet's people are to be under the protectorate of "the prince that shall come," the final Antichrist, who will deceive and betray them, turn into a cruel oppressor, interdict the worship he had helped them to re-establish and covenanted to protect, set up an idol of his own in the temple of Jehovah and bring about a series of abominations, hardships and desolating impieties, as if hell itself had been let loose upon the world.

But his career of wickedness will be short. Three and. a half years is the limit of it. And then is "the consummation," when all that has been fore-determined shall be executed on the terrible Desolater. And with his destruc-tion is the accomplishment of the seventy sevens, when transgression shall be ended, sin finally shut up, all former iniquity buried, an everlasting right-eousness brought in, all sacred vision and prophecy vindicated and fulfilled and a holiness of holinesses installed.

Great, awful, transcendent revelation! What a light it throws over all the ages of time! How true to the minutest particular in what of the period spanned has already passed! How sublime and overwhelming the demon-stration it gives of the reality of inspiration, of the goodness and severity of God, of the Messiahship of Jesus, of the guilt of rejecting Him and of the infal-lible certainty of Jehovah's word!

And why, then, will men persist in disbelieving the truth and divinity of books that come to us with such manifest authentications?

And why, again, will men continue to disown and reject Jesus Christ, in whom the sacred prophecies have been so astoundingly fulfilled, and the sad consequences of rejecting whom confront us every day in every Jew we meet and in every glance we cast upon Judea and Jerusalem?

And why will men be so blinded and slow to believe all that is written as to persevere in discrediting the things foretold of the future, though they stand written with equal plainness in the very same records and revelations so much of which has already been realized to the very letter?

Lecture Twelfth - The Picture Filled in; or, the Vision by the Hiddekel

Daniel 10:1-21 and 11:1-35.

THE part of the Book of Daniel on which we now enter embraces what rationalists and skeptics have most objected to, as arguing its non-genuineness. But if we were even to allow that certain portions of these two chapters have marks of a more recent origin than the time of Daniel, it does not therefore follow that the great body of the Book is not what it professes to be.

It is generally known that this Book, in the Greek version, once contained much which has long since been set aside by critics and the Church as not at all a part of it. The beginning once contained the Apocryphal History of Su-sanna and the Elders; the third chapter once contained the Apocryphal Song of the Three Hebrew Children in the fiery furnace; and at the end once stood the Apocryphal story of Bel and the Dragon. On very good grounds these things have been thrown out, as not belonging to the genuine ancient Book of Daniel. And it may be, as some orthodox and believing critics think, that even the present Hebrew text, particularly in the chapters now before us, embraces some things which possibly were not written by Daniel.

The questions have been asked — Why is it that the Book is so profuse, detailed and repetitious in its descriptions of the times of the Greek empire in Syria, and of those times only? Why is it that the composition, in dwelling on those times, is in the most prosaic style of human annals? Why is it that this minute description of events stops so suddenly short in Maccabean days? And why is the whole remainder of the prophetic portion of the Book so magnificently grand in outline, and just these two chapters are mostly so different? A recent writer on Daniel (Bosanquet) thinks that we have reason to thank skeptical critics for having drawn attention to these remarkable phenomena, and has come to the conclusion that the portions of this Book whence most offence has been taken were once mere marginal commentary, applying Daniel's prophecies to the times of Antiochus Epiphanes, which was accidentally taken up into the text by some copyist or transcriber, who failed to notice or note that it was no part of the original Danielle record.

The particular passages falling under this suspicion are chapter x. 1, 15-21, and chapter xi. 1, 5-35. By omitting these passages it is claimed that we have the pure, original Book of Daniel, not only freed from many objections raised by infidelity against its genuineness, but in clear, connected and thoroughly self-consistent form. And as there is really nothing of doctrinal importance in these particular paragraphs, and their omission in no wise maims the clearness, sublimity and worth of these prophecies in general, as received by the Church, it is held that there is no occasion for any one to be the least disturbed in case these particular items should be shown to have come from some other hand than that of the illustrious sage and courtier of Babylon and Medo-Persia.

The first verse of chapter x. certainly bears the appearances of being the remark of some commentator. It cannot be denied that the matter, style and form of it answer to those of a man writing down his own opinion of Daniel's vision. It reads precisely like the uninspired headings to the chapters in our English Bibles, whilst what follows reads quite differently. It is not according to the way in which Daniel elsewhere expresses himself, and seems to be at variance with other statements of the Book. It extends Daniel's life to 'the third year of Cyrus," whereas the conclusion of the first chapter speaks of him as continuing only "unto the first year." It says that Daniel "understood the thing, and had understanding of the vision," whereas Daniel himself, at the end of it (chap. xii. 8), remarks, "I heard, *but I understood not."* It says, 'the thing was true," seemingly meaning that events had turned out as foretold, just as the later Jews would say in remarking upon the prophecy, inasmuch as they believed it fulfilled in the times and doings of Antiochus Epiphanes; but Daniel could not so speak of his predictions, since he did not live to see them fulfilled; and he does not elsewhere use such language, though the angel repeatedly said that he came to show him the truth. By locating this vision in the reign of Cyrus, it also introduces some question in identifying the four succeeding kings of Persia in accordance with the record of chap. xi. 2-4, which would be entirely obviated by the omission of this verse. There is also an internal and circumstantial coherence between the references and statements which follow it and the particulars given in the preceding chapter, which this verse apparently breaks and dissevers, so as to render an intelligent explanation harder and more doubtful. The study, fasting and "words/' referred to by the angel in chap. x. but for this verse would inevitably be taken as identical with what was referred to in chap. ix. Daniel there tells us of his penitential devotions, at the beginning of which he had the revelation of the seventy sevens apportioned out upon his people and the Holy City; and he here would seem to be telling us that this fasting and prayer lasted "three full weeks," at the end of which he had the further revelation which is described in the remaining portions of the Book. And when the angel in ver. 12 says, *"From the first day that thou didst set thine heart to understand, and to chasten thyself before God,"* he seems to refer specifically to the particulars stated in chap. ix. 2-4.

So, again, the section from ver. 15 to the end of the chapter, inclusive of ver. 1 of chap. xi. is thought to be a continuation of this alleged comment. The prophetic manner is adopted, but that was common with the later Jews when they wished to give weight and sacredness to their discourse, whilst the statements furnish a series of particulars singularly flat in character as well as somewhat peculiar in contents. Whether from Daniel or not, it is largely a paraphrastic repetition of what was said elsewhere. It also introduces a style of colloquy found only here.

The section contained in vers. 5-35 of chap. xi. has been, from the time of Porphyry, the great stumbling-block with regard to this wonderful Book. It has about it the marks of an inferior style of composition not in harmony with the rest of this magnificent production. In despite of its minuteness, it is also very barren of prophetic matter not otherwise and more consistently embraced in chaps, vii. and viii., along with chap. xii. It is sadly jejune and unedifying in comparison with the undisputed Danielle prophecies, in that it deals with the affairs and doings of a few petty kings, queens and insurrections, which for the most part have very little connection with the grand current either of history or prophecy. That it refers to the Ptolemies and the Seleucidse, particularly to the Seleucid despot, Antiochus Epiphanes, there can be no doubt; but the appearances are as if written by some one applying the prophecies after the events, and as if meant to be nothing more than a paraphrastico-prophetic application of the true Danielle predictions. Such is a fair statement of the facts and arguments in the case.

For my own part, I have very little sympathy with that spirit which is for ever at work to revise, correct and expurgate the text of what the Church has for so many, many ages received and treated as part of her most sacred Books. I believe that much that is done in this line is presumptuous, uncalled-for and in the highest degree irreverent. In most instances it is in the interest of some false doctrine, the skeptical pride and selfishness of the human heart seeking to make God's word square with the philosophies and notions of depraved human thinking. Biblical criticism has its place, and needs to be diligently cultivated. It may also now and then serve to set the Church right on some particulars evidently different from what many may have rested in as settled. Nor should we ever fail to be concerned to have a pure text in those Books which we hold so sacred, and correct readings of that text. We cannot be safe in matters of our faith without it. But the danger is rather not to receive too much, but to receive too little, and to quibble and tinker where there is no real occasion for it. This super-exaltation of what men call "the critical sense" — the claim of a sort of intuitive perception of what is Bible and what is not which would rule out or rule in at its own sovereign pleasure, as if it could not be mistaken — is not what we need for these days of unfaith. It is only properly dealt with when rebuked and resisted as impious and absurd.

A few years ago there was a short poem found on a blank leaf of an early copy of the works of John Milton in the British Museum. It was apparently signed "J. M." It was published as perhaps the production of Milton, and a thousand critics set to work to decide the question of its authorship. Learned men and adepts pronounced it a genuine Miltonic composition, and agreed that Milton only could have woven "the subtle melody" of its lines. Others, equally wise and experienced, declared it mere rubbish, and that Milton never could have written it except "in his dotage.' And so the controversy went on, and still remains, with no prospect that criticism or all the "critical sense" in the world will ever be able to settle whether Milton wrote it or not. How great, therefore, are the presumption and conceit of a certain school of philologists, critics and literary experts who claim to be able to tell, by intuition or internal evidence alone, just what chapters and verses of each particular writer in the Scriptures are from him, and what not! Wearily picking up out of grammars and vocabularies the dried bits of dead languages, and utterly unable to pronounce a word of them as the people who spoke them, they fancy they can feel and detect all variations of construction, phrase or idea pertaining or not pertaining to each author, and hence take upon themselves to expurgate the Sacred Scriptures, and to cast out this or the other Book or passage from the Canon on no other ground than that so their "critical sense" decides. And yet here was a poem in the plain English which we all speak — a poem written in London, in the time of John Milton — which Englishmen, countrymen of Milton, his fellow-townsmen, familiar with every line he ever wrote, critics, experts, themselves poets, cannot tell whether it is John Milton's or not! Away with such pretensions whereby to revise and reconstruct our sacred Books, which have stood the tests of so many ages! If the best "critical sense" of the best English experts cannot settle from internal evidence whether a poem in the tongue which they have known from their cradles is Milton's or not, is it not worse than ridiculous — yea, wicked — for men to presume in this way to decide that this paragraph or that in any given Book of Holy Scripture does not belong to it? Let us ever beware of being led by such a manner of dealing with what we have every reason to honor and respect as the inspired record of God's word.

In the case before us but little difference would be made in the actual contents of these wonderful revelations whether we accept or omit the particular sections to which reference has been made. The only questions really dependent on the decision one way or the other are: (1) Whether Daniel lived to the third year of Cyrus, or only to the first year; (2) whether this vision by the Hiddekel was at the termination of the season of penitential devotion referred to in chapter ix. 3, 4, or at the termination of another such a period about four years later; (3) whether the Magian seven-months' usurper, the pseudo-Smerdis, is to be rated in the prophetic list of Persian kings or not; and (4) whether all the minute details touching the period of the Maccabees, or only the main outlines, were included in the original Danielic predictions. But for the possibility of letting go what, after all, may be a genuine part of the Book of "Daniel the prophet," and for the ill use that might be made of such a precedent, it would not involve much either way to allow that there has here been some taking into the text of what was not in it as it came from Daniel's pen. Whether we omit or retain the sections designated, the sublimer contents and entire substance of this Book remain untouched.

The prophet here tells of a long and devout season of fasting and prayer to which he had given himself. He informs us that it lasted "three full weeks;" that in those days "he ate no pleasant bread, neither did flesh or wine come into his mouth, nor did he at all anoint himself as at other times; and that at the end of these three weeks, in the twenty-fourth day of the first month, he was by the side of the great river Hiddekel, now known as the Tigris. Whether he had removed his residence from the court to this place, or whether he had selected it only as a quiet retreat for these special devotions, cannot be fully determined from the record. The probabilities are that he came hither for the great penitential observances of which he speaks. At least, he was by the side of the great river, far away from the scenes of court-life, when the three weeks of his devout fastings terminated.

Lifting up his eyes, he was greeted with an overpowering vision. Before him stood a being in man's form, clothed in linen and girded with gold. His body was like the beryl — like the bluish-green, prismatic light. His face was as the appearance of lightning, insufferably bright. His eyes were as burning flame. His arms and his feet were like burnished brass, and the voice of his words had the volume and majesty of the shoutings of a multitude. The description answers so fully to the appearance of the Saviour to John in the first vision of the Apocalypse that many think it was the Son of God himself who here manifested himself to the prophet. It also resembles the apparition of Christ to Saul of Tarsus, in that only Daniel saw the vision, while others about him did not see it, though filled with dread and terror on account of it, so that they fled and hid themselves, leaving the prophet entirely alone. Weak as he was from his long fast, and anticipating nothing of the sort, Daniel was completely overwhelmed by the suddenness and transcendent glory of the vision. There remained no more strength in him. All the excellences of his personal appearance collapsed, and he sank into a state next thing to death.

This shows how merciful it is in God to veil over the spiritual world from our fleshly sight. Were He to lift that veil, it would be impossible for flesh and blood to sustain itself under the "weight of glory." The presence of this apparition threw Daniel into the condition almost that of one dead. He heard the words of the glorious Being before him, but he was in a swoon, "in a deep sleep," lying with his face to the ground. Nor could he rise till touched by the strengthening hand of iho heavenly visitor and told to stand upright. And even when he regained his feet, he shook with dread and "stood trembling." We sometimes wish that we could have some of the experiences of the prophets in seeing the visions they saw and recorded, but it is because we fail to note through what sufferings of soul and body these revelations have come out through them. We think of the glory of what they saw and heard and felt, but overlook the terrific jarrings of all the framework of their earthly nature which were the price of these revelations. It is a mercy that we may profit by them without the dreadful experiences which attended the giving of them. Think how Moses did "fear and quake;" how Jacob at Bethel was thrilled and terrified at the realization of what had occurred to him there; how Isaiah was unmanned and made to cry out as one about to sink into annihilation at the glory he describes; how Paul was blinded, sickened and disabled by Christ's appearance unto him; how John fell down as dead at the voice and apparition which greeted him at the beginning of the Apocalypse; and through what dreadful horrors and disturbances of body, soul and spirit these wonders and revelations were vouchsafed through these sublimely-favored men! Daniel would perhaps have ceased to live to tell us of this vision had not a heavenly hand revived and strengthened him against the overwhelming terribleness of what he beheld. And rather than envy these singularly-favored men, we should be moved to thank God that He has given to us the full benefit of these marvellous disclosures without having to experience the awfulness which the giving of them wrought in those through whom they came.

The object of this vision was to reveal to Daniel a still fuller account of the fortunes of his people "in the latter days;" that is, in the mysterious future, extending down to the end of this present world. And to this revelation the whole remaining part of this Book is devoted.

If it was "in the third year of Cyrus," as stated in the superscription to this tenth chapter, that Daniel had this vision, two years had already passed since the decree permitting the Jews to return to rebuild their temple. In answer to the question why Daniel did not go up with his fellow-countrymen, it is usually replied that he was then very old; that the return yet involved much to be done in order to final success, for which his presence in Persia was more necessary than his presence in Jerusalem; and that he was in place and high consideration as an officer and councillor of state, and could be of much more service in watching and directing the affairs of the government under whose protection his brethren were returning than by leaving his place to accompany them. He was, at all events, most profoundly and devoutly concerned about the future of his people, and it was in answer to these anxieties that this glorious apparition came.

In explaining to Daniel the object of his coming this heavenly messenger proceeds to make those remarkable statements in regard to the offices and doings of the angels. Whether we omit or retain what is given of the conflicts among these spiritual orders in the latter part of the chapter, the same view of things is nevertheless implied in what this angel tells of his detention in coming to Daniel. Ver. 13. It is ever true that the histories of this world always have a background of spiritual agencies. The Scriptures everywhere represent the angels as largely participating in the divine government of the world and in the whole ongoing of earthly affairs. There are such things as guardian angels, who are more concerned in what comes to pass than any of us suspect. And among these active unseen potencies there are both good and bad, often in conflict with each other. We are here shown individual angels standing at the head of individual kingdoms, and in opposition to them, at the head of the Israelitish theocracy, Michael, one of the first or highest princes. In alliance with him, and opposed to the spirits of the world, there is another angel, whom a certain writer designates as the good spirit of the Gentile world, whose object is to promote the realization of God's plan of salvation among the Gentiles. It was natural that this angel should be sent to reveal to Daniel the fate which the powers of the world were preparing for the people of God; and he here lets the prophet catch a glimpse of the invisible struggles between the angelic princes as to who should exert the determining influence on the worldly monarch — whether the God-opposed spirit of this world, or the good spirit whose aim it is to further the interests of God's kingdom.

We are wont to speak in a spiritualizing way of a struggle between the good and evil principles in man, but Holy Scripture teaches us to regard the matter as a substantial reality. (See 1 Sam. xvi. 13-15; 1 Kings xxii. 22.) The Satanic influences, of which we have more particular knowledge through the language of Jesus and His apostles, are not essentially different from what is here told. The glorious angel who appears to Daniel had a struggle of three weeks with the evil angel at the head of the Persian monarchy, and only by Michael's help overcame him and gained superior influence over the Persian king. He also had on hand a further struggle of the same kind with the same prince-angel of Persia. After that he was to encounter the prince-angel of Grecia, in which no great success, even with Michael's help, was foreshadowed. The intimation was in this way given that the Persian kings would be favorable to Israel, and perhaps also the Greeks, but that then would come an adverse change. (See Auberlen on *Daniel and St. John*, pp. 56-58.)

The angel then proceeds (in chap. xi. 2-4) to state the course of things in its outward manifestations. From the time Daniel had this vision four kings were yet to hold dominion in Persia prior to the beginning of the transfer of power, when adversities were again to come. If it was in the third year of Cyrus that Daniel received this revelation, the three Persian rulers next succeeding him, as enumerated in Ezra iv., are — (1) "Ahasuerus," the son of Cyrus, who in secular history is called Cambyses; (2) 'Artaxerxes" — not the one mentioned by Nehemiah, but the Magian usurper, the pseudo-Smerdis, who in the absence of Cambyses seized the government, but came to a disgraceful end after a reign of but seven months; (3) Darius Hystaspes, son of Cambyses, the same from whom, in the twentieth year of his reign, came the commission to Nehemiah for the rebuilding of Jerusalem. In case the statement in the first verse of the tenth chapter be taken as a later addition, the time of this vision would date in the first year of Darius the Mede, the Astyages of profane history; and thus the brief usurpation of the pretended Smerdis would drop out of the count of the proper kings of Persia; which would seem to be the most reasonable. The succession would then stand— (1) Cyrus, (2) Cambyses, (3) Darius Hystaspes. Here, then, in either way of reckoning, we have the three kings whom the angel said would yet stand up in Persia subsequent to the time at which Daniel had this vision.

But a fourth is referred to and specially singled out from the rest as preeminently rich, and as he who should make a most noted attempt at the subjugation of Greece. The word is, "And the fourth shall be far richer than they all: and by his strength through his riches he shall stir up all against the realm of Grecia." It is agreed that this can refer to none other than Xerxes, son of Darius Hystaspes, who was the fourth Persian emperor after Darius the Mede, dropping out the pseudo-Smerdian usurpation, and the fourth from Cyrus, counting the usurper in.

Xerxes, who was the husband of Queen Esther, was by far the richest of all the Persian kings. Justin says of him that when his armies were swelled in numbers sufficient to drink rivers dry his wealth still remained unexhausted. In this respect he, and only he, fits to the prophecy. And when it is further said of this fourth king, "By his strength through his riches he shall stir up all against the realm of Grecia," we look in vain for any other Persian emperor to whom it will apply, whilst in Xerxes all was fulfilled to the letter. His father, Darius Hystaspes, had proudly styled himself 'King of the Continent," but the more ambitious son aspired to be *King of the World*. In a council of his government it was resolved to march throughout all Europe, and reduce the whole earth under one empire." Four entire years (three after the conquest of Egypt) were consumed in the preparations for this expedition. Nations were laid under contribution, and a force of infantry, cavalry, charioteers, ships of war and transports by land and sea was gathered and equipped which was the most enormous ever moved in one body by mortal man. Perhaps not less than five millions of men were directly included in this tremendous expedition, all bought up by the riches of the king and set in motion against Greece, and thence to press their conquests over the whole European world. The battles of Thermopylae, Marathon and Salamis were the result, in which a stunning blow was inflicted on Persia from which it began to sink to its final fall.

In so far, then, the words of the angel were most accurately fulfilled, the climax of Persian dominion reached, and a decadence of it commenced. beyond which the prophecy does not specially follow it.

Leaving off the Persian history with Xerxes, the angel at the same time spoke of the rising of another king, who 'should rule with great dominion, and do according to his will.' It is not said where he would rise or whence he should come; only that he was to be some other than a Persian king. But as he had just spoken of a great Persian campaign against Greece, the result of which is not given save that there the thread of Persian history is dropped, the natural suggestion is that we are to look toward Greece for this new and mighty conqueror. And there, indeed, we find him in the person of Alexander the Great, who in resentment of the invasion of Xerxes, though long after, "overran the Persian empire from the Hellespont to the Indus, and from the Oasis of Ammon to the deserts beyond the Jaxartes.' On this point also agreement is general. The prophecy fits "the great Emathian conqueror," and none other. "When he shall stand up," said the angel, "his kingdom shall be broken;" and so the mighty Macedonian dominion was suddenly shattered by the early death of Alexander when in the very height of his triumphs. His empire was severed to the four winds, being divided into four monarchies. It did not go to his posterity, but to four of his generals, whose wars and contentions about it both limited and weakened it, so that it was no longer "according to his dominion." Nor was it to abide even in these four divisions. The angel said it would be plucked up and become the possession of still others; which was also finally fulfilled in the aggressions and conquests of the Romans. It is really marvellous to see with what accuracy history has filled out the sketch of events which was given to Daniel at the beginning, when it was utterly impossible for any human foresight or calculation to anticipate what was to come.

Having thus, by a few masterly strokes, brought down the thread of history to the times of the divided form of the Macedonian empire, the narrative drops off into those minute particularizations respecting "the king of the south" and "the king of the north," their intrigues, wars and abominations, at which so many Biblical critics have taken offence, and out of which expositors have been able to make so little. These references denote the successive sovereigns of the two monarchies north and south of the Holy Land — that is, Syria and Egypt — between which, for scores on scores of years, the Jews were made to suffer as between two millstones.

"The king of the south" (ver. 5) is Ptolemy Lagus of Egypt. The prince who becomes strong above him, with great dominion, is Seleucus Nicator, one of Ptolemy's satraps, who separates to himself and becomes "the king of the north." The descendants of these and their strifes are treated of in the Books of the Maccabees, and make up the chief story as here given. In the course of the narrative it is not always the same individual monarch who is called "the king of the north" or "the king of the south," but those who happen to be in power at the time in Syria or in Egypt. These two divisions of the Macedonian empire were always more or less at variance and war for the whole one hundred and fifty years of their existence. They formed compacts and made intermarriages, but always to be broken and to fail in the end; the Jews all the while being disadvantaged, robbed, and often overrun by one or the other, and greatly oppressed and destroyed, till it came to the infamous reign of Antiochus Epiphanes, whose history and doings I gave on another occasion.

But with all the tribulations thus to come upon the prophet's people in those evil times, God was to be at the helm, neither suffering them to be overwhelmed nor allowing their afflictions to be without profit. For their sins, apostasies and infidelities the hand of judgment was to be lifted against them. Oppressors were to rule over them; flatterers were to beguile and deceive them; plunderers were to rob them; and the godless were to cast down their priests, profane their temple, stop their sacrifices, carry away their children into slavery and spoil them in every violent manner. Many of themselves were to prove traitors to their holy covenant, sell holy things for a price and join with the hosts of the adversary against their own flesh and blood. And multitudes were to be mowed down with the sword, burned with fire or driven to the wilds in untold wretchedness. But still God's eye was to be over them, and all was to be overruled for good. The wickednesses of the many were to make others the better. The fires were to purge and brighten the faithful and true, as well as to torture and consume the transgressors. Some were still to know their God, and be made strong and do exploits. The abounding faithlessness was to call forth better instruction, that the truth might not utterly die out. Through all the dark night of their tribulations there were promises and hope of a better morning. When God lets the wicked have their way, it is that He may destroy them utterly; but when He chastises His people, it is to purify and redeem them.

Nor are God's chosen ones alone in their conflicts with the ills and trials of time. The Eternal Father maketh angels His ministers to the heirs of salvation. In loving sympathy and untiring patience celestial princes stand at the seats of earthly power, and watch and guard, and exert their mysterious agencies to moderate and shape the counsels of the mighty and to hinder and thwart the ill thoughts of oppressors, that Jehovah's faithful ones may profit by their endeavors. With the evil principalities they struggle, and press their way to bring messages of comfort, assurance and hope to penitent suppliants, to show the superior greatness and glory of our God, to throw light upon the scene of gloom and to herald a blessed outcome to the dutiful and true. The chariots of the Lord are thousands of thousands, even thousands of angels, and as the mountains are round about Jerusalem, so these are camped round about them that fear God. Michael, the one like God, with all the holy princes of the invisible world, is on the side of the good, and stands for the children of the covenant, and exerts the mightier activity as the tide of trouble comes to its flood.

And how transient, at best, are the riches, power and glory of the wicked! All the wealth and greatness, pomp and grandeur, with which Xerxes went forth against Greece, how did it melt away before the energy of a few brave patriots of the land of freemen! How soon were all his armed myriads brought to naught! And all those astounding triumphs v f Alexander, what were they? what did they profit him? How suddenly they disappeared in the drivelling strifes of those who came after him! Brethren, there is no abiding riches but riches toward God — the riches of faith, obedience and humble trust in Him. 'All flesh is as grass, and all the glory of man as the flower of grass. The grass withereth, and the flower thereof falleth away: but the word of the Lord endureth for ever." Whosoever is built upon that Word is planted on everlasting security. His fortune is immortal. His triumph is for eternity.

"Pilgrim of earth, who art journeying to heaven!
    Heir of eternal life! child of the day!
Cared for, watched over, beloved and forgiven!
    Art thou discouraged because of the way?

"Weary and thirsty, no water-brook near thee,
    Press onward, nor faint at the length of the way;
The God of thy life will assuredly hear thee;
    He will provide thee thy strength for the day.

"Break through the brambles and briers that obstruct thee,
    Dread not the gloom and the blackness of night;
Lean on the Hand that will safely conduct thee,
    Trust to His eye to whom darkness is light,

"Be trustful, be steadfast, whatever betide thee,
    Only one thing do thou ask of the Lord —
Grace to go forward wherever He guide thee,
    Simply believing the truth of His word."

Lecture Thirteenth - The Reign of the Antichrist; or, the Wilful King

Daniel 11:36-45.

AN able living writer on this Book of Daniel says: We Christians look for an Antichrist yet to come. Our Lord forewarned of him and his deceivableness. St. Paul describes such an one as Daniel speaks of. Isaiah had before foretold of him and his destruction. Good and evil have grown together all through this world's history — all good foreshadowing and concentrating in

Him and His kingdom who alone is good, and all evil, having its diverse counterparts in the more signal manifestations of evil, culminating at last in the highest antagonism to good and God in the person and dominion of the Antichrist. Even apart from revelation, it is, in itself, in conformity with human nature and the laws of things that, as good intensifies to a grand consummation of good, so will evil also intensify to a grand consummation of evil. (See Puseys *Lectures,* pp. 91, 92.) The world is made up of light and shadow, the one always accompanying the other; and as the light increases the shadows deepen; till, when the King of glory comes to crown and establish the good. He will be confronted with the king and head of all wickedness, wrought up to the summit of lawlessness and blasphemy at which its doom shall come.

Hence wrote the venerable apostle John: "Little children, it is the last time: and as ye have heard that Antichrist shall come, even now are there many antichrists; whereby we know it is the last time. He is Antichrist that denieth the Father and the Son...Every spirit that confesseth not that Jesus Christ is come in the flesh is not of God: and this is that spirit of Antichrist whereof ye have heard that it should come; and even now already it is in the world...For many deceivers are entered into the world who confess not that Jesus Christ is come in the flesh. This is a deceiver and an antichrist." 1 John ii. 18, 22; iv. 3; 2 John 7.

Hence also Paul wrote to the Thessalonians: "Let no man deceive you by any means; for that day [of Christ] shall not come, except there come a falling away first, and that man of sin be revealed, the son of perdition, who exalteth and opposeth himself above all that is called God, or that is worshipped; so that he as God sitteth in the temple of God, showing himself that he is God. Remember ye not that when I was yet with you I told you these things? And now ye know what withholdeth that he might be revealed in his time. For the mystery of iniquity doth already work; only He who now letteth [hindereth] will let [hinder] until He [the Hinderer] be taken out of the way; and then shall that Wicked be revealed, whom the Lord shall consume with the spirit of His mouth, and shall destroy with the brightness [*epiphany,* manifestation] of His coming [*parousia,* presence]; even him [the Wicked One] whose coming is after the working of Satan with all power and signs and lying wonders, and with all deceivableness of unrighteousness in them that perish; because they received not the love of the truth that they might be saved." 2 Thess. ii. 3-12.

A still more circumstantial account of this final monster is given in the Apocalypse, where John, speaking of the last things to take place in this world, says: "I saw a beast rise up out of the sea, having seven heads and ten horns, and upon his horns ten crowns, and upon his heads the name of blasphemy. And the dragon [that old serpent, called the Devil] gave him his power, and his seat, and great authority. And all the world wondered after the beast. And they worshipped the dragon which gave power unto the beast, and they worshipped the beast, saying. Who is like unto the beast? Who is able to make war with him? And he opened his mouth in blasphemy against

God, to blaspheme His name, and His tabernacle, and them that dwell in heaven. And it was given him to make war with the saints, and to overcome them: and power was given him over all kindreds, and tongues, and nations. And all that dwell upon the earth shall worship him, whose names are not written in the book of life of the Lamb slain from the foundation of the world. If any man have an ear, let him hear." With this beast there is also a prophet, "who doeth great wonders, so that he maketh fire come down from heaven on the earth in the sight of men, and deceiveth them that dwell on the earth by means of those miracles which he had power to do in the sight of the beast, saying to them that dwell on the earth that they should make an image to the beast. And he had power to give life unto the image of the beast, that the image of the beast should both speak and cause that as many as would not worship the image of the beast should be killed. And he caused all, both small and great, rich and poor, free and bond, to receive a mark in their right hand, or in their foreheads; and that no man might buy or sell," save he that had the mark, or the name of the beast, or the number of his name." Rev. xiii.

And what is thus minutely pictured in the New Testament was also very fully foreshadowed in the Old. Wherever we look we find some image and fore-intimation of this great evil power running parallel with the predictions and promises concerning the Seed of the woman and the Messiah of the chosen people. In every murderous oppressor or son of Belial that came, or was to come, upon the field of history in opposition to the children of God, from Cain to Nimrod, Pharaoh, Amalek, Midian, Goliath and the kings of Babylon and Assyria, the sacred prophets ever saw another and final consummation of them all, just as they saw in Moses, Joshua, Gideon, David, Solomon, Cyrus or others of their class the pre-intimations and types of that great, final, consummate and eternal Saviour, Redeemer and Conqueror of hell and death set before us in the person and administrations of the anointed and enthroned Jesus of Nazareth. "We accordingly find the whole diction of their prophecies always taking on the imagery and coloring of the final outcome, no matter who or what may be the immediate subject in the foreground. Thus, the filthy dreamers of the last times, who despise dominion and speak evil of dignities, and bring on the terrible scenes of the final judgment, are only Cain and Balaam the more fully developed in their followers, and constitute the ultimate body of those sons of perdition included already in the prophecies of Enoch on the other side of the Flood. (See Epistle of Jude.) That proud and oppressive Lucifer of Isa. xiv. which did weaken the nations and made the world to tremble, but goes to the pit without burial, and that 'Assyrian" of Isa. xxx. on whom falls the lighting down of the devouring fire of God's wrath, even "the king" for whom Tophet is ordained of old, are more emphatically and truly the final Antichrist than any of those types of him found in the ancient oppressors of Israel. So too the idol shepherd of Zech. xi., who, while professing to protect and feed God's flock, does but eat their flesh and tear them in pieces; and so that impious and lawless confederation of the kings of the earth in the second Psalm which the Lord is to have in derision, and dash to pieces like pottery with a rod of iron, that He may set up His King on the holy hill of Zion. However any of these descriptions may have been realized in the past, they all, with many more which might be adduced, go forward in their full height and significance to that heading-up of all evil in the last period of our world known under the expressive Scriptural name of *the Antichrist,* who is all other antichrists in one, and who meets his end by the revelation of Jesus himself.

Hence the firm belief of all the Christian Fathers was that there is yet to come a development and impersonation of Antichristianism more dreadful than any that has ever yet been seen on earth, and which shall be destroyed only in the great day of God Almighty. Hence Barnabas wrote concerning "the season of the Wicked One," whom the Son of God shall "abolish" when He shall come to judge the ungodly. (*Epist.,* 15.) Hence Irenaeus gave it as part of the Christian faith that "Antichrist, who, being endued with all the power of the devil, shall come, not as a righteous nor as a legitimate king subject to God, but an impious, unjust and lawless one — as an apostate, iniquitous and murderous — as a robber, concentrating in himself the Satanic apostasy, setting aside idols to persuade that he himself is God, raising up himself as the only idol, embodying the varied falsities of the other idols, that those who worship the devil by means of other abominations may serve himself by this one idol, lifting himself above all that is called God, and tyrannously setting himself forth as God in the temple at Jerusalem, and shall be destroyed by the coming of our Lord." (*Contra Her.,* 5, cap. 25, 26.) So also Origen (*Contra Cels.,* 6, 45) and Lactantius (*Inst. Epit.,* 71) and the Fathers in general. The great Augustine says: "He who reads, though being half asleep, cannot fail to see that the kingdom of Antichrist shall fiercely, though for a short time, assail the Church before the last judgment of God shall introduce the eternal reign of the saints." (*Civ. Dei,.* torn. xx. 23.)

And this Antichrist it is who is described to us in the passage now before us. As early as three hundred and fifty years after the apostles Jerome wrote of it, and said: "Our people" — the Christians of his day — "consider all these things to be spoken of Antichrist, who is to come in the last time." Luther writes: "This prophecy applies entirely, as all expositors unanimously agree, to the Antichrist, whose spirit is the pope, but whose body is another, who corporeally oppresses, destroys and persecutes the congregation of the Lord." Many modern interpreters understand it as referring to Antiochus Epiphanes, and to him only; but as Kliefoth has rightly observed, "What is here said of *the king* far transcends, in all its dimensions, the measure of Antiochus." That this Seleucid tyrant and despoiler of the Jews is embraced in the description may be readily admitted; but the relation of Antiochus to *"the king,"* upon whom the emphasis here falls, is no more than that of Cyrus to Christ, or that of the destruction of Jerusalem by the Romans to the end of the world. The one is simply the typical forerunner of the other. Identity or the confinement of the portrait to Antiochus is never once to be thought of, unless we can arrange to transfer him clown to the still-pending period of the resurrection of the dead, to which the time of this monster is so specifically assigned.

Whoever this king may be, or from whatever quarter he may come, he is the last representative of the bestial world-power that ever bears rule upon earth. The terms of the angel's description, particularly as continued in the succeeding chapter, establish this beyond mistake. He is to "prosper till the indignation be accomplished" — till God's angry visitations on the Jews for their sins are finally and for ever exhausted and ended — which is manifestly not yet the fact. In the ninth chapter the angel had said that "desolations are determined" — desolations which "make desolate even until the consummation;" and he here says that this king shall prosper for the doing of "that that is determined." His prosperity must therefore run to the consummation. And so in the next chapter the time of his doings is specifically noted as contemporaneous with the period of the great tribulation — the period when the woes of the prophet's people are to reach a perpetual end — the period when every one written in the Book shall be delivered — the period when the many who sleep in the dust of the earth shall be raised to life again — the period when the scroll of prophecy shall be exhausted by fulfilment — "the time of the end" — "the end of the days," when Daniel shall stand in his lot. The character assigned to this king, and the manner in which the angel introduces him as *"the king,"* identifies him with the little horn which comes up after the ten kings in the first vision (chap. vii. 23-26), and with the 'Ming of fierce countenance and understanding dark sentences" in the second vision (chap. viii. 21-25), and with "the prince that shall come," who makes a covenant with many for seven years, and in the midst of the seven breaks it and desecrates the temple with abominations, as stated in the third vision (chap. ix. 26, 27). But the power spoken of in each of those instances extends to the termination of all mere human rule on earth — to the sitting of the judgment — to the time when transgressors are come to the full — even until the consummation.' He must therefore be the very last of this world's powers.

And so again, whoever this king may be, and from whatever quarter he may come, he is an individual person, the same as Cyrus, Cambyses, Darius Hystaspes, Xerxes or Alexander; for he is designated in precisely the same way, by the same angel, in the same continuous narrative. Also, in the previous visions he is spoken of with reference to personal features and qualities which must pertain to an individual man, and cannot be fairly interpreted of a continuous succession of monarchs or operators. He is specially styled "the prince that is to come," in distinction from the kingdom or people whom he is eventually to command and represent. Nor can any one read the account of him given in the text, or in other passages descriptive of the same potency, without receiving the impression that he is some one remarkable individual personage. And the terms in which the duration of his power is expressed, which no solid exegesis can extend over seven years, make it quite certain that it is *one man* — not a long succession of men — who is the subject of this prophecy.

Antichrist indeed exists in all time, but only as a working spirit which has not yet come to its final development and concentrated embodiment. Hence John said that in his day already there were "many antichrists;" and hence Paul said that when he wrote "the mystery of iniquity" did already work. And so it has been working in all ages in false doctrines and in the varied oppositions to Jehovah's rule, kingdom, people and word. In this sense the oppressive and destructive pagan governments of old time were antichrists, and Popery and Mohammedanism are antichrists, and all heresies, infidelities, philosophies, systems or governments antagonistic to God's truth and to Jesus Christ as the only Lord and Saviour of man are antichrists. But they are not *the Antichrist,* except in spirit, in type, in modified and not fully-matured form; just as Christ was in the institutes, hope and spirit of God's believing people in the ages before He was born, and as He is still in and with His Church prior to His awaited revelation in the fulness and majesty of His glory and power. But as Christ is to come in person, to be revealed with His saints, to appear, to be manifested in a visible and open display of himself to all eyes, so Paul tells us that the Man of Sin, the Son of Perdition, is to be revealed, to show himself, to be manifested in a corresponding apocalypse. And when antagonism to God, His Christ, His truth. His people and His kingdom stands thus finally revealed, it is ill the person of one individual man, who is the embodiment of the devil and all sin, to offset and supersede the incarnation of God and all good in Jesus Christ, *our King.* So all the Fathers of the early Church unanimously understood the matter, and so the Jewish interpreters of the Old Testament explained about the *anti-Messiah.* There are many germinant and precursory antichrists, but *the Antichrist* is one individual person.

Whence this king is to come cannot perhaps be definitely decided in the present state of Biblical interpretation. Some think that he will be a Jew of the tribe of Dan, for the reason that Dan is described as "a serpent by the way," and as none of the one hundred and forty-four thousand sealed ones referred to in the Apocalypse (chap, vii.) are taken from Dan. Others are quite confident that he will at least be an Oriental in general character, and will take his rise from one or the other of the four divisions of the dominion of Alexander. Many are very sure that he will in some way succeed to the Roman emperorship, as he is said (in Rev. xvii.) to be the eighth, and of the seventh head of the last beast, which last beast is Rome, and these heads are kings or forms of government. Rev. xvii. 7-11. Others think that he is some one of the great deceased representatives of iniquity, by Satan's power resurrected from the dead, as he is said to "ascend out of the bottomless pit," out of the Hadean abyss, and to have received a deadly wound, from which he had ceased to be, and yet is entirely recovered. Rev. xiii. 3, 12; xvii. 8. It is impossible to decide between these opinions. It may turn out that all of them are founded in truth. But it is quite certain that he is no ordinary personage — that he is, to a great extent, a supernatural being, energized with all the subtlety and power of Satan, and accompanied with the power of working miracles. Paul says expressly that he will manifest himself by "the working of Satan, with all power, and signs and lying wonders' (2 Thess. ii. 9); and John foresaw him attended with the doing of "great wonders," even to the making of fire drop from heaven and the giving of life and speech to a metallic image. Rev. xiii. 13-15. His power, his seat and his great authority, it is specifically stated, are given him by the dragon (Rev. xii. 9; xiii. 2), just as the angel said to Daniel, "his power shall be mighty, but not by his own power." Chap. viii. 24. Thus Satan proposed to give to Christ "all the kingdoms of the world, and all the glory of them." Jesus declined the tempting proposal, but the devil eventually finds one to accept it on the prescribed terms, and thus comes the Antichrist, for the chastisement of the guilty world and the hopeless perdition of every one who espouses his cause.

Let us turn now to the more particular delineation of this monster and his career as given in the passage immediately before us.

The angel abruptly introduces him as *"the king."* With the same abruptness and in the same words Isaiah, in two different places (Isa. xxx. 33; lvii. 9), introduces him. The implication is not only that he is to bear rule as an earthly monarch, but that he is so peculiarly and pre-eminently the wielder of all earthly dominion as to be the one consummate sovereign of all time, whose distinction from all other kings is so great and marked that there is no danger of confounding him with them. He is *the king* who stands as the main figure of all earthly potencies, and fills out to its final fulness the entire prophetic picture of this world's sovereignty.

"And the king shall do according to his will." This is a statement of profoundest import. Wilfulness is the essence and soul of sin. Wilfulness was its characteristic from the beginning. Wilfulness was the sin of fallen angels, and it was the sin of Adam. Nor can the fullest development and maturity of sin exceed this doing according to one's own will. It is here given as the fundamental thing in the character of the Man of Sin. And let the lesson not be lost upon us. All people are full of wilfulness. They show it from earliest childhood till they die. Many even admire it as manliness and virtue. But there is nothing more antichristian — no sum or enormity of crime that can go beyond it. The very impersonation of all sin only does according to his own will. The devil himself does no more. And if people will be free-thinkers and freedoers, acknowledging no law but their own natural choice and pleasure, they should remember that they are doing exactly what makes the Antichrist Antichrist, and thus mark themselves as belonging to his foul herd. The Christian's law is not his own will, but God's will — God's will alone, always and in everything, bringing every thought into captivity to Christ. If it be not so with us, we are not of Christ, but of Antichrist; for all the piled-up guilt of that Wicked One is nothing more than doing according to his own will. At present God does not allow men fully to act out their will. By His providence He throws restraints about them and hinders them from going beyond certain limits. If it were not for this, society would soon go to utter ruin. But the time is coming when that which hindereth shall be taken out of the way, and the

haters of the truth be given over to act out their own perverseness to the full. Satan's cheats being preferred to Jehovah's pure and righteous rule, God will permit him to bring about all his plans, that he may delude them to the utmost. And when it comes to the supreme enthronement of man's own hell-inspired will, it is the Antichrist complete.

The results are naturally to be anticipated. *The king will exalt himself.* The doctrine of man's native dignity, and the pratings about the sublime capabilities and powers of unregenerate human nature, will yet destroy the world. The kingdom is for the poor in spirit. The inheritance of the earth is for the meek. The royal road to exaltation is humility. Whatever differs from this is Antichrist; and Antichrist means certain damnation. Whosoever is proud and self-exalting, thereby takes part and position with Antichrist, endorses him, enacts him. And when selfish pride is once seated in the heart there are no bounds to which it will not go if left unhindered.

The angel says of this king, *"he shall magnify himself,"* not only above every man, but *"above every God."* Even "the God of gods," the great Jehovah himself, is singled out for special blasphemy and defiance. Some have pronounced the Antichrist an atheist, but he is not so much the denier of God's existence as the setter-up of himself to be the greater god, the true god of Nature's powers, the rival of Omnipotence, the superior of the Great Eternal. The mere thought of such pretensions makes one tremble. And yet to these heights of guilty presumption and untruth does the proud self-will of man lead. Not the God of his fathers, not that Holy One of whom every pious woman for four thousand years desired to be the mother, nor any god or divine thing, can command the least respect or consideration from this wilful man, *"for he shall magnify himself above all."* O ye people of unbelief and irreligion, who despise worship and hate sacred things, and disdain to honor the Lord God of your fathers, and care nothing for the eternal Powers! behold with whom you identify yourselves, whose cause it is that you abet, and to what your impiety is the initiation!

But, with all his irreligion, this king is still a patron of worship. Man cannot do without some deity. In the estate or place of God *he shall honor the god of Mauzzim* — the spirit-forces which energize the doings of the wicked and animate all wars and tyrannies — a deity which his fathers never knew, or any other worshippers — a power of which he claims, perhaps, to be the embodiment and representative, as lie really is. Strange fact! even the most impious have their pieties. Those who look upon all established religion as superstition, and therefore will have none of it, are yet the most basely superstitious. Denying the God who made them and the Son of God who died for them, and putting themselves above all that is called God, they yet pay devotion to gods which they themselves invent. Trampling beneath his feet the worship of the Father and the Son, and vainly supposing himself the superior of both, Antichrist still has a god, a god of his own creation, wh.om he puts into Jehovah's place and honors with gold, silver, precious stones and pleasant things — a god whose temples are military munitions, and whose apostles are sheriffs and centurions, with sword and branding-iron to burn their master's name into the flesh of men, and to cut off the heads of those who decline such an obedience. Thus shall he do with his strange god. The professed abolisher of superstition becomes the patron of devil-worship, and employs the wealth and sword of empire to enforce the foulest abominations that ever disgrace or afflict our world. And such god-makers and devil-worshippers are all they who count it superstition to reverence and adore Him who made and sustains all things. They abolish Jehovah as a myth, and set up shrines in adoration of the incarnations of hell!

And along with the impieties and blasphemies of this man, the angel also speaks of injustice, misrule. persecution and a devilish generosity. Honoring his infernal god with gold and silver and precious stones and pleasant things, he shall do his will with the strongholds, helped by the power of Satan, and give glory, riches and dominion to those who acknowledge and confess his deity. No one shall be of account in his day but those who worship the devil-power. The lands shall be seized and divided to them, and they shall have the rule, the honor and the offices as the rewards of their horrible devotions. Thus will the idol shepherd eat the fat of the flock which he had covenanted to protect, driving peace and order from the earth, and rendering it impossible to live in his dominions without accepting and abetting his awful abominations.

People are slow to believe it, but when right religion is trampled and despised every violence and disorder comes. If men will put the rule of Heaven out, they necessarily put the confusion of Hell in. Apostasy brings the Antichrist, and the reign of the Antichrist is the overturning of all the foundations on which the social economy of the world rests, entailing a condition of trouble the greatest that has ever been or ever will be thereafter. Wars, outrages and bloody confusion shall mark the days as they pass. From the south and from the north nation shall be dashed against nation and power fight with power, and country after country sink beneath the overwhelming flood of violence and desolation. Because men reject the only saving truth, strong delusion shall sway them to a damnation begun already while yet living and acting in this world. The spirits of devils take the place of the Spirit of God, and "go forth unto the kings of the earth and of the whole world, to gather them to the battle of that great day of God Almighty," when the wine-press of the Divine Wrath shall be trodden till the blood flows in depth to the horses' bridles for two hundred miles! Rev. xiv. 19, 20; xvii. 14; xix. 11-21.

Alas! alas! how little do men dream of the horrors they are preparing for the world by their apostasies from God, His word. His Son, His ordinances and His service, and by the Satanic philosophies which they persist in putting in the place of His holy revelations! When it is too late to undo the dreadful mischief they will see their folly. Fain would we pray and preach and entreat that mankind may not be so deluded; but the masses have already sold themselves to the devil, broken away from all sacred influences, ruptured the ties of heavenly obligation, and no hope remains save for the few who perchance may be snatched as brands from the burning pile.

But it is not possible that such a monstrosity of arrogance and iniquity should long continue. Though he plant the tabernacles of his palaces between the seas in the glorious holy mountain, and sit in the temple of God as verily the Almighty himself, "he shall come to his end, and none shall help him." His god of Mauzzim fails him, after all. There is a mightier God, whose right it is to reign, and who will reign. He who wears upon His vesture and upon His thighs the name written, **Lord of lords and King of kings,** shall at the last extremity uncover himself, accompanied with all the glorified battalions of his saints, and rain down hail and fire and brimstone on the hosts of the adversary, whilst hell opens its mouth to engulf the great Deceiver, who goes down alive into a lake of fire. Zechariah tells the story more fully where he says: "Then shall the Lord go forth, and fight against those nations, as w4ien He fought in the day of battle. And His feet shall stand in that day upon the Mount of Olives, which is before Jerusalem on the east, and the Mount of Olives shall cleave in the midst thereof...And the Lord shall be King over all the earth." Zech. xiv. Thus shall that Wicked One be overwhelmed, "whom the Lord shall consume with the spirit of His mouth, and destroy with the brightness of His coming." 2 Thess. ii. 8.

Are there, then, any signs or symptoms from which we may legitimately infer the near coming of any such a state of things in our world? I believe that there are, and that they are both many and evident. Though multitudes believe and preach that the age in which we live is the most glorious and hopeful that was ever known, and consider that we are now on the very threshold of a grand jubilee of universal intelligence, brotherhood and liberty for all men, in which the golden dreams of so many ages are about to be fulfilled in the onward flow of human improvement and progress, it is in the very principles and foundations on which all this is hoped and prognosticated that I see the coming of the Antichrist. If men would only sift it to the real elements of which it is made up, they could not fail to detect in it the very spirit out of which the divinely-predicted Man of Sin must come.

If men will look at what is most lauded and gloried in as the intellectual greatness of our times, they will find it summed up in a vaunting materialism, which finds its life and crown in inspections and manipulations of the lower elements, till it has come to be concluded in leading circles that everything is derivable from slime, without a personal God or need of revelations from Him. This is the spirit of the prevailing philosophies — of the popular theories of education, politics and legislation — of the noisy reforms which propose to do away with human ills without the word and ordinances of Jehovah — and of many of the most favored religious activities, which boast of having outgrown the ancient creeds, and are eating away the vital substance of all sound doctrine. We have only to dig down into the inner kernel of modern thought and feeling in order to find lodged there, in one form or another, and more or less swaying the whole spirit of the age, a doctrine which enthrones, adores and worships *Progress* as the great hope of the world, holds man to be an ever-improving growth, and practically accepts evolution as the bringer of a glorious reign of wisdom, peace and blessedness yet to come in this present world, without need of any kingdom to be brought to us from the heavens or any changes by the miraculous power of God. This is the sum of the teachings of scientists, of the theories of government and law, and of the popular theologies. Even the faith held by most professed Christians is but the aggregate of changeable and growing sentiments, ever throwing off the old and putting on the new, rather than the fixed literal revelations of God, which are the same for all ages alike. In other words, the heart, pulse and ruling ideas of our times exhibit all the indications of that very apostasy, or "falling away," which Paul fore-announced as the forerunner, beginning, spirit and cause of the Man of Sin and his disastrous revelation. The seed is planted and growing, and meets in our age a congenial season for rapid development and speedy maturity.

Accordingly, also, we everywhere and in all circles and teachings hear about *the Coming Man*. The idea is treated somewhat jestingly, but it is not a mere fancy, myth or play on words. It expresses something which is inlaid in the theories and principles which, in one shape or another, are governing the thinking and expectations of the great mass of the most active and potent existing mind. The feeling and constant implication in the noisiest as well as the most subtle of modern demonstrations is, that nothing is settled; that the great problems of human life, including society, government, philosophy and religion, all yet remain to be solved; that what has hitherto been taken as final authority is not final, and no authority at all; that there remains to be wrought out a thorough reconstruction in ail earthly affairs on other foundations than those which have served mankind in past ages; and that there must come a new order of the social fabric, with new regulating forces, exhibiting another style of man in all the relations of life. And, as things now go, what the majority ordains and determines will be. But when that Coming Man, who is thus developing, comes, he can be none other than this very Man of Sin, the Lawless One, the Antichrist, foreseen and foretold by the holy prophets; for the final, concentred maturity of human progress, cut loose from the time-honored laws and institutes of Jehovah, is the Antichrist. And with this manifest and inevitable tendency of things before our eyes, and the accepted thinkers of the world, including many among the most influential in the professed Church of God, abetting the conceit as man's great hope, ignoring the proper Christ of our salvation, and virtually denying both the Father and the Son by the philosophies they entertain, what is it that we see but the preparing of the way for the Antichrist and the manifest token of the nearness of his revelation? What the leaders of mankind thus unitedly covet and labor for as the goal of the race must come, and much sooner, perhaps, than they anticipate; but the result will be the sorest plague the earth has ever felt, bringing with it all the disasters of the last great catastrophe. *Principles* are living things, and must work out what is in them; and when we see them in-rooted in all the forces and activities most potent in human society, we may be sure of what is coming. Only the miraculous intervention of Omnipotence can hinder it. And as God has fore-announced that He will not interfere to thwart these last experiments of the apostate race — that His Spirit shall not always strive with men — nay, that He will take out of the way that which hindereth, — doubt of the near fulfilment of all that the prophets have fore-told about the last years of this present world must disappear. Details are needless where the principles are so manifest, so earnestly embraced and so universally pursued.

Yes, brethren, God is about to deal with the earth as He never before has dealt with it, and everything is maturing for the day of trial. Men are busy with their plans, and think to work out sublime results by their endeavors and agencies. They are fondly hoping soon to see the world set right, all so-cial and religious questions gloriously adjudicated, by the growing intelli-gence of the world. They are joyously expecting ere long to behold all disabil-ities removed, and all the hardships which oppress the many done away, through the ever-improving machinery of education, evangelization, benevo-lence, freedom and popular legislation. They mean it well, and often throw into it an amount of zeal and devotion which proves that they are sincere. But their hopes are falsely grounded. They reason from a mistaken philoso-phy. The only regeneration of the world the Scriptures tell of is of a different order and comes in quite another way. This humanitarian rationalizing, which so tortures the divine word to bring it into accord with human wishes, and all this building on the reforms, efforts and agencies of men, will fail. It is in a line which makes a Saviour for the world who is not the Christ, but the Antichrist. People embrace it for good, and devote themselves to it as the very spirit of the Gospel as distinguished from the rejected letter; but it is the evil genius of our times, by which Satan would deceive, if possible, the very elect. So far from bringing the expected triumph of good and blessedness, it will eventually embody itself in one great head, whom it will take for its champion, who supplants the Christ and introduces all the anarchy and mis-rule of hell. It is the spirit of self-redemption, baptizing itself with the Sav-iour's name and usurping the Saviour's prerogatives, whilst it really rejects Him and His glorious coming from its scheme, and with songs of a nearing paradise beguiles to a hopeless perdition. It is the great snare of Satan by which he is captivating the world, and will effectually captivate it to its de-struction. It is the last great temptation of God's people, by which myriads on myriads shall be drifted to eternal shipwreck. And this is that Antichrist whereof ye have heard that he shall come. May the Lord save us from his subtleties!

Lecture Fourteenth - The Final Outcome; or, the Great Consummation

Daniel 12: 1-13.

WE now approach the conclusion of this Book of wonders. A grand panorama of empires, revolutions, oppressions, deliverances, crimes, punishments and special interferences from Heaven and from Hell — a sketch of all the great mysteries of Jehovah's providence in all time — has been passing in review before us, and we now come to the last scenes, to the final outcome, to the great consummation of the whole. Brief glimpses of the end have been greeting us at each great crisis in the prophetic narration, for in God's doings the beginnings always include the end, as the end presupposes all that goes before it, but our attention is now to be occupied entirely with that consummation itself.

It is a little unfortunate that this chapter has been severed from what immediately precedes it, since it is really not only the continuation of the address of the same speaker, but the accompaniment and sequel of the same subject. This dividing of the Bible into chapters and verses is, for the most part, the work of modern printers, not of the inspired authors; and bad work has often been made of it. The separation, if any, should be at the end of the third verse, and not here. The very first words in this last chapter refer what follows them to exactly the same period of that which was foretold in the latter part of the chapter before it. We there had an account of the still future Antichrist, and all that is here given also belongs to his time.

Some are of opinion that it is not for man to understand these predictions. In the eighth chapter (26) the angel directed the prophet to 'shut up the vision,' seeing it was for a period in the far future; so also in the fourth verse of this last chapter, having completed his account of things to come, the angel said, "But thou, O Daniel, shut up the words, and seal the book, even unto the time of the end;" and again, in verse 9, he said, "the words are closed up and sealed till the time of the end." This has been taken to mean that the prophet was to conceal what was said, and to hide it from all human understanding, until the time of its fulfilment. But whilst a perfect understanding of these predictions may not be reached until their fulfilment makes them plain, the meaning of these expressions is the very reverse of what some thus attach to them. If the command was that these things should be made incomprehensible, it is impossible to see why the revelation was given at all. Besides, there is an object assigned for this shutting up and sealing, which, so far from preventing the prophecy from being understood, was so to protect it that men might come to it and increase their knowledge and understanding of it; for this is the real sense of the words rendered "many shall run to and fro, and knowledge shall be increased." If the shutting up and sealing of the prophecy was the excluding of it from man's understanding, this growth of knowledge

143

concerning it would be an impossibility. We must therefore look for some other meaning of this shutting and sealing which shall better accord with other features of the record. Fortunately, we find similar language used in Isaiah (viii. 6), where the sense is the very reverse of hiding or obscuring. God there says, "Bind [or shut] up the testimony, seal the law among my disciples;" but the succeeding verses show that this shutting and sealing had reference to the authentication of the testimony and law of God as the proper and only rule to which the people were to come for wisdom and direction, as it is added, "To the law and to the testimony: if they speak not according to this word, it is because there is no light in them." The shutting up and sealing of law and testimony was not the rendering of it unintelligible, but the securement to it of its true office, place and authority as the established test of righteousness and correct information. And of this sort was the shutting up and sealing of what the angel made known to Daniel. Because it was true and from God, therefore the command was to secure it well, give it authentically, and arrange for its perpetual preservation as an authoritative word from Heaven, that people in after times might consult and study it, and thereby increase in the knowledge of the divine plans and purposes. The idea of the angel was, that the whole matter was now complete, certified and true beyond all addition or change, and was so to be treated. Just as valuable official documents intended to direct and inform successive generations are carefully engrossed and secured and held inviolable against all tampering, that they may be preserved entire and transmitted uncorrupted to all whom they concern, so and in this sense and spirit was Daniel to shut up and seal the words of this Book. It was not that no one should understand them, but that we might have them in all their authoritative certainty, be sure of their divine contents and find in them a right knowledge of God's revelations. He was to close up and seal the Book, that no additions or curtailments might be made in it, that it might not be in any wise changed, but that it might be kept sacred and secure for all time, as a veritable communication from God, that men may search it through and through, and thus learn ever more and more of the Almighty's purposes. "Secret things belong unto the Lord," and with those we may not' presume to meddle, "but those things which are revealed belong unto us and our children for ever, that we may do all the words of this law." Deut. xxix. 29. Let no one, therefore, suffer himself to be deluded into the belief that what we have been deducing with so much directness from these sacred predictions is but the empty speculation of man, and not the veritable revelation of the Lord. The interests we all have at stake are too many and too momentous for us to turn a deaf ear to what the Almighty in His goodness has thus given us for our learning. Nor is the world so rich in lights and guides that we can afford to do without what comes to us with so evident a seal of the Almighty.

I. Proceeding, then, to the matter now immediately before us, we may note, in the first place, that the time of the Antichrist will be a time of unexampled distress. The text says, "It shall be a time of trouble, such as never was since there was a nation even to that same time." Jeremiah says of it, "Alas! for that day is great, so that none is like it: it is even the time of Jacob's trouble." The Saviour speaks of it where He says, "Then shall be great tribulation, such as was not since the beginning of the world to this time, no, nor ever shall be."

This trouble will be more or less upon all people then living on the earth, but the description here relates more especially to the prophet's people, the seed of Abraham, whose fortunes the angel said (x. 14) he had come to make known. Hence Jeremiah calls it pre-eminently "the time of *Jacob's* trouble." The principal scene of it is "the Holy City," which can be none other than Jerusalem, The Antichrist enters into "the glorious land," plants "the tabernacles of his palaces between the seas in the glorious holy mountain," takes away "the daily sacrifice," and sets up the abomination of the Desolater on some part of the temple; all of which goes to identify Palestine as unmistakably the chief seat of these troubles.

But this necessarily implies that the Jewish people will then have been largely restored, with their temple rebuilt and their old ritual again established. This is a point upon which many doubt, but upon which sacred prophecy is as clear and full as upon any other subject. That "race of the weary foot," which has been scattered and tossed anion": the nations for these eighteen hundred years, yet as distinct still as when Aaron was their priest or David their king, and never taking root in any land, is everywhere spoken of in the Scriptures as reserved for Palestine, and Palestine as reserved for it. And it is especially under the first three and a half years of the reign of the Antichrist that this return and re-establishment of the Jews and their ancient services will occur. Seven years is the Antichrist to reign, even the last seven of those seventy sevens divided out upon Daniel's people and the Holy City. That term begins in the conclusion of a solemn compact between him and many of the Jews (see chap. x. 27) — a league of friendship and mutual support and protection — a covenant in which the Jewish people agree to accept him as their great patron, king and Messiah, in fulfilment of those words of the Saviour, "I am come in my Father's name, and ye receive me not: if another shall come in his own name, him ye will receive." John v. 43. The implication is, that under and in pursuance of this league the Jews will return, rebuild their temple and restore the old order, which has now been so long interrupted. Those first three and a half years of the Antichrist or this pseudo-Messiah will accordingly be very prosperous years for the Jews, at least in a temporal point of view. Their population, wealth and enterprise will be enthusiastically directed toward the old homesteads of their fathers and their holy city. With a rapidity unprecedented the most wonderful improvements will spring up in Palestine and Jerusalem. Considering the facilities of our times and the vast resources of this people, we can easily see that if word, duly certified and believed, were to go forth from their wealthiest and most influential representatives that their Messiah has come with great authority, power and miracle to fulfil for them in Jerusalem all that they have this while been carnally dreaming about him, it would, in a few short years, transmute the city of David into the greatest centre of interest, wealth and influence in our world. And so sacred prophecy fore-announces that it will be.

But the idol shepherd of these deluded people will soon prove himself the monster Desolater, from whom they shall come into the severest tribulations ever experienced by their race in any period of its existence. Accepted as Messiah, he shall claim to be God, abolish the Jehovah-services which he assisted to restore, seize the temple for the worship of his own image, escheat the lands, to be given as rewards to his miscreant adherents for acknowledging his god of Mauzzim, and allow no one to bear rule, own property, buy or sell except such as accept the branding of hand or forehead with his mark and the mark of his infernal deity. Those who were deceived into the acceptance of him as their Savior, at the end of the first three and a half years will find themselves in covenant with hell and death, utterly helpless in the hands of the most monstrous tyrant that ever lived, compelled to become undisguised and openly-branded worshippers of the devil, or lose every foot of ground they own, every office of authority they hold, every means of livelihood, every protection in all that is dear in life, every possession on which the hand of wilful power can be laid, and life itself, except as it shall be secreted in the desolate places of the mountains and wilderness, not daring to let itself be seen by any of the minions of the devilish power which then shall reign.

Nor shall this state of things be only for a few days, weeks or months, but for full three and a half years. In not less than six different places, and in almost as many different ways, is this declared in the prophecies, including both Testaments. It is for "a time and times and the dividing of time" (Dan. vii. 25) — "It shall be for a time, times, and an half" (xii. 7) — "the holy city shall they tread under foot forty and two months" (Rev. xi. 2) — "the woman fled into the wilderness, a thousand two hundred and threescore days" — for "a time, and times, and half a time" (xii. 6, 14) — "and power was given him to continue forty and two months" (xiii. 5). All these passages refer to one and the same period of oppression and trouble under the Antichrist, and in each instance the measure is three and a half years, dating from the breaking of the league and the suspension of the daily offering to the destruction of the monster by the revelation of Jesus Christ. Our Lord ministered on earth three and a half years, and the Antichrist shall enact his Satanic ministry for the same length of time.

The effect of all this bitter experience is likewise stated by the angel. It is the old story over again. Human nature is the same whatever may be the times or administrations. People think if things were so or so, the truth would take hold on all hearts, and leave none so bad as to resist it; but they only dream. "If they hear not Moses and the prophets, neither will they believe, though one rose from the dead." In all ages and under all dispensations some get their eyes open and turn their hearts unto the Lord, but the multitude is ever blind and unconvertible. And so it will be even under the extraordinary scenes of the great tribulation. Many shall be purified and made white, and proved to be genuine people of God. Afflictions are sent to test and bring out our faith. Gold is refined and purified by taking it through the furnace. But the mass of men are made no better from their afflictions. Our own times illustrate how such things work. Everybody is bemoaning the sorrowful state of business and of affairs in general. The wails of distress and lamentation meet us continually on all hands. Ills of all sorts are said to be multiplying. But are the people improved? Do they not live on as they always have done? Are not the masses much the worse for it? Look at the playhouses and shows and places of amusement, and see if they are not more thronged than ever. Observe our avenues and pleasure-resorts on Sundays, and note the expenditures and profanations of the Lord's Day by all ranks of society. Even professed Christians, who cannot spare a dollar for the cause of Christ, have plenty to spend on their lusts and vanities, and are only the more lavish and unscrupulous in ministering to their own whims and pleasure as times become more pressing. The many are only hardened in crime instead of being humbled to penitence. And so it will be even when the great woes of God's judgments come. "The wicked shall do wickedly," and be only the more wicked and reckless, and shut their eyes and ears and hearts all the tighter against the truth. They "shall not understand," because they love themselves and their own perverse ways too well to admit better instruction, preferring to risk everlasting damnation to the letting go of a jot of their sins, till the great horrors of the Almighty's wrath engulf them for ever! So much, then, for this time of sorrows.

II. Note now, in the second place, that the time of the Antichrist is the time when Michael, the great prince over the children of the prophet's people, shall stand up in their behalf. Some think this the Lord Jesus himself. If so, then the glorious one who appeared to the prophet in chapter x. cannot be the Son of God. But these are questions that need not be discussed. Michael is one of those mighty spiritual princes connected with the administrations of God in our world. He is one of the first or highest of these holy Powers. Jude calls him "the archangel." John beheld him in command of angels in the great conflict with the dragon. He is manifestly one of the most exalted, if not the very highest, of all celestial Powers, next to Eternal Godhead. And to him particularly is assigned the direction of the affairs relating to the Jewish people from the beginning to the end. Hence the account of his disputation with the devil about the body of Moses, whilst he here appears, in the very closing years of time, as the great prince who stands for the children of the prophet's people, especially for such of them as have the prophet's faith and spirit, and thus prove themselves Israel, and not only *of* Israel.

This standing up of Michael includes a variety of administrations not here specified. They are elsewhere described, especially in the Apocalypse. Among the transactions of that time of wonders we read of a peculiar ministry in the hands of an angel from the sun rising, having the seal of the living God, with which he seals one hundred and forty-four thousand servants of God from among the Israelitish peoples. Rev. vii. These were thenceforward secured against many of the plagues with which the rebellious children of men are then to be visited. Rev. ix. 4. So we read again of special heavenly ministrations, the giving of testimony and the measuring of the temple, the altar and the worshippers therein. Rev. x. 11; xii. 1, 2. To the same list of these extraordinary manifestations belong the prophetic career and doings of the two Witnesses, who prophesy for three and a half years, whom I have elsewhere shown to be two celestial personages, even Elijah and Enoch, as understood by the early Church, and who alone, of all then upon earth, are able to cope with the infamous Antichrist. (See Rev. xi. 3-13, and my *Lectures on the Apoc. in loc.*) So, for those who are compelled to fly to the wilderness because they cannot consent to worship the beast or to receive his mark, there is also a marked divine manifestation. There is a place prepared of God, and a miraculous feeding of them in their seclusion till the Desolater comes to his end. Along with the rest is the sanctification of those dreadful sorrows to the purifying and making white of many to whom these trials were needful; also the war with Satan, which succeeds in casting him down from the aerial spaces (Rev. xii. 7-13); but, above all, the fulfilment of what was shown the prophet in the first vision (chap. vii. 9-12) — to wit, the sitting of the judgment, the opening of the books and the giving of the beast to the burning flames. All this, and perhaps more, is included in this standing up of Michael for the children of the prophet's people, or is directly connected with that standing up. The word of the angel is, that at that time every one found written in the book shall be delivered. And this is simply the summation of the completed result, in the accomplishment of which all these particulars have their part and place.

It stands out, therefore, as a most thoroughly authenticated Scriptural truth that God is not yet done with the Jewish people as such. While this present dispensation lasts they are in a state of disinheritance. We are now living in "the times of the Gentiles." The Jew at present has no privileges beyond or above those of other men. If he will repent of his sins, lay aside his conceit and self-righteousness and believe on the Lord Jesus Christ as the only Saviour of men, he can have salvation the same as any other mortal; but he has no other rights and no higher privileges than the Gentile, on whom he looks with so much scorn and contempt. But when "the times of the Gentiles are fulfilled" and the dispensation that now is comes to its close, for the fathers' sakes he shall again come to the front. Michael the archangel shall stand up for him. And for those of his blood and lineage who shall be found written in Jehovah's book shall come a deliverance from all disabilities, of which there shall be no more forfeiture for ever. For "Thus saith the Lord God; Behold, I will take the children of Israel from among the nations, whither they be gone, and will gather them on every side, and bring them into their own land: and I will make them one nation in the land upon the mountains of Israel; and one king shall be king to them all: and they shall be no more two nations, neither shall they be divided into two kingdoms any more at all: neither shall they defile themselves any more with their idols, nor with their detestable things, nor with any of their transgressions: but I will save them out of all their dwelling-places, wherein they have sinned, and will cleanse them: so shall they be my people, and I will be their God. And David my servant shall be king over them; and they shall have one shepherd: they also shall walk in my judgments, and observe my statutes, and do them. And they shall dwell in the land that I have given unto Jacob my servant, wherein your fathers have dwelt; and they shall dwell therein, even they, and their children, and their children's children forever: and my servant David shall be their prince for ever. Moreover, I will make a covenant of peace with them; it shall be an everlasting covenant with them: and I will place them, and multiply them, and will set my sanctuary in the midst of them for evermore. My tabernacle also shall be with them: yea, I will be their God, and they shall be my people. And the nations shall know that I do sanctify Israel, when my sanctuary shall be in the midst of them for evermore." Ezek. xxxvii. 21-28.

A mighty sea of ills and judgments, tears and recompenses for sin, still lies between Israel and that continent of peace and glory. God hath an account of indignation against that people for their impieties, which must first expend itself upon them and be paid off to the last. "Zion shall be redeemed with judgment, and those of her that return with righteous visitations." God will put them in the crucible, and sit as a refiner and purifier of silver, to purify the sons of Levi and purge them as gold and silver, that they may offer unto Jehovah an offering in righteousness. By the fires of unexampled trial He will purge away their dross and take away all their tin, that He may restore their judges as at the first, and their counsellors as at the beginning, and realize the complete fulfilment of all for which the angel said the seventy sevens have been divided out upon that race. Chap. ix. 24. At thirty days, or at most seventy-five clays, from the fall of the Antichrist, all that blessedness will have been reached. The consummation shall have come for Israel.

III. Note now, in the third place, that the time of the Antichrist is also a time of blessed resurrections. It is sometimes supposed that the ancient people of God knew little or nothing about the resurrection of the body, but this is a great mistake. Paul says that the Jews of his time allowed that there should be a resurrection of the dead, both of the just and of the imjust. He declared before Agrippa that it was the great hope in all the incessant services of the twelve tribes of Israel to attain to the resurrection of the just. He also affirmed of some who suffered for the faith in former ages that they refused deliverance from torture, "that they might obtain a better resurrection.' All through the Old Testament the references are numerous and plain touching the rising up again of those who have fallen under the power of death and the grave. And here the voice comes to us from Babylon, attested by the angel of God through Daniel the prophet, that in the same period in which the Antichrist shall be revealed, "many of them that sleep in the dust of the earth shall awake." It is not a figurative resurrection that is spoken of, for it is "to everlasting life." It is not a spiritual resurrection, but a resurrection of bodies, for spirits are not sleepers in dust of the earth. It is not a general or universal resurrection, but eclectic and particular, for it is predicated only of "many" — many *of,* or many *from among* — leaving others of whom it is not predicated. This *"many,"* as Rabbi Saadiah says, are the few, the lesser number, as where it is said "many brought gifts," "many of the people of the land became Jews," "many will entreat the favor of the prince." It seems to be implied in the passage that all the dead shall rise again in some form, at some day, but that at first only a portion of the sleepers in the dust shall awake. So in the first Psalm, though the wicked are to rise in their time, they do not rise or stand up in judgment with the congregation of the righteous. So also in the Apocalypse (xx.) there is a "first resurrection," consisting of those who are to be priests of God and of Christ, and over whom the second death has no power; whilst "the rest of the dead live not again until the thousand years are finished." Hence some of the very best Hebraists here translate, "And many from among the sleepers in the dust of the earth shall awake; these [the many who awake] unto everlasting life; but those [the rest of the sleepers, who awake only at some other time] unto shame and everlasting abhorring." But whether this be the precise sense or not, the words assert a bodily resurrection of many asleep in the ground, to whom this awaking is a high and blessed distinction. If it does not precede the resurrection of the wicked in point of time, as I am persuaded that it does, it certainly differs from and exceeds it in character; for it is to everlasting life, whilst the other is to everlasting dishonor, abhorring and contempt.

Great and awful has been the reign of death! Who can tell the associations of grief and pain, of dismay and agony, of streaming tears and broken hearts, of blasted hopes and ruined phms, of speechless misery and shattered reason, of desolate homes and bleeding affections, of darkness, misery and gloom, which throng around that chilling word — *death?*

Everywhere and in everything is death — resistless, gloomy, all-levelling *death.* Its subjects mingle with the soil of every clime and crowd the hidden depths of every sea. Nearly two hundred generations, with all their power, have gone down under its dark dominion, without a single representative left. And every tick of the clock, through all the hours and days and nights and weeks and months and years, without cessation, is the death-knell of scores of mortals, swept from friends and homes to the silent world of them that sleep in the dust of the earth.

But those sleeping myriads shall not sleep for ever. There yet shall come a trumpet-voice before which even death shall cower and all his bands dissolve. Rocky vaults and sepulchres, though sealed for ages and to the living lost, and all the deep incisions in "God's Acre," and all the hidden places whither the dead have been borne or laid away by loving hands, shall open to set their tenants free. All the dingy doors of the grave shall be lifted from their hinges, and all within be called to bid farewell for ever to all the mould and dampness of that sombre realm. For thus saith the holy apostle: "I would not have you to be ignorant brethren, concerning them which are asleep, that ye sorrow not, even as others which have no hope. For if we believe that Jesus died and rose again, even so them also which sleep in Jesus will God bring with Him...For the Lord himself shall descend from heaven with a shout, with the voice of the archangel, and the trump of God: and the dead in Christ shall rise first: then ye which are alive and remain shall be caught up together with them in the clouds, to meet the Lord in the air: and so shall we ever be with the Lord. Wherefore comfort one another with these words." 1 Thess. iv. 13-18.

Yea, and even before the Antichrist shall enact the wickednesses which bring the miseries of the great tribulation, this grand awakening and translation of the saints shall begin. Many, by reason of their unwatchfulness and unreadiness, will be obliged to linger in the world with the wicked and the unbelieving, and feel something of the woes of that time of trouble, till they have healed their deficiencies, washed their flesh-stained robes and made them white in the blood of the Lamb. Rev. vii. 9-17. But there are some to whom the Saviour's promise is, "Because thou hast kept the word of my patience, I also will keep thee from that hour of trial, which shall come upon all the world." Rev. iii. 10. When He was yet on earth He left command with promise: "Watch, and pray always, that ye may be accounted worthy to escape all these things that shall come to pass, and to stand before the Son of man." Luke xxi. 36. That which hinders the revelation of the Antichrist is the presence of Christ's true Church, in whom is the power of the Holy Ghost, and for whose sake and in answer to whose prayers Jehovah's providence is so ordered as to restrain the violence of Satan and the wrath of the wicked. It is only when this Hinderer is taken away that "that Wicked [One] shall be revealed." 2 Thess. ii. 7, 8. And if we ask in what manner that taking away is to be effected, the answer is given by the Saviour himself: "In that night there shall be two in one bed; the one shall be taken, and the other shall be left. Two women shall be grinding together; the one shall be taken, and the other left. Two men shall be in the field: the one shall be taken and the other left." And when the listening disciples asked whither these should be taken, the answer was: "Wheresoever the body is, thither will the eagles be gathered together;" that is, to Christ, on whose slain body the saints are nourished, and who will then be in the heavenly spaces where Paul says His people are to meet Him. Luke xvii. 34-37.

IV. Note also, in the fourth place, that then shall men receive their eternal rewards. The word of the angel is, "They that be wise shall shine as the brightness of the firmament, and they that turn many to righteousness, as the stars for ever and ever." We are now in the mere vestibule of our being:. There is another and an eternal life to which it leads. That life is not a mere spirit-life, but a resurrection-life — a life which succeeds the sleep in the dust of the earth. The bringing up again of our fallen bodies, or a mighty change equivalent to it, must first occur, before the sons of God enter upon their glories. Daniel was to go his way in the ordinary course of earthly duty and experience, and peacefully rest in his grave till "the end" should come, and only "at the end of the days" was he to stand in his lot, or be raised up to enjoy his portion. So Paul, at the end of his race, wrote to his son Timothy: "I am now ready to be offered, and the time of my departure is at hand. I have fought a good fight, I have finished my course, I have kept the faith: henceforth there is laid up for me a crown of righteousness, which the Lord, the righteous Judge, shall give me at that day." 1 Tim. iv. 6-8. It is a mistake to suppose that Christians, when they die, enter at once upon their final places and rewards. Those rewards and places are not yet ready for them, nor will they be till Christ comes again in the glory of His manifested kingdom; neither are they yet ready for those rewards. The souls of departed saints whilst in the disembodied state, though at rest in paradise and in conscious blessedness, are not in the exercise of the full functions of life, for which the presence of the body is necessary. Hence the supreme importance of the doctrine of the resurrection of the body in all proper presentations of the Christian system. Everything waits for and depends on "the redemption of our body" (Rom. viii. 23), which does not occur till Christ is ready to take to himself His great power and reign. Hence Peter writes to the suffering saints: "When the chief Shepherd shall appear, ye shall receive a crown of glory that fadeth not away." 1 Pet. v. 4. If there were to be any crowning of the saints prior to that time, he would have said so. But when Christ who is our life shall appear, *then* shall we also appear with Him in glory. And great shall be the portion of the true and faithful.

Very little is said of the final destiny of the wicked. It is not important that we should know much on that subject. And blessed will those be who never find out what it will be. A few words tell the story with sufficient ampleness. They also are to be brought up again from their sleep in the dust of the earth, but their resurrection will be a disgrace, not a glorification, and all the eternity of their being will be an abhorrence and contempt. On the other hand, how bright and cheering is the imagery which sets forth the destiny of the good and faithful!

Contemplate the pure blue sky which arches over us, and has bent its fair circle round our world ever since man was made. How beautiful in the rosy dawn of morning, lit up with the joys of incoming day and spreading out its arms of welcome to the rising king of light! How sublime at high noon, flooded with brightness from horizon to horizon, and lifted up like some great celestial dome whose arches seem to spring from eternity to eternity to make a tabernacle for the sun! How serenely sweet at sunset, spread out like an inverted sea of liquid glass and gold, tinging all the earth with the mellow radiance of its glory! How unspeakably charming and solemn in the silent midnight, looking like the apparition of some vast supernal city with its myriad lamps lit and twinkling with immortal fires! Could anything be more excellent, more beautiful, more cheering, more perfect? Six thousand years has it thus stood. Clouds have many a time overspread its face, but they have not dimmed it. The fumes and smoke and dust of earth's cities, battles and commotions again and again have risen against it, but it is still untarnished. Ages on ages have snowed their years upon it, but not a wrinkle, not a mark of decay, have they there produced. Storms on storms have driven over it with their fury and thunder, but they have not rent it. Changes on changes have worked their way into everything else, but no alterations have they wrought in this. It bends over us at this hour as beautiful, benignant and blessed as when God looked upon it at the first and said it was "very good." And such and so glorious is to be the portion of the wise. *"They shall shine as the brightness of the firmament."* Like it, their home shall be on high. Like it, they shall be incorruptible, peaceful, beautiful, perfect, as if they had always been sons of the sky. Like it, their cheering, enlightening and benignant glory shall envelop the earth with blessedness from age to age for ever. Every faithful man of God is a child of light. Jesus pronounces His people "the light of the world." In this life their light is often dim. Shadows, clouds, crags and hills frequently intercept its radiance, and sometimes the flame burns low, as if ready to expire. But this dull twilight is the herald of a coming noon, when all obstructions shall be surmounted, and all obscurations left far beneath, whilst the ethereal glow of heavenly brightness pours out its flood of peaceful splendors in an everlasting flow!

Contemplate, again, those sparkling lights which shine like polished gems in the canopy above us. How beautiful their light and the sublimity and variety of their glory! How they attract our eyes, and seem to kindle corresponding fires in our hearts! How we are drawn and charmed by them as the crown-jewels of the universe! And thus have they been blazing in the smiles of God for all these many, many ages. The flowers wither, the rainbow fades, but these never lose their immortal beauty, and abide as fresh and glorious as when they sang together the great birth-hymn of the world. They change their places, but they never cease their shining nor ever lay aside their glory. No convulsions can ever disturb the eternal calm of their beauty. Even when "the powers of the heavens shall be shaken" their serene magnificence will abide unharmed, their brightness undiminished, their splendor sempiternal. And so they that turn many to righteousness shall shine, even *"as the stars for ever and ever."* The men and women who have been God's light-bearers in a world of darkness shall be His lights eternally. The fame and glory of apostles and prophets, evangelists and martyrs, reformers and confessors, and the honor of those who have stood, labored and suffered for the truth of God in every age, shall never wane, never pass away. All the mysterious changes of the day of judgment will only increase their exaltation and make their names the more illustrious. Every minister, missionary, teacher and instrument of the enlightenment and salvation of the benighted and the lost, if faithful on earth, is to have eternal place in heaven, luminous as the stars and for ever beyond all the vicissitudes, defilements, disasters or accidents of time. Oh, the glory, the sublimity, the untold dignities and honors to be inherited by the humble and self-denying teachers of salvation! To be set by God's own hand in God's own heavens! to shine as everlasting stars! to sparkle as illustrious gems in the firmament of Jehovah's power! to be the glory-bearers of His eternal excellency! to shine His radiance through celestial spaces! to be

God's imperishable lights for heaven itself. His stars for ever and ever! What a portion to be put within the reach of poor feeble children of the earth! How the objects of this world's ambition dwindle and shrink in comparison! What toils, what sufferings, what sacrifices of self is it not worth! What is all the joy, comfort, honor, wealth and glory that can possibly be crowded into this brief earthly life which it would not be a blessed privilege to lay down for such a destiny! To be but a fragment, a jot, a particle of the firmament of God is a glory fit to be purchased at any price; but to be its eternal stars, the very jewels of the realm of light, the objects of undying interest and admiration in supernal worlds — here is a wealth of magnificence by the side of which all other greatness is as nothing!

Nor are the conditions hard on which these sublimities of human destiny depend. True, a genuine wisdom is required. It is *"the wise,"* only the wise, who are thus to shine. There is much that passes for wisdom which is not such in reality. Men call those wise who are skilled in physical science, worldly philosophy, politics, law, finances, trade and human erudition; but if this be all, even the wisest need to become "fools," that they may be wise. Knowledge is not wisdom, especially if it be mere secular knowledge. Knowledge is only one of the tools of wisdom, and all thinking or enlightenment which concerns itself only with earthly interests, gains, progress and comfort fails of true wisdom. People may know much, and make themselves very familiar even with God's works and attributes, and still be in utter soul-ignorance. Wisdom is the heart's knowledge of God himself. Behold, the fear of the Lord, that is wisdom: and to depart from evil is understanding." To be "wise" we must give up sin and self, and learn to fear, love and trust in God above all things. No man is wise who settles his confidence on what must perish. No man is wise who has made no provision for eternity. No man is wise who puts the Lord his Maker out of his calculations, or fails to award Him His rightful place and authority in the universe. True wisdom and eternal life is this: to know God, and Jesus Christ whom He hath sent. And to this wisdom only is eternal glory linked. This wisdom God also wills that we should have, and has arranged every facility for us to acquire. He hath spoken that we may learn of Him, drink in His light, and by fellowship with His Spirit become like Moses on the mount, like Stephen in his dying moments, yea, like Christ in His transfiguration, illuminated with celestial radiance and brightened with the glory that shall never fade. He desires that all men should turn with all their heart to Him and His saving truth in Christ Jesus, and, having turned, to exert themselves to turn others also. He expects all whom He has called and redeemed to take active part in bringing the erring and lost to the same light and salvation. And where this wisdom and devotion are, there the glories of which the angel speaks will surely follow.

Ah, yes, dear friends, as we live and labor in this world, so shall be our eternal future. The life to come will be good and glorious or evil and disgraceful just as our present lives are fashioned to the truth or turned away from it. As we now direct ourselves, we determine the complexion of our eternity. By the deeds we here perform we lay the outlines and draw the features of that body which we shall for ever wear. Just as we shape our behavior on earth we prepare germs for our graves which the resurrection will develop into the brightness of the firmament and into the glory of the everlasting stars, or into that which shall be to us and all beings an unmitigated and unending abhorrence. Oh, mighty and momentous thought! How should it search and awaken our souls! Take it with you, and, as you value immortal blessedness, never suffer it to be forgotten. And may that God who hath revealed these stupendous wonders make it a living truth in every heart, to shape and guide us in all the activities of this life, that, with the holy Daniel, we may each stand in our lot at the end of the days!

And now, "unto Him that loved us, and washed us from our sins in His own blood, and hath made us kings and priests unto God and His Father; to Him be glory and dominion for ever and ever. Amen."

It will be order then,
   Under the sceptre of a holy King,
Each creature, low and high, angels and men,
   To the great concord sweetly ministering.
Self-will unknown, true harmony restored,
Happy obedience to the righteous Lord;
The multitude of wills all lost in One —
The Will that rules from the eternal throne;
Disorders, strifes, confusions, groans and cries
Then ended in the endless harmonies.

A Critically-Revised Translation of the Book of Daniel

Chapter I

In the third year of the reign of Jehoiakim, king of Judah, came [1] Nebu-chadnezzar, king of Babylon, to Jerusalem and besieged it. (2) And the Lord gave Jehoiakim, king of Judah, into his hand, and a part of the vessels of the house of God; and he brought them [2] to the land of Shinar, to the house of his god; and he brought the vessels into the treasure-house of his god.

(3) And the king commanded Ashpenaz, the chief of his eunuchs, [3] that he should bring of the sons of Israel, both of the royal seed and of the nobles, (4) kids, in whom was no blemish, and of good appearance, and apt in all wisdom, and quick in knowledge, and ready of understanding, and who have ability in them to stand [4] in the palace of the king; and that he should teach them the learning and the language of the Chaldeans. (5) And the king allot-ted to them a daily portion of the dainties of the king, and of the wine of his drinking, that he might nourish them three years, and that at the end thereof they might stand before the king. (6) Now among them were of the sons of Judah, Daniel, Hananiah, Mishael, and Azariah. (7) And the prince of the eu-nuchs gave names to them; and he gave to Daniel the name of Belteshazzar; and to Hananiah, of Shadrach; and to Mishael, of Meshach; and to Azariah, of Abednego. [5]

(8) And Daniel purposed in his heart that he would not defile himself with the dainties of the king, and with wine of his drinking; and he entreated of the prince of the eunuchs, that he might not defile himself. (9) And God gave Daniel faor and tender regard in the sight of the prince of the eunuchs. (10) And the prince of the eunuchs said to Daniel, I fear my lord, the king, who hath appointed your food and your drink; for why should he see your faces more sad than those of the lads who are of your age, and why would ye en-danger my head to the king? (11) And Daniel said to the Melzar, [6] whom the prince of the eunuchs had set over Daniel, Hananiah, Mishael, and Aza-riah, (12) Prove thy servants, I beseech thee, ten days; and let them give us of the vegetables [7] that we may eat, and water that we may drink. (13) And let our countenance be looked upon before thee, and the countenance of the lads that eat the dainties of the king; and as thou shalt see, deal with thy servants. (14) And he hearkened to them in this matter, and proved them ten days. (15) And at the end of ten days, their countenance appeared fairer and fatter in flesh, than all the lads that did eat the dainties of the king. (16) And the Melzar took away their dainties and the wine of their drinking, and gave them vegetables. (17) And as for these four lads, God gave to them knowledge and skill in all learning and wisdom; and Daniel had understand-

ing in all visions and dreams. (18) And at the end of the days, when the king had said he should bring them in, the prince of the eunuchs brought them in before Nebuchadnezzar. (19) And the king conversed with them; and among them all was found none like Daniel, Hananiah, Mishael, and Azariah; and they stood before the king. (20) And in every matter of wise understanding concerning which the king inquired of them, he found them ten times better than all the scribes and enchanters that were in all his kingdom. (21) And Daniel continued unto the first year of Cyrus the king.

[1] came,— so *Hävernick, Uwald, Stuart, Hitzig* and *Hofmann;* marched, — *Kranichfeld, Keil* and *Hengstenberg.*
[2] them — *i.e.* the vessels, — *Keil, Stuart;* including Jehoiakim, — *Hitzig, Kranichfeld.*
[3] *or* courtiers.
[4] To serve.
[5] Ahed-neho, —Uitzig, Keil, Lenormant, Fuller.
[6] Overseer or steward.
[7] Seeds, such as peas, beans, and the like.

Chapter II

And in the second year [1] of the reign of Nebuchadnezzar, Nebuchadnez-zar dreamed dreams, and his spirit was troubled, and his sleep failed him. (2) And the king commanded to summon the scribes and the enchanters, and the sorcerers and the Chaldeans, that they might show the king his dreams; and they came and stood before the king. (3) And the king said unto them, I have dreamed a dream, and my spirit is troubled to know the dream. (4) And the Chaldeans said to the king in Aramaean, [2] O king, live for ever, tell thy serv-ants the dream, and we will declare the interpretation. (5) The king an-swered and said to the Chaldeans, The decree is made known [3] by me; if ye will not make known unto me the dream and the interpretation thereof, ye shall be cut to pieces and your houses shall be made a dunghill. (6) But if ye declare the dream and the interpretation thereof, ye shall receive from me gifts, riches, and great honor; therefore declare the dream and the interpre-tation thereof. (7) They answered a second time and said. Let the king tell his servants the dream, and we will declare the interpretation. (8) The king an-swered and said, I know of a truth that ye would gain time, wholly because ye see the decree is made known by me. (9) Which dream, if ye will not make known unto me, one decree [4] is for you; for ye have prepared lying and corrupt words to speak before me, till the time be changed; therefore tell me the dream, and I shall know that ye can declare the interpretation thereof. (10) The Chaldeans answered before the king, and said, There is not a man upon the earth, who is able to declare the matter of the king; because [5] no great and powerful king has asked a thing like this of any scribe, enchanter, or Chaldean. (11) And the thing which the king asks is weighty, [6] and there is none other who can declare it before the king, except the gods, whose dwelling is not with flesh. (12) Because of this the king was angry and exceedingly wroth; and commanded to destroy all the wise men of Babylon. (13) And the decree went forth, that the wise men should be slain; and they sought Daniel and his companions to be slain. (14) Then Daniel answered with counsel and wisdom to Arioch, the chief of the body-guard of the king, who was gone forth to slay the wise men of Babylon. (15) He answered and said to Arioch, the powerful one of the king. Why is the decree so urgent [7] from the king? Then Arioch made the matter known to Daniel. (16) Then Daniel went in and besought the king that he would give him time, and he would declare the interpretation to the king.

(17) Then Daniel went to his house and made the matter known to Hananiah, Mishael, and Azariah, his companions; (18) even, that they might seek compassion of the God of heaven concerning this secret; that they might not destroy Daniel and his companions with the rest of the wise men of Babylon. (19) Then was the secret revealed unto Daniel in a vision of the night; then Daniel blessed the God of heaven. (20) Daniel answered and said,

Blessed be the name of God, from everlasting to everlasting,
For wisdom and might are his.
(21) And he it is who changeth the times and the seasons.
Who removeth kings and setteth up kings,
Who giveth wisdom to the wise
And knowledge to them that know understanding.
(22) He revealeth the deep and secret things;
He knoweth what is in the darkness,
And the light dwelleth with him.
(23) Thee, O God of my fathers, do I thank and praise;
For thou hast given me wisdom and might,
And now thou hast made known unto me
That which we sought of thee;
For thou hast made known unto us the matter of the king.

(24) Therefore Daniel went to Arioch, whom the king had appointed to destroy the wise men of Babylon; he went and spake thus to him: Destroy not the wise men of Babylon; bring me in before the king, and I will declare unto the king the interpretation. (25) Then Arioch brought Daniel before the king in haste, and thus spake to him, I have found a man of the sons of the captivity of Judah, who will make known unto the king the interpretation. (26) The king answered and said to Daniel, whose name was Belteshazzar, Art thou able to make known to me the dream which I have seen, and the interpretation thereof? (27) Daniel answered in the presence of the king and said, The secret which the king has asked, the wise men, the enchanters, the scribes, the astrologers, are not able to declare unto the king. (28) But there is a God in heaven, who revealeth secrets, and he hath made known to the king, Nebuchadnezzar, what shall be in the latter days. Thy dream, even the

visions of thy head upon thy bed, was this. (29) As for thee, O king, thy thoughts came up upon thy bed, what should be hereafter; and He who revealeth secrets hath made known to thee what shall be. (30) But as for me, this secret is revealed to me, not by wisdom which I have more than any living, but that they might make known the interpretation of the king, and that thou mightest know the thoughts of thine heart.

(31) Thou, O king, sawest, and behold, a great image stood before thee; this image was great, and its brightness excellent, and its appearance terrible. (32) This image — its head was of pure gold, its breasts and its arms of silver, its belly and its thighs of brass, (33) its legs of iron, its feet partly of iron and partly of clay. (34) Thou sawest until a stone was cut out without hands, and it smote the image upon its feet of iron and clay, and crushed them. (35) Then was crushed at once the iron, the clay, the brass, the silver, and the gold, and they became like the chaff of the summer threshing-floors; and the wind carried them away, and no place was found for them; and the stone which smote the image became a great mountain and filled all the earth. (36) This is the dream; and we will tell the interpretation thereof before the king.

(37) Thou, O king, king of kings, to whom the God of heaven hath given the kingdom, the power, and the strength, and the glory; (38) and wherever the sons of men dwell, the beast of the field and the fowl of the heavens hath he given into thine hand, and hath made thee to rule over them all — thou art the head of gold. (39) And after thee shall arise another kingdom inferior to thee, and another, a third kingdom of brass, which shall rule over all the earth. (40) And the fourth kingdom shall be strong as iron; as iron breaks in pieces and crushes everything, even as iron which dashes in pieces, all these will it crush and bruise. (41) And since thou sawest the feet and the toes, part of potter's clay and part of iron, the kingdom shall be divided, and there shall be in it of the firmness of iron, because thou sawest the iron mixed with miry clay. (42) And since the toes of the feet were partly of iron and partly of clay, the kingdom shall be partly strong and partly brittle. (43) Since thou sawest iron mixed with miry clay, they shall mingle themselves with the seed of men; but they shall not cleave one to another, behold, even as iron doth not mingle itself with clay. (44) And ii the days of these kings the God of heaven shall set up a kingdom which shall never be destroyed; and the kingdom shall not be left to another people; it shall crush and bring to an end all these kingdoms, and it shall stand for ever. (45) Forasmuch as thou sawest that the stone was cut out of the mountain without hands, and that it crushed the iron, the brass, the clay, the silver, and the gold, the great God hath made known to the king what shall be hereafter; and the dream is certain, and the interpretation thereof faithful.

(46) Then the king, Nebuchadnezzar, fell on his face, and worshipped Daniel, and commanded that they should offer an oblation and sweet odors unto him. (47) The king answered Daniel and said. Of a truth it is, that your God is a God of gods, and a Lord of kings, and a revealer of secrets, because thou hast been able to reveal this secret. (48) Then the king promoted Daniel, and

gave him many great gifts, and made him ruler over all the province of Babylon, and chief of the governors over all the wise men of Babylon. (49) And Daniel requested of the king, and he appointed Shadrach, Meshach, and Abed-nego over the administration of the province of Babylon; and Daniel was in the gate of the king.

[1] second year, but also the fourth. See Exposition.
[2] The language here changes from Hebrew to Aramaean, which continues to the end of chapter vii.
[3] made known, published, — *Kranichfeld, Zöckler, Kliefoth, Keil;* The word has gone out, — *Gesenius, Hävernick, Lengerke, De Wette, Stuart;* The matter is gone from me, — *Theodotion, Vulgate, Luther, Bertholdt;* The word from me stands firm, — *Peshito, Aben Ezra, Saadiah, Winer, Hengstenberg.*
[4] decree, sentence, — *Vulgate, Luther, Zöckler, Keil, Gesenius;* one thing is your purpose, — *Theodotion, Lengerke, Hitzig, Stuart, Maurer.*
[5] because, — so *Zöckler, Keil, Stuart, Driver;* wherefore, — *Gesenius, Lengerke.*
[6] weighty, hard, — *Cheyne, Driver.*
[7] harsh, — *Cheyne, Driver.*

Chapter III

Nebuchadnezzar the king made an image of gold; its height was threescore cubits, its breadth, six cubits; he set it up in the plain of Dura, in the province of Babylon. (2) And Nebuchadnezzar the king sent to assemble the satraps, the governors, and the pashas, the judges, the treasurers, the counsellors, the lawyers, and all the rulers of the provinces, to come to the dedication of the image which Nebuchadnezzar the king had set up. (3) Then the satraps, the governors, and the pashas, the judges, the treasurers, the counsellors, the lawyers, and all the rulers of the provinces, were assembled to the dedication of the image which Nebuchadnezzar the king had set up; and they stood before the image which Nebuchadnezzar had set up. (4) And a herald cried with might. To you it is commanded, ye nations, tribes, and languages, (5) at the time that ye shall hear the sound of the horn, flute, harp, sackbut, psaltery, symphony, [2] and all kinds of music, ye shall fall down and worship the golden image which Nebuchadnezzar the king hath set up. (6) And whoever shall not fall down and worship, shall at the same moment be cast into the midst of the furnace of burning fire. (7) Therefore at the time when all the nations heard the sound of the horn, flute, harp, sackbut, psaltery, and all kinds of music, all the nations, tribes, and languages fell down and worshipped the golden image which Nebuchadnezzar the king had set up.

(8) Wherefore, at the time, men who were Chaldeans came near, and accused the Jews. (9) They spoke and said to Nebuchadnezzar the king, O king, live for ever. (10) Thou, O king, hast established a decree, that every man that shall hear the sound of the horn, flute, harp, sackbut,])saltery, and bag-

pipe, and all kinds of music, shall fall down and worship the golden image; (11) and whoever shall not fall down and worship shall be cast into the midst of a furnace of burning fire. (12) There are men, who are Jews, whom thou hast appointed over the affairs of the province of Babylon, Shadrach, Meshach, and Abed-nego; these men, O king, have not regarded thee; they serve not thy gods, and the golden image which thou hast set up they do not worship.

(13) Then Nebuchadnezzar in rage and fury commanded to bring Shadrach, Meshach, and Abed-nego; then these men were brought before the king. (14) Nebuchadnezzar spoke and said to them, Is it of design, O Shadrach, Meshach, and Abed-nego, that ye do not serve my gods, nor worship the golden image which I have set up?

(15) Now if ye be ready, that at the time when ye shall hear the sound of the horn, flute, harp, sackbut, psaltery, and bagpipe, and all kinds of music, ye will fall down and worship the image which I have made, it is well; but if ye will not worship, at the same moment shall ye be cast into the midst of the furnace of burning fire; and who is that god that shall deliver you out of my hand?

(16) Shadrach, Meshach, and Abed-nego answered and said to the king, O Nebuchadnezzar, we have no need to answer thee in this matter. (17) If it be, our God whom we serve is able to deliver us from the furnace of burning fire, and from thy hand, O king, lie will deliver. (18) And if not, be it known unto thee, O king, that we will not serve thy gods, nor worship the golden image which thou hast set up.

(19) Then was Nebuchadnezzar full of fury, and the form of his countenance was changed against Shadrach, Meshach, and Abed-nego; he spake and commanded that they should heat the furnace seven times above what it was wont to be heated. (20) And he commanded men, the most mighty of his army, to bind Shadrach, Meshach, and Abed-nego, in order to cast them into the furnace of burning fire. (21) Then these men were bound in their lower garments, their tunics, and their mantles, and all their clothing, and were cast into the midst of the furnace of burning fire. (22) Therefore, because the command of the king was urgent, and the furnace exceeding hot, the men who took up Shadrach, Meshach, and Abed-nego, them the flame of the fire slew. (23) And these three men, Shadrach, Meshach, and Abed-nego, fell down bound into the midst of the furnace of burning fire.

(24) Then Nebuchadnezzar the king was astonished, and rose up in haste; he spoke and said to his counsellors. Did not we cast three men into the midst of the fire, bound? They answered and said to the king. True, O king. (25) He answered and said, Lo, I see four men loose, walking in the midst of the fire, and there is no hurt to them; and the appearance of the fourth is like to a son of the gods. (26) Then Nebuchadnezzar came near to the door of the furnace of burning, fire; he spake and said, Shadrach, Meshach, and Abed-nego, ye servants of the most high God, come forth, and come out. Then Shadrach, Meshach, and Abed-nego came forth from the midst of the fire.

(27) And the satraps, the governors, and the pashas, and the counsellors be-ing assembled, they saw these men, on whose bodies the fire had no power, and the hair of their heads was not singed, neither were their lower gar-ments changed, nor had the smell of fire passed on them, (28) Nebuchadnez-zar spake and said. Blessed be the God of Shadrach, Meshach, and Abed-nego, who hath sent his angel, and delivered his servants who trusted in him, and transgressed the word of the king, and yielded their bodies that they might not serve nor worship any god except their God. (29) And by me a decree is made, that every nation, tribe, and language which shall speak blasphemy against the God of Shadrach, Meshach, and Abed-nego shall be cut to pieces, and his house be made a dunghill; because there is no other god who is thus able to deliver. (30) Then the king promoted Shadrach, Meshach, and Abed-nego, in the province of Babylon.

[1] lawyers,— so *Gesenius, Davies, Keil, Pusey, Zöckler.*
[2] symphony, a kind of bagpipe,— *Gesenius, Davies, Hitzig, Ewald, Zöckler, Keil.*
[3] a son of the gods,— so *Hengstenberg, Zöckler, Keil, Fuller;* a son of God, — *Hitzig, Ewald.*

Chapter IV

Nebuchadnezzar the king to all nations, tribes, and languages that dwell in all the earth; Peace be multiplied unto you. (2) The signs and wonders which the most high God has wrought with me it has seemed good for me to de-clare. (3) His signs, how great! His wonders, how mighty! His kingdom is an everlasting kingdom, and his dominion is from generation to generation. (4) I Nebuchadnezzar was at rest in my house, and flourishing in my palace; (5) I saw a dream, and it made me afraid, and the thoughts upon my bed and the visions of my head terrified me.

(6) And by me a decree was made to bring before me all the wise men of Babylon, that they might make known to me the interpretation of the dream. (7) Then came in the scribes, the enchanters, the Chaldeans, and the astrolo-gers; and I told the dream before them; but they did not make known to me the interpretation thereof. (8) But at last Daniel came before me, whose name is Belteshazzar, according to the name of my god, and in whom is the spirit of the holy gods; and before him I told the dream. (9) Belteshazzar, master of the scribes, because I know that the spirit of the holy gods is in thee, and that no secret presses [1] thee, tell the visions of my dream which I have seen, and the interpretation thereof. (10) And the visions of my head on my bed were these. I saw, and behold, a tree in the midst of the earth, and the height thereof was great. (11) The tree became great and waxed strong, and the height thereof reached unto heaven, and the sight thereof to the end of all the earth. (12) The foliage thereof was fair, and the fruit thereof much, and on it was food for all; under it the beasts of the field found shade, and the

fowls of the heaven dwelt in the branches thereof, and all flesh was fed of it. (13) I saw in the visions of my head on my bed, and, behold, a watcher, even a holy one, came down from heaven. (14) He cried aloud and said thus. Hew down the tree, and cut off its branches, cause its foliage to fall off, and scatter its fruit; let the beasts get away from under it, and the fowls from its branches. (15) But leave the stump of its roots in the earth, and with a band of iron and brass, in the tender grass of the field; and let him be wet with the dew of heaven, and let his portion be with the beasts in the grass of the earth; (16) let his heart be changed from that of a man, and let the heart of a beast be given him, and let seven times pass over him. (17) By the decision of the watchers is the decree, and by the command of the holy ones the demand, in order that the living may know that the Most High is ruler over the kin2:dom of men, and giveth it to whomsoever he will, and setteth up over it the humblest of men. (18) This dream I, king Nebuchadnezzar, have seen; and do thou, Belteshazzar, declare the interpretation thereof, because all the wise men of my kingdom are not able to make known unto me the interpretation; but thou art able, for the spirit of the holy gods is in thee.

(19) Then Daniel, whose name is Belteshazzar, was astonished for a moment, [2] and his thoughts troubled him. The king spoke and said, Belteshazzar, let not the dream or the interpretation thereof trouble thee. Belteshazzar answered and said. My lord, the dream be to them that hate thee, and the interpretation thereof to thine enemies. (20) The tree which thou sawest, which became great and waxed strong, and whose height reached unto heaven, and the sight thereof to all the earth, (21) and whose foliage was fair, and the fruit thereof much, and on which was food for all, under which the beasts of the field dwelt, and on the branches thereof the fowls of the heaven abode; (22) it is thou, O king, that hast become great and waxed strong, and thy greatness hath increased and reached unto heaven, and thy dominion to the end of the earth. (23) And whereas the king saw a Watcher, even a Holy One, coming down from heaven, and saying, Hew down the tree, and destroy it; yet leave the stump of its roots in the earth, and with a band of iron and brass in the tender grass of the field; and let him be wet with the dew of heaven, and let his portion be with the beasts of the field, until seven times pass over him; (24) this is the interpretation, O king, and it is the decree of the Most High, which is come upon my lord the king. (25) And they shall drive thee from men, and thy dwelling shall be with the beasts of the field, and they shall cause thee to eat grass as oxen, and they shall wet thee with the dew from heaven, and seven times shall pass over thee, until thou shalt know that the Most High is ruler over the kingdom of men, and giveth it to whomsoever he will. (26) And that they commanded to leave the stump of the roots of the tree, — thy kingdom shall be sure unto thee, as soon as thou shalt know that the Heavens do rule. (27) Wherefore, O king, let my counsel be pleasing unto thee, and break off [3] thy sins by righteousness, and thine iniquities by mercy to the poor, if it may be a lengthening of thy tranquillity.

(28) The whole came upon Nebuchadnezzar the king. (29) At the end of twelve months he was walking upon the royal palace of Babylon. (30) The king spake and said, Is not this great Babylon, which I have built for the house of the kingdom by the might of my power, and for the honor of my glory? (31) While the word was in the king's mouth, there fell a voice from heaven, O king Nebuchadnezzar, to thee it is spoken, — the kingdom is departed from thee. (32) And they shall drive thee from men, and thy dwelling shall be with the beasts of the field; they shall cause thee to eat grass as oxen; and seven times shall pass over thee, until thou shalt know that the Most High is ruler over the kingdom of men, and giveth it to whomsoever he will. (33) At that very moment [4] was the word fulfilled upon Nebuchadnezzar, and he was driven from men, and did eat grass like oxen, and his body was wet with the dew of heaven, until his hair grew like that of eagles, and his nails like those of birds.

(34) And at the end of days, I, Nebuchadnezzar, lifted up mine eyes unto heaven, and mine understanding returned unto me, and I blessed the Most Higli, and Him who liveth for ever I praised and honored, whose dominion is an everlasting dominion; and his kingdom is from generation to generation. (35) And all the inhabitants of the earth are counted as nothing; and he doeth according to his will in the army of heaven, and among the inhabitants of the earth, and there is none who can stay his hand or say to him, What doest thou? (36) At the same time, my understanding returned to me; and for the honor of my kingdom, my glory and splendor returned to me, and my counsellors and my lords sought me, and I was established in my kingdom, and excellent majesty was added unto me. (37) Therefore I, Nebuchadnezzar, praise and exalt and honor the King of heaven, for all his works are truth, and his ways judgment; and those who walk in pride he is able to abase.

[1] presses, — i.e. is too difficult for.
[2] a moment, — so *Keil Stuart, Gesenius, Füerst, Davies*; one hour,—*Zöchler, Michaelis, Hitzig, Kranichfeld*.
[3] break off, — so *Rashi, Geier, Starke, Hävernick, Lengerke, Kranichfeld, Keil, Stuart, Melanchthon* in Apol. Conf., Art. 111, 140, ed. Mü., p. 132; redeem,— *Vulgate, Saadiah, Aben Ezra, Bertholdt, De Wette, Hitzig, Zöckler, Gesenius, Raman Catholic Commentators*.
[4] See verse 19.

Chapter V

Belshazzar the king made a great feast to his thousand karris, and drank wine before the thousand. (2) Belshazzar, while tasting [1] the wine, commanded to bring the golden and silver vessels which his father Nebuchadnezzar had brought from the temple which was in Jerusalem, that the king and his nobles, his wives and his concubines, might drink out of them.

(3) Then they brought the golden vessels which had been taken out of the temple of the house of God which was in Jerusalem, and the king and his nobles, his wives and his concubines, drank out of them. (4) They drank wine and praised the gods of gold and of silver, of brass, of iron, of wood, and of stone.

(5) At that very moment came forth fingers of a man's hand and wrote over against the candlestick upon the plaster of the wall of the palace of the king; and the king saw the end of the hand which wrote. (6) Then the king changed his color, and his thoughts troubled him, and the joints of his loins were loosed, and his knees smote one against the other. (7) The king cried aloud to bring in the enchanters, the Chaldeans, and the astrologers. The king spake and said to the wise men of Babylon, Whoever shall read this writing and declare to me the interpretation thereof, shall be clothed in purple, and have a chain of gold about his neck, and shall rule as the third in the kingdom. (8) Then came in all the wise men of the king; but they were not able to read the writing, nor make known to the king the interpretation thereof (9) Then was King Belshazzar greatly troubled, and his color was changed upon him, and his nobles were astonished. (10) The queen, on account of the words of the king and his nobles, came into the banquet-house; the queen spoke and said, O king, live for ever; let not thy thoughts trouble thee, nor thy color be changed. (11) There is a man in thy kingdom in whom is the spirit of the holy gods, and in the days of thy father [2] light and understanding and wisdom, like the wisdom of the gods, was found in him; and king Nebuchadnezzar, thy father — thy father, O king — appointed him master of the scribes, the enchanters, the Chaldeans, the astrologers, — (12) inasmuch as an excellent spirit and knowledge and understanding to interpret dreams, show mysteries, and dissolve knots [3] was found in the same Daniel, whom the king named Belteshazzar; now let Daniel be called, and he will declare the interpretation.

(13) Then was Daniel brought before the king. The king spoke and said, Art thou that Daniel, who art of the sons of the captivity of Judah, whom the king, my father, brought out of Judea? (14) And I have heard of thee, that the spirit of the gods is in thee, and that light and understanding and excellent wisdom is found in thee. (15) And now the wise men, the enchanters, have been brought before me, that they might read this writing and make known to me the interpretation thereof, and they were not able to declare the interpretation of the word. (16) And I have heard of thee, that thou art able to make interpretations and dissolve knots; now if thou art able to read the writing and make known to me the interpretation thereof, thou shalt be clothed in purple, and have a chain of gold about thy neck, and shalt rule as the third in the kingdom.

(17) Then Daniel answered and. said before the king. Let thy gifts be to thyself, and give thy rewards to another; yet I will read the writing unto the king, and make known to him the interpretation. (18) O thou king, the most high God gave Nebuchadnezzar, thy father, the kingdom and the majesty and

the glory and the honor; (19) and for the majesty that he gave him all nations, tribes, and languages trembled and feared before him; whom he would
he slew, and whom he would he kept alive; and whom he would he set up,
and whom he would he put down. (20) And when his heart was lifted up, and
his spirit hardened in pride he was deposed from the throne of his kingdom,
and they took his glory from him; (21) and he was driven from the sons of
men, and his heart was made like the beasts, and his dwelling was with the
wild asses; they caused him to eat grass as oxen, and his body was wet with
the dew of heaven; till he knew that the most high God ruled over the kingdom of men, and that he appointeth over it whomsoever he will. (22) And
thou his son, O Belshazzar, hast not humbled thine heart, notwithstanding
thou didst know all this; (23) but thou hast lifted up thyself against the Lord
of heaven; and the vessels of his house have been brought before thee, and
thou and thy nobles, thy wives and thy concubines, have drunk wine out of
them; and thou hast praised the gods of silver and of gold, of brass, of iron, of
wood, and of stone, which neither see, nor hear, nor know; and the God, in
whose hand thy breath is, and whose are all thy ways, hast thou not glorified.
(24) Then was the end of the hand sent from before him; and this writing
was written. (25) And this is the writing that was written, *Mené, Mené, Tekél,
Upharsín.* (26) This is the interpretation of the word; *Mené,* God hath numbered thy kingdom, and finished it; (27) *Tekél,* thou art weighed in the balances and art found wanting; (28) *Perés,* thy kingdom is divided, and is given
to the Medes and Persians.

(29) Then commanded Belshazzar, and they clothed Daniel in purple, and
put a chain of gold on his neck. and made proclamation concerning him, that
he should rule as the third in the kingdom.

(30) In that night was Belshazzar, the king of the Chaldeans, slain. (31) And
Darius the Median took the kingdom, being about threescore and two years
old.

[1] Tasting, enjoying, drinking so as to feel its effects.
[2] father — *i.e.* grandfather. See Exposition, pp. 139, 148.
[3] dissolve knots — *i.e.* explain difficult subjects.

Chapter VI

It seemed good to Darius to set over the kingdom one hundred and twenty
satraps, who should be over the whole kingdom; (2) and over them three
presidents, of whom Daniel was one; that these satraps might render an account unto them, and the king have no loss.

(3) Then this Daniel outshone the presidents and satraps, because an excellent spirit was in him, and the king thought to set him over the whole
kingdom.

(4) Then the presidents and satraps sought to find occasion against Daniel
on the part of the kingdom, but they were not able to find any occasion or

corruption, inasmuch as he was faithful, and not any fault or corruption vas found in him. (5) Then said these men. We shall not find any occasion against this Daniel, except we find it against him concerning the law of his God. (6) Then these presidents and satraps ran together with tumult to the king and said thus unto him, O king Darius, live for ever. (7) All the presidents of the kingdom, the governors and satraps, the counsellors and pashas, have given counsel that the king should establish a statute and make a firm decree, that whoever shall ask a petition of any god or man for thirty days, except of thee, O king, he shall be cast into the den of lions. (8) Now, O king, establish the decree, and sign the writing, that it be not changed, according to the law of the Medes and Persians, which altereth not. (9) Because of this. King Darius signed the writing and the decree.

(10) And Daniel, when he knew that the writing was signed, went to his house; and his windows were open in his chamber toward Jerusalem, and he kneeled upon his knees three times in a day, and prayed and gave thanks before his God, because he had done so before this. (11) Then these men rushed forward and found Daniel praying and making supplication before his God. (12) Then they drew near and spoke before the king concerning the decree of the king: Hast thou not signed a decree that every man that shall ask of any god or man for thirty days, except of thee, O king, shall be cast into the den of lions? The king answered and said: The word is firm, according to the law of the Medes and Persians, which altereth not. (13) Then answered they, and said before the king: Daniel, who is of the sons of the captivity of Judah, doth not regard thee, O king, nor the decree which thou hast signed, but three times in a day doth he make his petition. (14) Then the king, when he heard the word, was greatly displeased with himself, and set his heart on Daniel to deliver him; and he labored till the going down of the sun to deliver him. (15) Then these men ran together with tumult unto the king, and said unto the king. Know, O king, that the law of the Medes and Persians is, that no decree nor statute which the king establisheth may be changed. (16) Then the king commanded, and they brought Daniel and cast him into the den of lions. The king spoke and said unto Daniel, May thy God, whom thou servest continually, deliver thee! (17) And a stone was brought, and placed upon the mouth of the den; and the king sealed it with his signet, and with the signet of his nobles, that the matter [1] concerning Daniel might not be changed.

(18) Then the king went to his palace, and passed the night fasting; neither were concubines [2] brought before him; and his sleep fled from him. (19) Then the king arose at early dawn, when it was light, and went in haste to the den of lions. (20) And when he drew near to the den, he cried with a distressed voice unto Daniel; the king spoke and said to Daniel, O Daniel, servant of the living God, is thy God, whom thou servest continually, able to deliver thee from the lions? (21) Then Daniel spoke with the king: O king, live for ever. (22) My God hath sent his angel, and hath shut the mouth of the lions, and they have not hurt me; inasmuch as before him innocency was found in me; and also before thee, O king, have I done no harm. (23) Then the

king was exceeding glad within himself, [3] and he commanded that they should take Daniel up out of the den. And Daniel was taken up out of the den, and not any hurt was found on him, because he trusted in his God. (24) And the king commanded, and they brought those men who had accused Daniel, and they cast into the den of lions them, their children, and their wives; and they had not come to the bottom of the den before that the lions had the mastery of them and had broken their bones to pieces,

(25) Then Darius, the king, wrote to all the nations, tribes, and languages who dwelt in all the earth; Peace be multiplied unto you. (26) By me a decree is made, That in every dominion of my kingdom men tremble and fear before the God of Daniel; for he is the living God, and endureth for ever, and his kingdom shall not be destroyed, and his dominion shall be unto the end. (27) It is he that delivereth and rescueth, and who doeth signs and wonders in heaven and on earth, who hath delivered Daniel from the power of the lions.

(28) And this Daniel prospered in the reign of Darius and in the reign of Cyrus the Persian.

[1] matter, — so *Zöckler, Keil;* purposes, — *Gesenius, De Wette, Hävernick, Lengerke, Stuart, Ilaurer, Kliefoth.*
[2] concubines, — so *Gesenius, Dietrich, Tregelles, Davies, Keil, Stuart, Zöckler,* etc.
[3] within himself, — so *Stuart, Gesenius, Maurer, Lengerke, Strong, Davies.*

Chapter VII

In the first year of Belshazzar, king of Babylon, Daniel had a dream and visions of his head upon his bed; then he wrote the dream, he told the sum of the matters. (2) Daniel spoke and said:

I saw in my vision by night, and behold, the four winds of the heaven broke forth upon the great sea.

(3) And four monstrous beasts came up from the sea, diverse one from another. (4) The first was like a lion, and it had the wings of an eagle; I saw until the wings thereof were plucked, and it was lifted up [1] from the earth, and made to stand on the feet like a man, and the heart of a man was given to it.

(5) And behold, another beast, a second, like to a bear, and it raised up on one side, and three ribs were in its mouth between its teeth, and thus they said to it, Arise, devour much flesh.

(6) After this I saw, and behold, another, like a panther, and it had upon its back four wings of a bird; and the beast had four heads, and dominion was given to it.

(7) After this, I saw in the visions of the night, and behold, a fourth beast, dreadful and terrible, and strong exceedingly; and it had great teeth of iron; it devoured and broke to pieces, and stamped the remnant under its feet; and it was diverse from all the beasts that were before it; and it had ten horns.

(8) I was considering the horns, and behold, there came up between them another little horn, and three of the first horns were rooted out from before

it; and, behold, eyes like the eyes of a man were in this horn, and a mouth speaking great things. (9) I saw until the thrones were set, and the Ancient of days did sit, whose garment was white as snow, and the hair of his head like pure wool; his throne flames of fire, his wheels burning flame. (10) A stream of fire issued and came forth from before him; thousand thousands ministered to him, and ten thousand times ten thousand stood before him; the judgment was set, and the books were opened. (11) 1 saw then because of the voice of the great words which the horn spoke; I saw until the beast was slain and its body destroyed, and given to the burning fire. (12) And as to the rest of the beasts, their dominion was taken away; and continuance of their lives was given them for a season and time.

(13) I saw in the visions of the night, and behold, with the clouds of heaven One like the Son of man came, and he approached the Ancient of days, and they brought him near before him. (14) And to him was given dominion, and honor, and a kingdom, that all nations, tribes, and languages should serve him; his dominion is an everlasting dominion, which shall not pass away, and his kingdom one which shall not be destroyed.

(15) As for me, Daniel, my spirit was grieved in the midst of my body, and the visions of my head troubled me. (16) I drew near to one of them that stood by, that I might ask of him the certainty of all this. And he told me, and made me know the interpretation of the words.

(17) These monstrous beasts, which are four, are four kings, which shall arise from the earth. (18) And the saints of the Most High shall receive the kingdom, and shall possess the kingdom for ever, even for ever and ever.

(19) Then I desired the truth concerning the fourth beast, which was diverse from all of them, exceeding terrible, whose teeth were of iron, and its claws of brass; which devoured, broke to pieces, and stamped the remnant under its feet; (20) and concerning the ten horns that were on its head, and the other one, which came up, and before whom three fell, and that horn, even it, had eyes, and a mouth that spoke very great things, and its aspect was mightier than that of its fellows. (21) I saw, and that horn made war with the saints, and prevailed against them; (22) until the Ancient of days came, and judgment was given [2] to the saints of the Most High, and the time came, and the saints possessed the kingdom. (23) Thus he spoke, The fourth beast shall be the fourth kingdom on earth, which shall be diverse from all kingdoms, and it shall devour all the earth, and shall tread it down, and break it to pieces. (24) And the ten horns out of this kingdom are ten kings which shall arise; and another shall rise after them, and he shall be diverse from the first, and he shall overthrow three kings. (25) And he shall speak words against the Most High, and the saints of the Most High shall he vex, and he shall think to change times and law; and they [3] shall be given into his hand until a time and times and the dividing of time. (26) And the judgment shall sit, and they shall take away his dominion, to consume and to destroy it, to the end. (27) And the kingdom, and dominion, and the greatness of the kingdom under the whole heaven, shall be given to the people of

the saints of the Most High; whose kingdom is an everlasting kingdom, and all dominions shall serve and obey him. (28) Hitherto is the end of the matter. As for me, Daniel, my thoughts much troubled me, and my color changed upon me, but I kept the matter in my heart.

[1] lifted up, — so *Zöckler, Keil, Stuart;* taken away, — *Jerome, Theodotion, Rashi, Bertholdt, Hitzig.*
[2] was given, — so *Hengstenberg, Fausset, Wordsworth, Auth. Version;* done unto, — *Hitzig, Zöckler, Keil, De Wette.*
[3] They — *i.e.* the saints or things in general.
[4] the matter, — the word, — *Ewald, Zöckler, Keil.*

Chapter VIII

[1]

In the third year of the reign of Belshazzar the king, a vision appeared to me, to me, Daniel, after that which appeared to me at the first. (2) And I saw in a vision, and it came to pass, when I saw, that I was in Shushan, the palace, which is in the province of Elam; and I saw in a vision, and I was by the river Ulai.

(3) And I lifted up my eyes, and saw, and behold! a ram standing before the river, and he had two horns; and the two horns were high, but one was higher than the other, and the higher came up last. (4) I saw the ram pushing westward, and northward, and southward; and none of the beasts could stand before him, neither could any deliver out of his hand; and he did according to his will, and became great. (5) And I was considering, and behold, a he-goat came from the west on the face of all the earth, and touched not the earth; and the goat had a notable horn between his eyes. (6) And he came to the ram which had two horns, which I had seen standing before the river, and ran to him in the heat of his power. (7) And I saw him when he approached near the ram, and he was enraged at him, and smote the ram, and broke to pieces his two horns; and there was no power in the ram to stand before him, and he cast him down to the earth, and stamped upon him, and there was no deliverer to deliver the ram out of his hand. (8) And the he-goat waxed exceeding great; and when he had become great, the great horn was broken; and for it came up four notable ones [2] toward the four winds of heaven.

(9) And from one of them came up out of littleness [3] one horn, and it waxed exceeding great toward the south, and toward the east, and toward the glorious [4] land.

(10) And it waxed great, even to the host of heaven; and it cast down to earth some of the host and of the stars and trampled upon them. (11) Even to the Prince of the host did he magnify himself, and by him the daily service [5] was taken away, and the dwelling-place of his sanctuary was cast down. (12) And a host was placed over [6] the daily service by means of transgression, [7] and it [8] cast down the truth to the ground; and it did and prospered.

(13) And I heard a holy one speaking, and one holy one said to the certain one who was speaking, How long shall be the vision of the daily service and the transgression of the desolater — the giving up of both the sanctuary and the host to be trampled upon? (14) And he said unto me. Unto two thousand and three hundred evening-mornings; then shall the sanctuary be justified.

(15) And it came to pass, as I, I Daniel, was seeing the vision, that I sought a meaning, and behold, there stood one before me like the appearance of a man. (16) And I heard the voice of a man between the Ulai, and he called and said, Gabriel, make this man to understand the vision. (17) And he came near where I stood, and as he came, I was afraid, and fell on my face; and he said to me, Understand, O son of man; for the vision is to the time of the end. (18) And as he was speaking with me, I was in a deep sleep on my face, on the earth; and he touched me, and caused me to stand upright. (19) And he said. Behold, I will make thee to know what shall be in the last time of the indignation; for at the appointed time is the end.

(20) The ram which thou sawest having two horns are the kings of Media and Persia. (21) And the shaggy goat is the king of Greece; and the great horn which is between its eyes, that is the first king. (22) And that it was broken and four stood up in its stead, four kingdoms shall stand up out of the nation, but not with his power. (23) And in the last time of their kingdom, when the transgressors shall have come to the full, a king of hard countenance and understanding intrigues shall stand up; (24) and his power shall be mighty, but not by his own power; and he shall destroy wonderfully, and shall prosper and do, and shall destroy the mighty and the holy people. (25) And through his cunning he also shall cause deceit to prosper in his hand, and he shall magnify himself in his own heart, and unexpectedly shall he destroy many; and against the Prince of princes shall he stand up, but he shall be broken to pieces without hand. (26) And the vision of the evening and the morning which was told, it is true; and do thou shut up the vision, for it shall be for many days.

(27) And I, Daniel, fainted and was sick for days; and I arose and did the business of the king; and I was astonished at the vision, and none understood it.

[1] With the beginning of this chapter the Hebrew language is resumed, in which all that follows is written.
[2] or, came up conspicuously four.
[3] out of littleness, — so *Keil, Maurer, Hofmann, Kranichfeld, Kliefoth, Zöckler;* one little horn, — *Lengerke, Stuart, Strong, Authorized Version.*
[4] glorious, — literally, the glory.
[5] daily service, — so Hengstenberg, Havernick, Hofmann, Kranichfeld, Kliefoth, Keil, Zöckler.
[6] a host was placed over, — so Stuart, Grotius, Michaelis; a host shall be given up together with, — *Keil, De Wette, Lengerke, Hävernick, Kranichfeld, Kliefoth, Maurer;* a host shall be raised against, — *Hitzig, Ewald, Zöckler, Kamphausen, Jerome, Luther.*

[7] by means of transgression,— so *Hitzig, Ewald, Zöckler, Stuart.*

[8] it — *i.e.* the horn.

[9] mighty, — so *Keil, Zöckler;* many, —*Stuart, Lengerke, Maurer, Kliefoth.*

[10] unexpectedly, — so *Keil, Stuart.*

[11] none understood it, — so *Keil,* etc.; I understood it not, — *Maurer, Hitzig, Kranichfeld, Kamphausen, Stuart.*

Chapter IX

In the first year of Darius the son of Ahasuerus, of the seed of the Medes, who was made king over the kingdom of the Chaldeans; (2) in the first year of his reign, 1, Daniel, understood by the Scriptures the number of the years concerning which the word of Jehovah came to Jeremiah the prophet, — to fulfil seventy years with respect to the desolations of Jerusalem. (3) And I set my face unto the Lord God, to seek prayer and supplications, with fasting, and sackcloth and ashes; (4) and I prayed to Jehovah my God, and made confession, and said:

O Lord, the great and dreadful God, who keepeth the covenant and mercy to them that love him and keep his commandments; (5) we have sinned, and have acted perversely, and have done wickedly, and have rebelled, and have departed from thy commandments and from thy judgments; (6) and we have not hearkened to thy servants the prophets, who spoke in thy name to our kings, our princes, and our fathers, and to all the people of the land. (7) To thee, O Lord, belongeth righteousness, but unto us shame of face, as at this day; to the men of Judah, and to the inhabitants of Jerusalem, and to all Israel, who are near and who are afar off, in all the countries whither thou hast driven them, because of their trespass which they have trespassed against thee. (8) O Lord, to us belongeth shame of face, to our kings, to our princes, and to our fathers, because we have sinned against thee. (9) To the Lord our God belong mercies and forgivenesses, for we have rebelled against him; (10) And we have not hearkened to the voice of Jehovah our God, to walk in his laws, which he has set before us by the hand of his servants the prophets. (11) And all Israel have transgressed thy law, and have turned back, that they might not hearken to thy voice; and thou hast poured upon us the curse and the oath which is written in the law of Moses, the servant of God, because we have sinned against him. (12) And he hath confirmed his words, which he spoke concerning us, and concerning our judges, who judged us, by bringing upon us a great evil, which hath not been done under the whole heaven, as it hath been done upon Jerusalem. (13) According to what is written in the law of Moses, all this evil has come upon us; and yet we have not made supplication before Jehovah our God, that we might turn from our iniquities and understand thy truth. (14) And Jehovah hath watched over the evil, and brought it upon us; for righteous is Jehovah our God concerning all his works which he doeth, and we have not hearkened to his voice. (15) And now, O Lord, our God, who hast brought thy people from the land of Egypt with a mighty hand, and hast made for thyself a name, as at this day; we have sinned, we have done wickedly. (16) O Lord, according to all thy righteousness, let thine anger and thy fury be turned away from thy city Jerusalem, thy holy mountain; for, on account of our sins and the iniquities of our fathers, Jerusalem and thy people are become a reproach to all around us, (17) And now, O our God, hear the prayer of thy servant, and his supplications, and cause thy face to shine upon thy sanctuary, which is desolate, for the Lord's sake. (18) O my God, incline thine ear, and hear; open thine eyes and see our desolations, and the city upon which thy name is called; for we do not lay down our supplication on account of our righteousness, but on account of thy great mercies. (19) O Lord, hear; O Lord, forgive; hearken and do; delay not, for thine own sake, O my God, for thy name is called upon thy city and upon thy people.

(20) And while I was speaking and praying, and confessing my sin and the sin of my people Israel, and laying my supplication before Jehovah, my God, concerning the holy mountain of my God, (21) even while I was speaking In prayer, the man Gabriel, whom I had seen in the vision at first, wearied wIth a swift course, reached me about the time of the evening oblation. (22) And he gave understanding and talked with me, and said, O Daniel, I am now come to instruct thee in knowledge. (23) At the beginning of thy supplication the word went forth, and I am come to tell thee; for thou art greatly beloved; therefore consider the word, and understand the vision.

(24) Seventy sevens are cut off' upon thy people and upon thy holy city to finish the transgression, and to seal up sins, and to make reconciliation for iniquity, and to bring in everlasting righteousness, and to seal vision and prophecy, and to anoint a holiness of holinesses. [1] (25) Know, therefore, and understand, from the going forth of the word to restore and to build Jerusalem unto Messiah Prince shall be seven sevens, and threescore and two sevens; it shall be restored and built with the street and fosse, [2] but in troublous times.

(26) And after the threescore and two sevens, Messiah shall be cut off, and nothing is to him; [3] and the people of the prince that shall come will destroy the city and the sanctuary; and its [4] end shall be with a flood, and unto the end shall be war, [5] a decree of desolations.

(27) And he [6] shall confirm a covenant with many for one seven; and in the middle of the seven he shall cause the sacrifice and the oblation to cease, and upon a wing of abominations shall be the desolater, even until the consummation, and that determined shall be poured upon the desolater. [7]

[1] See Exposition.
[2] fosse, — so *Gesenius, Herzfeld, Ewald, Zöckler;* aqueduct, — *Grotius, Pusey.*
[3] See Exposition, pp. 249, 250. Cf. *Hofmann, Hengstenherg, Kranichfeld, Kliefoth, Calvin, Ebrard, Pusey, Vulgate.*
[4] its — *i.e.* the city and sanctuary's, — so *Hengstenberg, Hitzig, Pusey, Hävernick, Auherlen, Delitzsch.*

[5] and unto the end shall be war, — so *Hengstenberg, Hitzig, Hävernick, Keil, Lengerke, Maurer, Pusey, Wieseler, Kranichfeld, Auberlen, Kliefoth, Stuart;* unto the end of the war, — *Rosenmüller, Hofmann, Ewald, Fuller, Zöckler.*

[6] he — *i.e.* the prince that shall come and become the desolater, — so *Bertholdt, Maurer, Wieseler, Ewald, Kranichfeld, Kliefoth, Stuart, Keil, Zöckler.*

[7] upon the desolater, — so *De Wette, Maurer, Davidson;* the terrible thing, — *Hitzig, Herzfeld, Ewald.*

Chapter X

[In the third year of Cyrus, king of Persia, a word was revealed to Daniel, whose name was called Belteshazzar; and the word was truth, and the warfare great; [1] and he understood the word, for understanding was given to him in the vision. [2]

(2) In those days I Daniel was mourning three whole weeks. (3) I ate no pleasant bread, [3] neither flesh nor wine came into my mouth, I did not so much as anoint myself, until three whole weeks were fulfilled. (4) And on the four and twentieth day of the first month I was by the side of the great river, which is Hiddekel; [4] (5) and I lifted up mine eyes, and saw, and behold, a man clothed in linen, and his loins girded about with fine gold of Uphaz; (6) and his body was like the beryl, and his face like the appearance of lightning, and his eyes like lamps of fire, and his arms and his feet like the lustre of polished brass, and the voice of his words like the voice of a multitude. (7) And I Daniel alone saw the vision; for the men who were with me saw not the vision; but a great quaking fell upon them, and they fled, hiding themselves. (8) And I was left alone, and I saw this great vision, and no strength was left in me; and my life-appearance was turned upon me to destruction, and I retained no strength. (9) And I heard the voice of his words; and when I heard the voice of his words, then was I in a deep sleep upon my face, and my face was toward the earth. (10) And, behold, a hand touched me, and it raised [5] me upon my knees and the palms of my hands. (11) And he said unto me, O Daniel, a man greatly beloved, understand the words which I speak unto thee, and stand upright; for unto thee am I now sent. And while he was speaking this word unto me, I stood up, trembling.

(12) And he said unto me. Fear not, Daniel; for from the first day that thou gavest thy heart to understand, and to humble thyself before thy God, thy words were heard, and I am come according to thy words. (13) And the prince of the kingdom of Persia withstood me one and twenty days; and, lo, Michael, one of the chief princes, came to help me; and I gained the victory [6] there, with the kings of Persia. (14) And I am come to make thee understand what shall befall thy people in the latter days, for the vision is yet for those days.

[7] (15) And while he was speaking unto me words like these, I set my face toward the earth and became dumb. (16) And, behold, one like the sons of men touched my lips; and I opened my mouth and spoke, and said to him

who stood before me; My lord, by the vision my distresses [8] are turned up-on me, and I have retained no strength. (17) And how can this servant of my lord speak with this my lord?

And as for me, straightway there remained no strength in me, neither was there breath left in me. (18) And one like the appearance of a man again touched me, and he strengthened me. (19) And he said, O man greatly be-loved, fear not; peace be unto thee, be very strong. And while he was speak-ing to me, I was strengthened, and said, Let my lord speak; for thou hast strengthened me. (20) And he said. Dost thou know why I am come unto thee? and now will I return to fight with the prince of Persia; and when I am gone forth, lo, the prince of Greece shall come. (21) But yet I will tell thee what is written in the book of truth; and there is no one who puts forth his strength with me against these, save Michael your prince.

[1] warfare great, — *Cheyne, Driver, Keil, Stuart, Zöckler, Maurer, De Wette.*
[2] See Exposition.
[3] pleasant bread, — *Keil, Stuart;* leavened bread, — *Hävernick, Lengerke, Maurer, Hitzig, Kranichfeld, Zöckler.*
[4] Hiddekel — *i.e.* the Tigris.
[5] raised, — *lit. shook.*
[6] I gained the victory, — *Luther, Geier, Winer, Gesenius, Hävernick, Keil, Fausset;* I maintained my place, — *Füller, Hofmann;* I was no longer needed, — *Ewald, Zöckler;* I remained or tarried, — *Vulgate, Dereser, Rosenmüller, Kranichfeld.*
[7] verses 15-21 and xi. 1. See Exposition, pp. 258-261.
[8] distresses, or pains, — *Cheyne, Driver, Gesenius, Davies, Zöckler, Keil, Fausset;* my joints trembled in me, — *Vulgate, Luther, Bertholdt, Hävernick, Füller;* ray features were changed, — *Ewald, Stuart.*

(Chapter XI)

(1) And I also, in the first year of Darius the Mede, stood to strengthen and confirm him. [1] (2) And now I will tell thee the truth.

Behold, three kings of Persia shall yet stand up; and the fourth shall ac-quire greater riches than they all; and when he is become strong, through his riches, he shall stir up all, toward the kingdom of Greece. (3) And a mighty king shall arise, and he shall rule a great dominion, and do according to his will. (4) And when he is risen up, his kingdom shall be broken, and it shall be divided toward the four winds of heaven; but not to his posterity, nor accord-ing to his dominion which he ruled; for his kingdom shall be plucked up, and shall be for others besides these. [2] (5) And the king of the south shall wax strong; but one of his princes [3] shall become stronger than he, and shall rule; his dominion shall be a great dominion. (6) And at the end of years they shall form an alliance; and the daughter of the king of the south shall come to the king of the north to make agreements; [4] but she shall not retain the power of the arm, neither shall he stand, nor his arm; and she shall be given up, and they that brought her, and he who begat her, and he that strengthened her in the times.

(7) And one of the branches of her roots shall rise up in his place, and he shall come against the army [5] and shall enter into the fortress of the king of the north, and shall do against them and prevail; (8) and he shall also carry into captivity to Egypt, their gods, with their molten images, with their precious vessels of silver and gold; and he shall withstand [6] for years the king of the north. (9) And he [7] shall come into the kingdom of the south, but he shall return into his own land.

(10) And his sons [8] shall stir up war, and shall assemble a multitude of great forces; and he shall come, and overflow, and pass through; aud he shall return and make war to his [9] fortress. (11) And the king of the south shall become greatly enraged, and he will go forth and fight with him, with the king of the north; and he [10] shall raise up a great multitude; but the multitude shall be given into his [11] hand. (12) And the multitude shall lift itself up, [12] and his [13] heart shall be elated; and he shall cast down tens of thousands, but he shall not become strong. (13) And the king of the north shall return, and he shall raise up a multitude greater than the first one, and at the end of times, years, he shall surely come with a great army and with much substance. [14] (14) And in those times many -will stand up against the king of the south; and the violent sons of thy people shall exalt themselves to establish the vision, but they shall fall. (15) And the king of the north shall come, and he shall cast up a mound, and take a strongly fortified city; [15] and the arms of the south shall not withstand, neither his chosen people, [16] neither shall there be any power to withstand. (16) And he who cometh against him shall do according to his will, and none shall stand before him; and he shall stand in the glorious land, [17] and destruction is in his hand. [18] (17) And he shall set his face to come with the strength [19] of his whole kingdom, and agreements [20] shall he make with him; and he shall give the daughter of women to him, to destroy it; [21] but it [22] shall not stand, neither be for him. (18) And he shall turn his face unto the isles, and shall take many; but a chieftain shall cause the reproach offered by him to cease, yea, his own reproach shall he cause to return upon himself. (19) And he shall turn his face toward the fortresses of his own land; and he shall skimble and fall, and not be found.

(20) And there shall stand up in his place one that shall cause a raiser of taxes to pass over [23] the glory of the kingdom; but in few days he shall be destroyed, but not in anger, nor in war.

(21) And in his place shall stand up a despised one, to whom was not given the honor of the kingdom; but he shall come unexpectedly, [24] and obtain the kingdom by dissimulations. (22) And the arms of the flood shall be swept from before him, and shall be broken, yea, also a covenant prince. [25] (23) And from the making of the covenant with him he shall do deceitfully; and he shall come up and prevail with a small people. (24) Unexpectedly shall he

come even upon the rich places of the province; and he shall do what his fathers have not done, nor his fathers' fathers; he shall scatter among them prey, and spoil, and riches; and he shall forecast his devices against strongholds, and that for a time. (25) And he shall stir up his power and his heart against the king of the south with a great army; and the king of the south shall be stirred up to war with a very great and mighty army; but he shall not stand; for they shall forecast devices against him. (26) And they who eat of his dainties shall destroy him, and his army shall overflow; and many shall fall down slain. (27) And both these kings' hearts are unto evil; and at one table shall they speak lies. But it will not succeed, for yet the end shall be at the time appointed. (28) And he shall return to his land with great riches; and his heart shall be against the holy covenant; and he shall do, [26] and return to his own land.

(29) At the time appointed he shall return and come toward the south; but not as the former shall the latter be. (30) For ships of Chittim [27] shall come against him; and he shall be discouraged, and return, and rage against the holy covenant; and he shall accomplish it; and he shall return and have an understanding with those who forsake the holy covenant. (31) And arms shall arise at his command, [28] and they shall pollute the sanctuary, the fortress, [29] and shall take away the daily service, and they shall set up the abomination that maketh desolate. [30] (32) And those who do wickedly against the covenant shall he corrupt by dissimulations; but the people who know their God shall become strong, and do it. (33) And they that be wise among the people shall instruct the many; and they shall fall by the sword, and by flame, by captivity, and by spoil, for days. (34) And when they shall fall, they shall obtain a little help; and many shall cleave to them with deceits. (35) And some of them that be wise shall fall, to try them, and to purify and to make them white, to the time of the end; because it is yet for the time appointed.]

(36) And the king shall do according to his will; and he will exalt himself and magnify himself above every god; and he will speak marvellous things [31] against the God of gods, and he will prosper until the indignation be accomplished; for what is determined shall be done. (37) Neither will he regard the God [32] of his fathers, nor the desire of women, nor will he regard any god; for he will magnify himself above all. (38) But in his place [33] will he honor the god of fortresses; [34] and a god whom his fathers knew not will he honor with gold and silver, and with precious stones and pleasant things. (39) And he shall do [35] to the strong fortresses with [36] a strange god; whoso [37] shall acknowledge him, he will increase with honor, and he will cause them to rule over the many, and he will divide the land as a reward. [38]

(40) And at the time of the end the king of the south shall push at him; and the king of the north shall storm against him, with chariot, and with horsemen, and with many ships; and he shall enter into the countries and shall overflow and pass over. (41) And he shall enter into the glorious land, and

many shall fall; but these shall escape out of his hand, Edom and Moab, and the chief of the sons of Amnion. (42) And he shall stretch forth his hand upon the countries; and the land of Egypt shall not escape. (43) And he shall rule over the treasures of gold and of silver, and over all the precious things of Egypt; and the Libyans and the Cushites shall be in his steps. (44) And rumors out of the east and out of the north shall trouble him; and he shall go forth in great fury to destroy and utterly to make away many. (45) And he shall plant the tents of his palace between the seas and the glorious holy mountain; and he shall come to his end, and none shall help him.

[1] him — *i.e.* Michael, — *Hofmann, Füller, Zöckler, Keil, Stuart, Rosenmüller; or,* Darius, — *Hävernick, Hitzig, Hengstenberg.*
[2] verses 5-35. See Exposition, pp. 258-264.
[3] but one of his princes shall become, — Keil, ZocMer, Ftvald, Hitzig, Stuart, Fausset.
[4] agreements,— *lit.* rights.
[5] against the army, — *Keil, Zöckler, Kranichfeld;* unto the [his] army, *Hitzig, Herzfeld, Kliefoth, Ewald, Stuart, Michaelis, Bertholdt, Lengerke;* he attained to might, — *Hävernick.*
[6] withstand for years the king, — *Bertholdt, Gesenius, Winer, De Wette, Kranichfeld, Keil, Peshito, Vulgate;* stand aloof from, — *Hitzig, Kliefoth, Ewald, Zöckler, Stuart, Hävernick, Lengerke, Maurer.*
[7] he — *i.e.* the king of the north, — so *Keil, Zöckler, Cheyne, Driver, Stuart.*
[8] his — *i.e.* the king of the north's.
[9] his — *i.e.* the king of the south's.
[10] he — *i.e.* the king of the north, — Keil, Fausset.
[11] his — *i.e.* the king of the south's, — Keil, Fausset.
[12] shall lift itself up, — Cheyne, Driver, Zockler, Keil.
[13] his — *i.e.* the king of the south's.
[14] substance — *i.e.* equipment.
[15] strongly fortified city, — *lit.* a city of fortifications.
[16] people — *i.e.* troops.
[17] glorious land, — *lit.* land of beauty.
[18] destruction is in his hand, — *Gesenius, Hitzig, Herzfeld, Zöckler, Keil;* it is wholly in his hand, — *Hävernick, Lengerke, Van Ess, Füller, Bertholdt, Dereser, Stuart.*
[19] with the strength, — *Theodotion, Luther, Auth. Ver., Geier, Hitzig, Kranichfeld, Keil, Zöchler;* against the strength — *i.e.* of the Egyptian kingdom, — *Michaelis, Hävernick, Lengerke, Maurer, Kliefoth, Stuart.*
[20] *lit.* rights; an agreement shall be made with him, — *Septuagint, De Wette, Hitzig, Grätz, Fwald, Zöckler, Stuart, Bertholdt, Dereser, Lengerke;* and upright ones shall be with him, and he shall succeed, — *Gesenius, Winer, Auth. Ver.; and* strong ones come with him, — *Fuller;* and uprightness with him, — *Hävernick, Kranichfeld;* with upright intention; and he shall do it, — *Keil.*
[21] to destroy it — *i.e.* the kingdom of Ptolemy, — *Stuart, Cheyne, Driver, Ewald, Grätz, Zöckler;* to destroy her, — *Michaelis, Bertholdt, Bosenmüller, Keil, Kranichfeld.*

[22] it — *i.e.* his plan, — *Stuart, Hitzig, Pusey, Zöckler, Füller, Lengerke, Maurer, Cheyne, Driver; she,* — *Keil, Fausset;* the land, — *Ewald.*

[23] one that shall cause...to pass over, — so *Cheyne, Driver, Stuart, Zöckler, Maurer, Keil.*

[24] unexpectedly, — *Gesenius, Lengerke, Cheyne, Driver, Keil, Zöckler.*

[25] covenant prince — *i.e.* a prince in league with him, — *Hengstenberg, Ewald, Cheyne, Driver, Stuart.*

[26] do — *i.e.* carry out his purpose, — *Hitzig, Herzfeld, Zöckler, Keil, Stuart.* **[27]** Chittim — *i.e.* Cyprus.

[28] his command — *lit.* from him.

[29] the fortress, — *Stuart, Cheyne, Driver, Keil, Zöckler.*

[30] horrible abomination, — *Hitzig, Herzfeld, Ewald.*

[31] marvellous things, *or,* wonderfully.

[32] God, or gods, — *Hitzig, Herzfeld, Zöckler, Keil, Stuart.*

[33] in his place, — so *Gesenius, De Wette, Kliefoth, Keil, Luther, Kranichfeld, Fuller;* on his pedestal, — *Hävernick, Lengerke, Maurer, Hitzig, Ewald, Stuart, Zöckler, Bertholdt.*

[34] fortresses, — so *Grotius, Michaelis, Gesenius, Hävernick, Lengerke, Maurer, Ewald, Hitzig, Stuart, Kliefoth, Keil, Zöckler, Cheyne, Driver;* Mauzzim, *a proper name,* — *Theodotion, Vulgate, Luther.*

[35] do — *i.e.* his will, — so *Keil, Stuart.*

[36] with — *i.e.* the help of, — so *Keil, Kranichfeld, De Wette.*

[37] whoso shall acknowledge him, he will, — so *Keil, Stuart, Cheyne, Driver, Zöckler.*

[38] as a reward,— so *Keil, Maurer, Kliefoth, Stuart, Cheyne, Driver, Zöckler.*

(Chapter XII)

(1) And at that time shall Michael stand up, the great prince, who standeth for the sons of thy people; and there shall be a time of distress, such as never was since there was a nation to that time; and at that time thy people shall be delivered, every one that is found written in the book. (2) And many [1] of them that sleep in the dust of the earth shall awake, these to everlasting life, and these to shame, to everlasting abhorrence. (3) And they that be wise shall shine as the brightness of the firmament; and they that turn the many to righteousness, as the stars for ever and ever.

(4) But thou, O Daniel, shut up the words, and seal the book, to the time of the end; many shall examine it, and the knowledge [2] shall be increased. (5) And I, Daniel, looked, and behold there stood two others, one on this bank of the river, and the other on that bank of the river. (6) And one said to the man clothed in linen, who was over the waters of the river, How long is the end of the wonders? (7) And I heard the man clothed in linen, who was over the waters of the river; and he lifted up his right hand and his left hand to heaven, and swore by Him that liveth for ever, that for a time, times and an half; and when he shall have ceased to scatter a part of the holy people, all these things shall be fulfilled. (8) And I heard, but I understood not; and I said. My

lord, what is the end of these things? (9) And he said. Go thy way, Daniel, for the words are closed up and sealed till the time of the end. (10) Many shall be purified, and made white, and tried; but the wicked shall do wickedly; and none of the wicked will understand, but they that are wise will understand. (11) And from the time when the daily service shall be taken away, and an abomination that maketh desolate set up, there shall be a thousand two hundred and ninety days. (12) Blessed is he that waiteth and Cometh to a thousand three hundred and five and thirty days. (13) But go thou thy way unto the end, and thou shalt rest, and rise up to thy lot at the end of the days.

[1] many — *i.e.* Not all (*the first resurrection*), — *Saadiah, Aben Ezra, Tregelles, Bush, Bertholdt, Kranichfeld, Füller, Kostlin, Fausset;* all (*general resurrection*), — *Hävernick, Hofmann, Anberlen, Zündel, Kliefoth, Zöckler.*
[2] knowledge — *i.e.* of it, of this prophecy,— *Luther, Lowth, Gill, Stuart, Zöckler, Wintle, Keil, Fausset, Wordsworth, De Wette, Tregelles, Van Ess, Vatican Text.*

List of Authors

In addition to the various ancient versions of the Book of Daniel, the following are the names of authors, volumes and articles more or less consulted and used in the preparation of this book, particularly in the revision of the translation, as referred to in the foot-notes to the revised text, as also in the Lectures themselves: —

Alexander, art. "Canon," Kitto's *Bibl. Cyclo.*

Allin, *Israel's Restoration,* London, 1855.

Allioli, *Die Heilige Schrift, mit der Vutgata,* 3d ed., Regensburg, 1865,

Ante-Nicene Christian Library, 26 vols., Edinburgh.

Armageddon, 3 vols., London, 1858.

Auberlen, *The Prophecies of Daniel and the Revelations of St. John,* New York, 1857.

Augustine, Aurelius, *Works,* 14 vols., Edinburgh.

Ayre, *Introduction to Old Testament,* vol. ii. of Horne's *Introd.,* eleventh ed., London, 1863.

Barnes, *Notes on the Book of Daniel,* New York, 1856.

Ben-Ezra, *The Coming of Messiah* (Irving), 2 vols., London, 1827.

Berg, *The Stone and the Image,* Philadelphia, 1856.

Berlenburger *Bibel,* 4 vols., 1726.

Bertholdt, *Daniel aus dem Heb. Aram, nen übersetzt und erklärt, 2 vols.,* Erlangen, 1806, 1808.

Bickersteth, *Works,* 16 vols., London, 1853.

Birks, *The Two Later Visions of Daniel,* London, 1846.

Bleek, *An Introduction to the Old Testament,* 2 vols., London, 1875.

Bloomsbury Lectures, 12 vols., London.

Bosanquet, *Messiah the Prince,* London, 1869.

Böttcher, *Ausführliches Lehrbuch der Heb. Sprache,* Leipzig, 1866-68.

Boyle, *The Inspiration of the Book of Daniel,* London, 1863.

Brooks, *The History of the Hebrew Nation,* London, 1841.

Browne, *Ordo Sseclorum,* London, 1844.

Bunsen, *The Chronology of the Bible* (Sayce), London, 1874.

Cheyne. *The Holy Bible, edited with Various Renderings and Readings,* London, 1876.

Cheyne, art. "Daniel," *Ency. Brit.,* ninth ed.

Cowles, *Ezekiel and Daniel,* with Notes, New York, 1867.

Cumming, *Lectures on the Book of Daniel,* 1854.

Daniel's Great Period, London, 1844.

Davidson, A. B., *An Introductory Hebrew Grammar,* second edition, Edinburgh, 1876.

Davidson, J., *Discourses on Prophecy,* London, 1875.

Davidson, S., art. "Canon," *Ency. Brit.,* ninth edition.

- *Introduction to the Old Testament,* vol. ii. of Horne's *Introd.,* tenth ed., London.

Davies, *A Compendious Hebrew and Chaldee Lexicon,* London, 1872.

- *Revised English Bible,* London, 1877.

Delitzsch, F., art. "Daniel," Herzog's *Ency.* In both editions (separate articles).

Donaldson, *The Apostolical Fathers,* London, 1874.

Driver, *The Holy Bible, edited with Various Renderings and Readings,* London, 1876.

___ *A Treatise on the Use of the Tenses in Hebrew,* Oxford, 1844.

Duncker, *Geschichte des Alterthums,* vierte Auflage, vol. ii,, Leipzig, 1874.

Ephrem the Syrian, *Select Works of,* Oxford, 1847.

Ernesti, *Concordantiae Bibliorum Germanico-Hebraico-Graecae,* Lipsiae, 1688.

Ewald, *Ausführliches Lehrbuch der hebr. sprache des A. Bundes,* die 7 Auflage, Gött., 1863.

Die Propheten des alten Bundes erklärt, 2 Bde,, Stuttgart, 1840-41,

- *History of Israel,* 6 vols, London, 1869.

Faber, *On the Prophecies,* 5 vols,, London, 1818.

Fairbairn, *On Prophecy,* Edinburgh, 1856.

Fausset, *A Commentary on Daniel, Critical, Experimental and Practical,* Philadelphia, 1876.

Fry, *The Second Advent,* 2 vols,, London, 1822,

- *Unfulfilled Prophecies,* London, 1835.

Fuller, *Commentary on Daniel,* in *Bible Commentary,* New York, 1876.

Füller, *Der Prophet Daniel erklärt,* Basel, 1868.

Fürst, *Hebräisches und Chäldäisches Handwörterbuch über das A. T.* (Davidson), 1867.

- *Chaldäischo Grammatik,* Leipzig, zweite Auflage, 1864.

Gaussen, *The Prophecies of Daniel Explained,* London, 1873.

Gesenius, *Hebrew Grammar,* from the 21st German edition, by Roediger, translated by Davies, London, 1869.

- *Thesaurus Linguae Hebraeae et Chaldaeae V. T.* (Roediger).

- *Lexicon Manuals Heb. et Chal. in V. T.* (Robinson).

Gesenius. *Hebräisches mid Chaldäisches Handwörterbuch über das A. T.,* 7te Auflage (Dietrich).

Gibbon, *Rome* (Milman), 6 vols.

Gill, *Exposition of Old Testament,* vol. iv.

Green, *A Grammar of the Hebrew Language,* third edition. New York, 1864.

Greswell, *Dissertations,* 4 vols., Oxford, 1837.

Guers, *Israel in the Last Days,* London, 1862.

Hale, *New Analysis of Chronology and Geography, History and Prophecy,* 4 vols., London, 1830.

Hävernick, *Kommentar über das Buch Daniel,* Hamburg, 1832.

- *Handbuch der hist. - Krit. einleitung in das A. T.,* 5 vols., Erlangen, 1836-54.

- Art. "Daniel," Kitto's *Bibl. Cyclo.*

Hefele, *Patrum Apostolicorum Opera,* Tübingen, 1855.

Hengstenberg, *Die Anthentie des Daniel,* Berlin, 1831.

- *Beiträge zur einleitung in's A.T.,* Berlin, 1831.

- *Christology of the Old Testament,* second ed., 4 vols., Edinburgh. 1864.

- *History of the Kingdom of God under the Old Testament,* 2 vols., Edinburgh, 1871-72.

Hertwig, *Tabellen zur einleitung in die Bücher des A. T.,* 2te Auflage, Besorgt von Kleinert, Berlin, 1869.

Hitzig, *Kurzgefasstes exeget. Handbuch zum A. T., das Buch Daniel,* Leipzig, 1850.

Hofmann, *Die 70 Jahre Jeremias und die 70 Jahrwochen des Daniel,* Nuremberg, 1836.

Hussey, *The Holy Bible, with a Brief Hermeneutic and Exegetical Commentary,* 3 vols., London, 1845.

Jahn, *Biblical Archaeology* (Uphara), second edition, Andover, 1827.

- *Hebrew Commonwealth,* London.

Kamphausen, in Bunsen's *Bibelwerk,* Leipsic, 1867.

Keil, *The Book of the Prophet Daniel,* Eng. trans., Edinburgh, 1872.

- *Lehrbuch der hist.-Krit. einleitung in die kanon. Schriften des A. T.,* Frankfort und Erlangen, zweite Aufgabe, 1859.

Keith, *History and Destiny of the World and the Church,* London, 1861.

Kelley, *Notes on Daniel,* London.

Kett, *History the Interpreter of Prophecy,* 3 vols., Oxford, 1799.

Kliefoth, *Das Buch Daniels übersetzt und erklärt,* Schwerin, 1868.

Kranichfeld, *Das Buch Daniel erklärt,* Berlin, 1868.

Lactantius, *Opera* Omnia, Lipsiae, 1739.

Layard, *Discoveries in Nineveh and Babylon,* New York, 1856.

Leathes, art. "Babylon," Kitto's *Bibl. Cyclo.*

Lengerke, *Das Buch Daniel verdentscht und ausgelegt,* Königsberg, 1885.

Lenormant, *Manual of the Ancient History of the East,* 2 vols., London, 1869.

Leopold, *Lexicon Hebraicum et Chaldaicum,* Lipsiae, 1832.

Lord, *The Theological and Literary Journal,* 13 vols.. New York, 1848-61.

Lowth, *Commentary upon the Prophecy of Daniel and the Twelve Minor Prophets,* 2 vols., London, 1726.

Luther, *Auslegung des Proph. Daniel,* Walch, vol. vi.

Maitland, *The Apostles' School of Prophetic Interpretation,* London, 1849.

Maurer, *Commentarius Grammaticus criticus in V. T.,* vol. ii., Lipsiae, 1836.

McCaul, *The Old Paths,* London, 1846.

McCausland, D., *The Latter Days of Jerusalem and Rome,* London, 1859.

Mede, Joseph, *Works,* London, 1677.

Melanchthon, *In Danielem Prophetam Commentarius,* Corpus Reformatorum, vol. xiii., 1846.

Michaelis, C. B., *Adnotationes philologico-exegeticae in Danielem,* Halle, 1720.

Michaelis, D. J. H., *Biblia Hebraica,* Halle, 1720.

Molyneux, *Israel's Future,* London, 1860.

Newton, B. Wills, *Prospect of the Ten Kingdoms,* London, 1849.

Newton, B. Wills, *Aids to Prophetic Enquiry,* 2 vols., London, 1853.

Newton, Bishop, *Dissertations on the Prophecies,* 1796.

Newton, Isaac, *Observations upon the Prophecies of Daniel and the Apocalypse of St. John,* London, 1733.

Nolan, *The Chronological Prophecies,* London, 1837.

Noyes, *A New Translation of the Hebrew Prophets,* fourth edition, 2 vols., Boston, 1868.

Oehler, art. "Kanon," Herzog's *Ency.,* first edition.

Olshausen, *Lehrbuch der Heb. Sprache,* Braunschweig, 1861.

Oppert, *Records of the Past, Assyrian Texts,* vols. vii. and ix., London.

Phillips, *A Syriac Grammar,* third edition, London, 1866.

Pirie, *Works,* 6 vols., Edinburgh, 1865.

Pusey, *Daniel the Prophet, Nine Lectures,* second edition, London, 1868.

Quarterly Journal of Prophecy (Bonar), 24 vols., London, 1849-72.

Rawlinson, G., art. "Babylon," Smith's *Bible Dict.* (Amer. ed.).

- *A Manual of Ancient History,* New York, 1871.

- *The Origin of Nations,* New York, 1878.

- *Herodotus,* 4 vols., N. Y., 1859.

- *Five Ancient Monarchies,* London.

Riggs, *A Manual of the Chaldee Language,* New York, 1866.

Roediger, *Chrestomathia Syriaca Dan. vii., cum Scholiis Ephraemi,* editio altera, Halle, 1868.

Rosenmüller, *Scholia in V. T.,* vol. X., Lipsiae, 1832.

Ruetschi, arts. "Babel," "Babylonia," Herzog's *Ency.,* first edition.

Rule, *Oriental Records,* Historical, London.

- *Oriental Records,* Monumental, London.

Sayce, arts. "Babylon," "Babylonia," Ency. Brit., ninth ed.

- *Records of the Past, Assyrian Text,* vols. vii. and ix., London.

Smith, George, *Records of the Past, Assyrian Texts,* vols. vii. and ix., London.

Smith, P., *The Old Testament History,* New York, 1875.

- *The Ancient History of the East,* New York, 1871.

Smith, R. Payne, art. "Daniel," *Bible Educator.*

Stanley, *Lectures on the History of the Jewish Church,* 3 vols.. New York.

Stier and Theile, *Biblia Polyglotta,* 5vols., Bielefeld, 1856.

Stuart, *A Commentary on the Book of Daniel,* Boston, 1850.

- *Critical History and Defence of the Old Testament Canon,* Andover, 1872.

- *Hints on the Interpretation of Prophecy,* Andover, 1842.

Suicer, *Thesaurus Ecclesiasticus, e Patrihus Graecis,* 2 vols., Amsterdam, 1728.

Taylor, *Daniel, the Beloved,* New York, 1878.

Tregelles, *Remarks on the Prophetic Visions in the Book of Daniel,* fifth edition, London, 1864.

Trevilian, *To Therion,* London, 1858.

Turner, *Studies, Biblical and Oriental,* Edinburgh, 1876.

Uhlemann, *Syriac Grammar,* translated by Hutchinson, second edition, New York, 1875.

Volck, arts. "Babel," "Babylonia," Herzog's Ency., second edition.

Westcott, arts. "Canon," "Daniel," Smith's Bible Diet. (Amer. ed.).

Wette, de, *Lehrbuch der historisehkritischen einleituny in die Bücher des alten Testaments,* fünfte Ausgabe, Berlin, 1848.

Wieseler, *Die 70 wochen und die 63 Jahrwochen des Propheten Daniel,* Gött., 1839.

Winchester, *On the Prophecies,* 4 vols., 1813.

Winer, *Lexicon Manuale Heb. et Chal. in V. T. Libros* (Havernick).

- *Chaldäische Grammatik,* 2te Ausgabe, Leipzig, 1842.

Wintle, *Daniel, an Improved Version Attempted, with Notes,* London, 1836.

Wordsworth, *The Book of Daniel, with Notes and Introduction,* London, 1871.

Zöckler, *The Book of the Prophet Daniel* (Lange), Eng. trans., edited by James Strong, New York.

Zündel, *Kritische Unfersuchungen über die Abfassungszeit des Buch Daniel,* Basle, 1861.